Wild Thyme and Saladelle

ALEXANDER MAITLAND

Wild Thyme and Saladelle

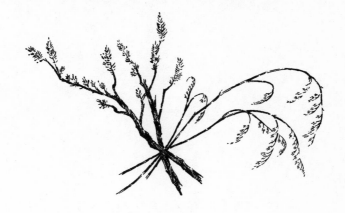

Journeys round Western Provence

Methuen

First published in Great Britain 1993
by Methuen London
an imprint of Reed Consumer Books Ltd
Michelin House, 81 Fulham Road, London SW3 6RB
and Auckland, Melbourne, Singapore and Toronto

A CIP catalogue record for this book
is available from the British Library

ISBN 0 413 63010 2

Typeset by Deltatype Ltd, Ellesmere Port
Printed in Great Britain by
St Edmundsbury Press Ltd, Bury St Edmunds, Suffolk

For Margaret

Contents

List of Illustrations

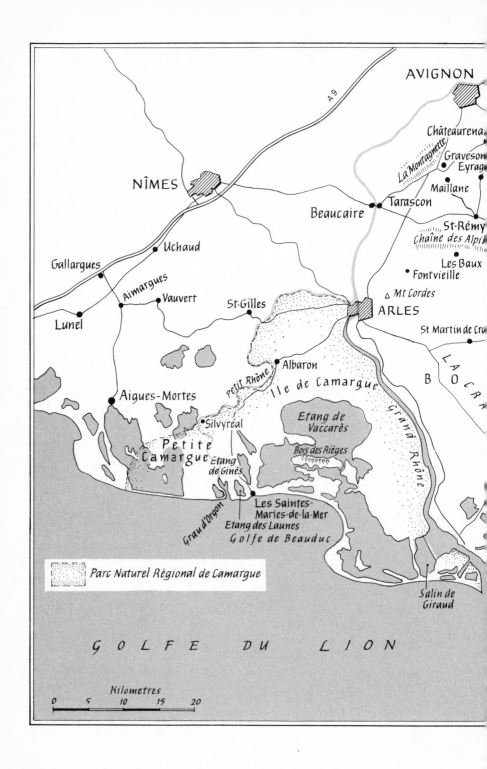

AVIGNON

Châteaurena

NÎMES

Graveson
Eyrag

La Montagnette

Maillane

Beaucaire   Tarascon

St-Rémy

Chaîne des Alpi

Uchaud

Gallargues

Les Baux
Fontvieille

Aimargues

Vauvert   St-Gilles

Lunel

△ Mt Cordes   ARLES

St Martin de Cra

B

L
A
C
R
A

Petit Rhône   Île de Camargue

Aigues-Mortes   Albaron

Grand Rhône

Etang de
Vaccarès

Silvyréal

Bois des Rièges

Petite
Camargue   Etang
de Ginès

Grau d'Orgon   Les Saintes-
Maries-de-la-Mer

Etang des Launes
Golfe de Beauduc

Salin de
Giraud

Parc Naturel Régional de Camargue

GOLFE   DU   LION

Kilometres
0   5   10   15   20

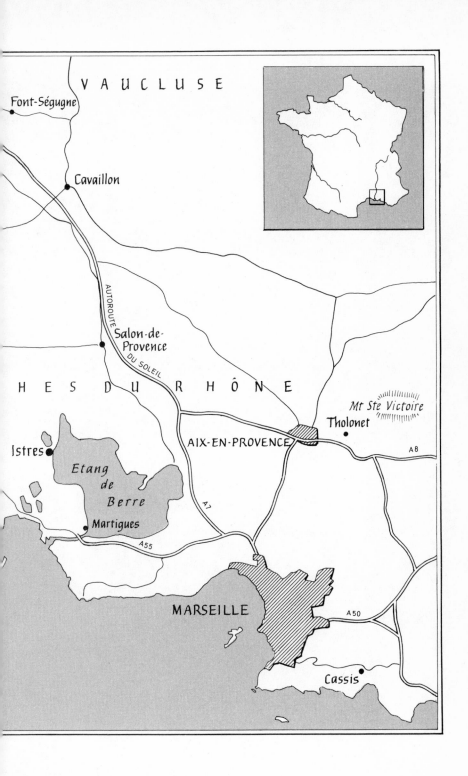

VAUCLUSE

Font-Ségugne

Cavaillon

AUTOROUTE

Salon-de-Provence

DU SOLEIL

HES DU RHÔNE

Mt Ste Victoire

Tholonet

AIX-EN-PROVENCE

A8

Istres

Etang
de
Berre

Martigues

A7

A55

MARSEILLE

A50

Cassis

Acknowledgements

I have great pleasure in acknowledging the advice and practical assistance given by the following individuals, learned societies, private and public concerns and others without whose generous involvement this book would have been infinitely more difficult to accomplish.

The Scottish Arts Council in 1984 awarded me a grant which aided my initial research in Avignon and the Camargue. Patrick Goyet, Répresantant Général, the late Pauline Hallam and Marc Humphries of the French Government Tourist Office, London, provided introductions, information and arranged accommodation for several visits, for which I am very grateful. Peter Mills and Christine Lagardère of French Railways Ltd, London, assisted my journeys to Provence and loaned me useful literature. Their help, like that of the French Government Tourist Office, has been invaluable. I likewise received helpful assistance from Charles Page and Julie Mitchell of British Rail International, and Sealink and Hoverspeed Ltd whose staff have aided various trips. Folly Marland of McCarta Ltd provided me with a very comprehensive selection of excellent maps. Hertz and Europcar Ltd assisted with car-rental in France.

I wish to thank the Librarian and staff of the Institut Français, London for much information and advice, and similarly the Librarians and staff of the Royal Geographical Society and the Kensington and Chelsea Public Libraries.

At the Tourist Office in Avignon I was assisted by the Directrice, Martha Walger, and her staff including Mariane Colomb. I wish especially to thank the Conservateur of the Palais du Roure, Avignon, Sylvain Gagnière for his courteous assistance and guidance in Provençal translations. The former Secretary-Archivist of the Roure, Mireille Bosqui and her husband, Marcel Bosqui, since 1984 have taken infinite trouble to further my studies of Provençal writers and artists. I cannot thank them sufficiently. I thank also Sabine

Barnicaud, Mme Bosqui's successor, who provided information and valuable insights and, together with her mother and daughter, entertained me very hospitably at their home near Les Saintes-Maries. My thanks are due also to M and Mme Laurent Aubanel for information on Provençal literature.

At Arles, the Directrice of the Tourist Office, Mme Valette, and her Deputy, Alain Marion, welcomed me and generously assisted in every aspect of my work and travels. Without Alain Marion's continual support, I could never have accomplished this task so expeditiously. Any thanks to him must be inadequate. Among my friends at Arles, I wish to thank the following for their boundless help and encouragement: Jennifer and André Lacote; Maité Dubosquet; Josette and Hervé Bourillon; Dominique Serena; Nicole Niel; Mme Castanet; Mme Marchand; Carole Boissy; Catherine Aubert; Françine Richard-Mathias; Alphonse Jalabert; Philippe Milhe; Mr and Mrs Izumo Hayashikawa of Kagoshima and Mr and Mrs Nishidome of Tokyo; Alain DePlanck and members of his family; Alexandru Ioan Florescu; Françoise and Yvan Audouard; Monique and Jean-Christophe Lassalle of the Hôtel-Gril Campanile; René Quenin; Jeanne Calment; M and Mme Matonnat; M and Mme Hubert Yonnet; Germaine Dibon; Eliane Mineff; Mme Boullin; Mme Palazon; Françoise and Hubert Nyssen; the administrators and staff of the Arles hospital and the Maison du Lac; the Librarian and staff of the Arles Médiathèque; Chantal Franco; Jean-Pierre Morize; Eugène Kuntz; Julian and Nelly Panichi; Yvonne and Jules Moulard-Lelée; Giselle Valiente; M and Mme Michel Albanac, François Astié and the staff of the Hôtel Jules-César; the Senator-Mayor of Arles, J.-P. Camoin; Charles Farine; Albert Lugassy of *Le Provençal*; and Silvie Aries of *Le Méridional*.

In Fontvieille, I was received and entertained very hospitably by Michel Gay and Marcel Fouque of the Galérie Saint-Michel. MM Gay and Fouque's contribution to my work cannot be overestimated. I am immensely grateful for everything they have done for me. I wish also to thank Lilette Ripert at Marseille; Andéri Macchia, President of the Fondation Louis Jou; Annie Plécy of the Cathédrale d'Images, Les Baux; and, at Lunel, Loretta and the late Jean Hugo. At Graveson, I received courteous assistance from the mayor, Raoul Bonjean; and at the Mas de Martin from Jean and Marie-Paule Chabaud. I must thank also Mme Barnier of Aix-en-Provence; and at Gallargues, Michel-Droit, René Théron, Marie-Thérèse and René Jouveau and Mireille and Bernard Hyacinthe. In Aigues-Mortes I received useful advice from Mlle Lawrence Rossi and Mme Bartelot. The mayor of Tarascon, Thérèse Aillaud, welcomed me there and I was further assisted by Michel Naval; Serge Popovitch; Robert Archet; and M and Mme Jean Lavalle.

I owe a very great debt of gratitude to my friends and colleagues at Les Saintes-Maries-de-la-Mer. Foremost, Henri and the late Riquette Aubanel: Henri Aubanel introduced me to many aspects of Camargue life, literature and traditions; to him and his late wife I offer my thanks, trusting that it will acknowledge, however insufficiently, their kindness to me over the years. I wish also to thank Marie-Caroline Aubanel, her sisters and brother, Jacqueline, Nerte and Pierre, for their unfailing hospitality and advice. At Les Saintes-Maries, I thank Pascale Maurel; Marie Delpy; Jacques Bon; M and Mme Nicolas Barrera; Marcel Taillet; the staff of the Musée Baroncelli; the curate of Les Saintes-Maries' church; M and Mme André Dupuis; René Baranger; M and Mme Henri Laurent; Marcel Mailhan; Mme Bellon; Anik Nou; Denys and Monique Colomb de Daunant; Florian de Daunant; Magali Dunant; M and Mme Bedot; and Raymond Bechet.

For permission to quote from one of her letters to me, I wish to thank Germaine Greer. The Comte and Comtesse de Maynard showed me much generous hospitality at Arles and guided my research on the Visconte Gaston de Luppé and Léopold Lelée. Further thanks are due to Yvonne Moulard-Lelée for allowing me to study her late father's books and paintings from her collection and for her encouragement and warm support. I thank Francisco Campbell Custodio and Ad. Donker (pty) Ltd for permission to quote from Roy Campbell's poem, 'Horses on the Camargue'. My thanks are also due to Bruce Hunter, Ann Mansbridge and to Methuen's editor, David Watson, who devoted considerable care to the preparation of this manuscript, for which I am very grateful.

My wife, Margaret, has accompanied me during several visits to Arles and the Camargue and her constant encouragement and perceptive advice on every aspect of my work have been invaluable. Her enthusiasm and support made all the difference during the months I spent writing the book in London.

There has been helpful assistance given by others over the years, whose names I have not mentioned and many pleasant intervals spent in the company of passers-by whose friendliness I shall not forget. To them all, I offer my grateful thanks.

The chain of circumstances which fired my interest in this region of southwest France began in 1956 when I first saw Albert Lamorisse and

Denys Colomb de Daunant's film, *Crin-Blanc*. Later I met the late Violet Tschiffely, the widow of A. F. Tschiffely, a friend of Roy and Mary Campbell. Through Mrs Tschiffely, I met Lord and Lady Polwarth. Jean Polwarth, a great-niece of R. B. Cunninghame Graham, introduced me to Loretta Hugo, who in turn introduced me to Henri and Riquette Aubanel. These events occurred over a period of more than twenty years; now, almost forty years after seeing *Crin-Blanc*, for the moment at least, my work on Rhôneland Provence and the Camargue has been completed.

'I know a bank whereon the wild thyme blows . . .'

Shakespeare,
A Midsummer Night's Dream

'J'ai lié à l'arçon de ma selle
un joli brin de "saladelle"
C'est une fleur de gardian . . .'

Joseph D'Arbaud

'C'est la Provence qui chante,
Le Languedoc qui combat.'

Introduction

In Provence, and the Rhôneland, where people are surrounded by so much beauty, beauty also tends to be widely appreciated and, what is more, one finds it is shared eagerly in ways which are often simple and touching. One morning, near the village of Maillane, I was admiring the hills of La Montagnette after a heavy shower of rain when an old man appeared suddenly out of nowhere and handed me a branch of thorn from which glistening red berries hung in brilliant clusters. 'Lovely aren't they?' he remarked in a matter-of-fact tone. 'You would almost think they were on fire.' And with that, he turned on his heel and vanished back the way he had come.

It is only a few months since I last returned from Provence, but already it seems like a lifetime. Last October, I abandoned the grey skies and cold of an English autumn and spent some months wandering the highways and byways of the Arles country and the Camargue. This is the area known officially as the Pays d'Arles and it also appears on maps of Provence as the Bouches du Rhône, which is its departmental name. The Rhôneland – what the novelist Marie Mauron has called La Rouanesse – is the triangle of Western Provence between Avignon, Arles and the Mediterranean, embraced by the Great and Lesser Rhône. Here the Rhône divides at the final stage of its

long journey from Lake Geneva, through France, towards the
sea.

I have made a number of visits to this beautiful region in the
past and its enchantment never wanes. Much of my time there
has been spent drawing and painting, or else merely lazing in the
sun. I find that the easy-going, cheerful tempo of Provençal life,
with its occasional bursts of unexpected, feverish activity, suits
my temperament very well indeed and it harmonizes perfectly
with my views on the relative importance of work and leisure.
Of course, I am not suggesting for a moment that the Rhôneland
folk are idlers: nothing could be further from the truth. In
general they work very hard, but their attitude to work is not the
same as ours in the north. In Provence, they tell you, 'Life is a
cadeau, a gift from God which is there to be enjoyed.' What they
dismiss sneeringly as the 'TGV life' – life in the fast lane, as
exemplified by the *train à grande vitesse* – of big northern cities
such as Paris and London, offers them little or nothing by way of
temptations. Paris is too impersonal and too sprawling for their
taste. They dislike intensely its noisy streets, traffic-jams and the
crowds of self-preoccupied, ill-mannered people who seem to
be always in a hurry. All this haste, to the southerner, appears
fairly pointless and actually uncivilized.

I have often been amused by the sharp contrast between
moments of repose and frantic activity such as one finds in the
Rhôneland. At Les Saintes-Maries in the Camargue, I once saw a
warning notice painted in large red letters on someone's
garage-door. The notice read: *Sorties – fréquentes et urgentes!* The
garage was in a quiet lane which was hardly ever used and I
doubt that the garage exit was blocked more than once or twice a
year by parked cars. What its owner was really saying was this:
when I want to use my car, you had better get out of the way and
be quick about it! This has much to do with the southern pace of
life in general. In a sandwich-bar or an *épicerie*, the assistant will
deal with your request for food as though his or her life
depended on it. Bread will be sliced, spread with butter and
filled with cold meat or cheese and thrust into your hands at
lightning speed. But the instant the transaction is complete and

you have pocketed your change, the shopkeeper relaxes and, assuming there is no one waiting to be served, is now quite happy to spend five or ten minutes chatting as though he had all the time in the world at his disposal.

People in a restaurant or a café who have devoted an hour or two to lunch make a rush for their cars, or leap astride a motorcycle and drive off at terrific speed to the office or their house which, if it is not quite next-door, is at most a few streets away.

In this way, the simplest and the most difficult tasks are soon accomplished and the maximum amount of time is left for the real business of life, such as conversation and the enjoyment of good food and wine. In Arles, I often heard people having a laugh at their own expense, remarking that here they worked for about three months a year, while the remaining nine months were spent *en travaux* – that is to say, thinking about work. While this is an exaggeration made in jest, it makes a neat distinction which in some ways may not be so far off the mark.

None of this is exclusive to Provence. You will find the same contrasts in Spain or Italy when you compare the pace of Madrid and Rome with life in the wilds of Estramadura or Calabria.

The southern lifestyle, as much as the wonderful attractions of strong sunlight and the Mediterranean scenery, has tempted generations of writers and artists who have come there in search of peace of mind, as well as exotic subjects. It is easy to see why this is so. Art and poetry are fundamentals of the Rhôneland. In our own day even, as much as in the past, artists and writers generally are appreciated here – unlike, for example, England where they are still regarded, sometimes quite openly, with misgivings. Whereas in England they say, he or she is an artist – humph! and mean artists are no better than the rest of us, in Provence they say, he's an artist – of course he is different and isn't that wonderful! If this sounds naïve to the point of absurdity, nevertheless I am convinced that it really is the case and, as the preceding long list of acknowledgements may suggest, I have found it proved again and again by personal experience, and the experiences of many others besides.

I

Night-train to Provence

Somewhere between Montélimar and Orange, shortly before daybreak, the overnight train from Calais ran into a belt of thick fog. In some places the visibility had been reduced to less than 50 metres. Except for a station signboard, a blurred flash of dimly illuminated lettering which my drowsy senses barely registered, there was nothing to indicate that we had arrived in Provence.

From my carriage window, I had only the vaguest impression of night slowly giving way to dawn. For several kilometres the railway tracks ran parallel to a stretch of country road. As the daylight increased, I made out the smokey-blue silhouette of some houses, ghostly images which sailed past in a gently undulating, wavelike motion, rapidly fading, and disappeared into the gloom.

I had decided to travel to Provence by the night-train purely and simply as a matter of convenience. There was no doubting that the night-journey had an appeal of its own – not least the pleasant surprise of waking up to find oneself in entirely different surroundings. Even the swathes of early morning mist had an eerie sort of charm. And yet, I missed the thrill of the changing countryside in broad daylight, the blue sky and the sunshine and the glorious Mediterranean landscapes flashing by.

It occurred to me that, had I travelled south by the afternoon TGV Express, I should have noticed the light as it intensified and became suddenly much brighter. As the light changed, so did the landscape. Where there had been wide-spreading fields with oaks and elms, there were instead pines and poplars and hedges of elegant cypress. By Valence, these changes became very obvious. The wild, tawny colour of the soil, the fields of sunlit vines, olive-trees and almonds, the farmhouses with crinkled red-tile roofs and the fantastic outcrops of bleached white rocks, told the instant you had crossed the northern frontier of Provence.

All things considered, I think it was the sudden boost to the city-dweller's jaded spirits given by the strong southern sunlight that made the greatest difference of all – especially to those of us accustomed to the weaker effect of the sun diffused by the polluted atmosphere of big cities such as Paris or London. Certainly it had been the poet Roy Campbell's desperate craving for 'clear pagan sunlight' which first drew him to Provence in the early 'twenties. Encouraged by his friend, Augustus John, Campbell came and savoured it. He lived in Provence for some years, working as a fisherman at Martigues, and a herdsman or *gardian* in the Camargue. He learned to speak the difficult *langue d'oc*, the lilting Provençal tongue, which enabled him to read the poetry of Mistral, Baroncelli-Javon and D'Arbaud, men of genius whose work – Mistral's excepted – is still hardly known outside the region.

A close friend of Roy Campbell introduced me, somewhat indirectly, to the world of these Rhôneland writers and artists, more than twenty-five years ago. Although I did not visit Provence for a long time afterwards, when I did go there eventually, I was, like Campbell, immediately smitten. The lives of the poets and artists fascinated me as much as the magnificent country where they lived and found their inspiration to write and paint. I resolved that one day, when I had enough time at my disposal, I would return to the Pays d'Arles and the Camargue – the country of bulls and rushing waves which I call the Rhôneland – and go in search of the poets, the painters and their wind-blasted, sun-drenched landscapes: Mistral, Baroncelli, D'Arbaud, Lelée, Pranishnikoff and others better known such as Daudet, Van Gogh and Cézanne.

My thoughts were rudely interrupted by the night-steward who rapped loudly at the compartment door and announced that in a few minutes the train would be arriving at Avignon. The noise woke the compartment's only other passenger, in the bunk above mine, a young French Air Force doctor who had joined the train at Amiens and was on his way to a radar base at Rocquebrune, close to Nice.

The previous evening, before turning in, the doctor and I had sat up talking for an hour and I had been somewhat taken aback to discover that he did not share my enthusiasm for Provence. Quite the opposite, in fact. He accepted rather grudgingly my liking for Arles and its surroundings; but he seemed truly aghast and astonished by my fascination for the Camargue. He gulped, adjusted his spectacles and straightaway began a heated, lengthy comparison between the North and South of France, a theme which, I soon gathered, he had expounded a good many times before.

Shading his eyes dramatically with the flat of his hand, the young doctor waxed rhetorical. (I ought to add, by the way, that he spoke to me in French and what follows is my rather inadequate effort at conveying the *profondeur* of his passionately-held convictions in English).

'In the South,' he exclaimed, 'I look out from my window and what do I see? Nothing but the blue waves, the blue sky and the palm-trees. *Quel ennui!* Moreover, it is the same every day. Always the blue sky and the sunshine. Always the little blue waves, so flat and lifeless. I feel sure that your Camargue must be like that. I love the wild sea of Brittany much better, when the tempest blows and she becomes like an angry lady!'

While the climates of Brittany and Provence really could not be compared, I admitted there was some similarity, however tenuous it might seem, between the wild waves of Biscay and the spate which gives La Rouanesse its name. Quoting my sturdy ally, Roy Campbell, I told the doctor that 'Rouan' was the river Rhône in Provençal. The word also signified a bull. In his now scarce monograph on *Taurine Provence*, published in 1932, Campbell noted that ' "Rouan" [is] a fighting bull in its prime: or figuratively, a wave that hurls itself forward. . . . There is much in common between the impetuous character of this headlong tawny river and the bulls of the Crau and the Camargue.'

The doctor graciously acknowledged these observations, but stuck firmly to his guns – and so did I. In the end, following the late Prime Minister Nehru's wise example, we agreed to disagree since, after all, the doctor like myself was perfectly entitled to his own opinion. But now the night's debate was forgotten in a flurry of polite farewells, as the doctor wished me a safe journey, pulled the blankets back over his head and rolled over in his bunk, determined to blot out the awful prospect of autumn on the Riviera with pleasanter dreams of his beloved Brittany coast lashed by the gales.

I shook my head, thinking of his world-weary bedtime lecture, as I stared out at Avignon's fog-bound suburbs, the hazy street-lights and the huge spectral forms of the modern apartment-blocks, factories and warehouses by the trackside.

But then, it was October – what the shopkeepers and hoteliers here called the *morte saison*, the season of falling leaves and falling-off trade, of migrating birds and departing tourists.

★

At Avignon, I found the station cafeteria at 6.30 am crowded with a scruffy assortment of young men and girls, a very catholic mixture of French, Moroccans and West Africans, lounging at the tables or stretched out full-length, fast asleep on the rexine-covered benches, under the hard neon light. Some of these youngsters looked deathly pale and drawn and their dilated pupils suggested that they might be users of drugs. These were Avignon's *demi-monde*, the out-of-work or shiftless nomads of the city's twilight zone with whom the tourists rarely came in contact. No effort had been made by the cafeteria's waiters to swab the dirty linoleum which lay awash with coffee-dregs and spilled beer and was littered with discarded cellophane wrappers and empty cigarette packets.

I decided to forego the cup of coffee I'd promised myself earlier and instead I crossed the dark forecourt and walked up the avenue Jean-Jaurès into the rue de la République in search of an hotel. The fog exhaled the damp musty smell of a long-disused attic and, with it, came a fine drizzle of rain which, to my great relief, did not last long. The bed-and-breakfast tariffs posted by the hotels along the main street were mostly far above the limit of my fairly restricted budget. But in due course, after tramping for an hour, I reached a pretty little *pension* in the rue Joseph-Vernet, with green louvred-shutters and pink geraniums in tubs by the entrance, where I was offered a modestly-priced room on the ground floor off a small courtyard at the rear.

I washed and shaved, unpacked my suitcase and then went upstairs to a first-floor foyer where a plump, fairhaired girl in ripped jeans served me with breakfast – bread and strawberry-jam, a tumbler of orange-juice and a pot of strong black coffee.

By about 9 o'clock, the fog had cleared and the sun shone from a cloudless blue sky.

I left the hotel and retraced my steps as far as the rue Saint-Agricol, off the place de l'Horloge which in Roman times had been Avignon's forum and now lies at the heart of the old city, inside the ramparts, close to the Palais des Papes. Inspired by the sunshine and mild air, restored by a good breakfast, I began to pay more attention to my surroundings. In the rue Joseph-Vernet, I made a note of a fine eighteenth-century wrought-iron gate which seemed worth sketching; at the foot of the rue Saint-Agricol, a burly greengrocer in a straw-boater setting up his displays of cabbages, fat white leeks and tomatoes; a trellis of scaffolding which cast its fretwork of shadow against the yellow-grey stones of Saint-Agricol's Church. I marked them all down as likely subjects, not forgetting the Librairie Roumanille, across the way, Avignon's most famous book-shop whose street-frontage and gilded signs have remained unaltered since the poet, Joseph Roumanille, established it 150 years ago.

The son of a market-gardener from Saint-Rémy-de-Provence, Roumanille together with Frédéric Mistral had been one of the original founders, in May 1854, of the celebrated society of Provençal poets and writers known as the Félibrige. The Librairie Roumanille had been a publishing house as well as a booksellers in those days. Now it was a veritable Aladdin's Cave for anyone interested in the history, literature and traditions of Provence. The shelves were lined with modern paperback editions of Roumanille's poetry, besides Mistral's and works by other less familiar writers such as Folco de Baroncelli-Javon, Théodore Aubanel and Joseph D'Arbaud, few of whose books are available in English translation. There were lavishly illustrated books on the Provençal landscape, architecture, bullfights and costumes. In a small room, a kind of inner *sanctum* at the back of the shop, were kept a number of first editions, many of them in sumptuously decorated leather bindings. In France, generally speaking, books tend to be expensive; and I noticed that even a quite modest paperback cost almost as much as a substantial hard-cover biography would in England.

I prowled about in the Librairie Roumanille for the better part of an hour, enjoying myself thoroughly. It was charming, and indeed typical, to find the owner's own affairs overlapping those of the shop. As a gesture to the computer age the owner,

Monsieur Siaud, went about the shop carrying a mobile telephone: but when he either made or received a call he invariably sat at his desk using the mobile like an ordinary handset. Madame Siaud, permed and very *chic* in a pair of short, flared, Black Watch-tartan culottes, had been writing down the details of my order, when suddenly she broke off to introduce me to her handyman, 'a treasure', who happened to poke his head round the door saying he had finished draining-down the central-heating system in the Siauds' apartment. Madame Siaud excused herself for a few moments while she dealt with the handyman. Meanwhile her secretary, Natasha, an eager young woman who blushed constantly and wriggled her toes, wrote my order on a slip of yellow paper. I was anxious to obtain a copy of *Folco de Baroncelli*, a biography of the Marquis by the late Henriette Dibon. I should have liked to meet Madame Dibon, whose *félibre* nickname 'Farfantello' means 'mirage', before she died at Avignon in 1984. Her discursive portrait of Folco, littered with anecdotes, had been based on their long friendship and, although uncritical, it provided a major source of information about this greatest of the Camargue's heroes. As recently as 1975 Folco was dismissed by one English writer as 'an eccentric in a lovable amateur fashion; an interesting man about whom there is little known'. The book was long out of print and would take time to find, but Natasha, blushing to the roots of her hair, assured me that if it hadn't arrived by the time I had to return to London, I would without doubt receive it before Christmas.

As it turned out, I left Avignon without it, nearly two months later. But Natasha had been as good as her word and a beautiful copy of *Folco de Baroncelli* was delivered to my flat by parcel post, on 22 December.

The Home of the Baroncellis

Roumanille's bookshop is only five minutes' walk from one of the most fascinating, though I suspect least well known buildings in Avignon, the Palais du Roure. Every year, hundreds of thousands of tourists flock to the vast imposing Palais des Papes and linger by the remains of Saint-Bénézet's famous bridge which the catchy lyric '*Sous le pont d'Avignon*' has immortalized. The visitors congregate at the many open-air café-restaurants surrounding the noble place de l'Horloge, all of which are close by. Yet a mere handful have heard of the Palais du Roure, hidden away in a sunless cobbled side-street behind the tiny place Louis Le Cardonnel, off the rue de la République.

After leaving the Librairie Roumanille, I spent the rest of the morning, and a good part of the afternoon, at the Roure where its Secretary-Archivist, Madame Sabine Barnicaud, guided me through the extensively-refurbished apartments, brought me up to date with items of local news and arranged a meeting with her predecessor, my old friend Madame Mireille Bosqui, the following afternoon.

Until 1909, when it was purchased by a constuction company, the Société Immobilière de Vaucluse, the Palais du Roure had been the ancestral home of the Baroncellis, Florentine aristocrats whose links with Avignon extended back to the beginning of the fourteenth century. Before the Great Schism in 1376, while Avignon remained the capital city of Christendom, Jehan de Baroncelli had served as a Serjeant-at-Arms under Pope Gregory XI. The former Hôtel de Baroncelli, known originally as the Taverne de L'Amourié, or Mulberry Tavern, was bought in 1469 by Pierre de Baroncelli, a merchant-banker, from his father-in-law, Alaman de Passis. The inventory of sale described the Tavern's layout on three floors around a galleried courtyard. The great hall, sparsely furnished with a dresser, two tressle-tables, some benches and a candelabra, led to seven bedrooms; the second-floor attics were used for storage. Pierre later acquired two adjacent properties and converted all three into a single dwelling. Much of this work was merely cosmetic and included the carved masonry porch, a series of stained-glass windows and a splendid beamed ceiling over the hall with coats of arms painted in green, gold and red. Since then, the Roure's austere Gothic north façade has remained substantially un-altered.

For years historians have disagreed over the meaning of the *bas-relief* of entwined branches sculpted in stone above the main entrance. It was once thought they represented oak, the family emblem of Cardinal Giuliano della Rovere – a friend of Michelangelo – who became Pope Julius II and built the nearby Collège du Roure in 1476. But it is now generally accepted that they were meant to represent mulberry, the symbol of the ancient Tavern. The Baroncelli arms can be seen in the vestibule and again, in red and white cobble-stones, in the street by the doorway.

During the seventeenth century the courtyard galleries were partly walled in and one of the original staircases was replaced by a fine Louis XIV stair with a wrought-iron balustrade leading from the entrance-hall to the first-floor salons, including the Salon des Batailles which the artist, Joseph-François Parroçel decorated in 1760. Finding the Salon des Batailles too sombre, a Baroncelli of the *ancien régime*, Alexandre-Joseph-Félicien, en-hanced the room with lavish gilding, scarlet panels and mirrors, after which it became known as the Salon Rouge. The Roure

survived the French Revolution and suffered none of the damage inflicted on the Palais des Papes by the military. Only its gardens were later destroyed to make way for a new road. But the Société Immobilière de Vaucluse inexplicably vandalized the house in 1909, tore out the eighteenth-century panelling and sold Parroçel's fine military paintings.

The present-day condition of the Palais du Roure and the formation of its unique archives, owed much to its last private owner, Jeanne de Flandreysy-Espérandieu, who rescued the house in 1918. She restored it and gave Folco de Baroncelli-Javon and his family a life tenancy of the remodelled second-floor apartments, where they continued to live at intervals until the Second World War.

It had been Folco de Baroncelli's daughter, Riquette, who first introduced me to the Roure and its rich, diverse collections of Provençal literature, archaeology and paintings. Folco, the last Baroncelli to occupy the Roure, captured my imagination and fired my interest in the traditional life of the region, mainly through the stories told to me by Riquette and her husband, the *manadier* Henri Aubanel. Folco de Baroncelli had been a poet and a close friend and collaborator of Frédéric Mistral, who led the mid-nineteenth-century renaissance of Provençal language, literature and traditions and in 1904 was awarded the Nobel Prize. Baroncelli had combined his gift for poetry with an active life, involving much hardship, as a breeder of Camargue fighting-bulls. His lifelong obsession with bulls and his passionate love for the Camargue in turn inspired his writing. He became an excellent horseman, stylish and fearless, with many feats of horsemanship to his credit, including a 280-mile ride on his bull-horse Sultan, from Les Saintes-Maries to Lyon and back in 1905.

Marie-Lucien-Gabriel-Folco de Baroncelli, the future Marquis of Javon, was born at Aix-en-Provence on 1 November 1869, the eldest of Raymond de Baroncelli and Henriette de Chazelles-Lunac's nine children. Folco's name as I have given it here is the correct version; but he was also known throughout the Rhôneland and the Camargue as Folco Baroncelli, Baroncelli-Javon, the Marquis de Baroncelli or simply as *lou marquès*. His first sight of the Camargue and its bulls, when he was five, was of seven *cocarde*-bulls, destined for Bouillargues, which the *gardians* had driven into a corral at Bellecote. The bulls and *gardians* as they galloped past was a spectacle which Folco never forgot.

After spending almost a decade as the editor of Frédéric Mistral's journal *L'Aiöli*, with Mistral's blessing, Folco devoted the remainder of his life to the Camargue where he continued to write poetry and breed fine bulls for the Course Camarguaise. In February 1895, he married Henriette Gabrielle Constantin and on 30 July 1899 the young couple came to live at the Mas du Marais, about 2 kilometres to the west of Les Saintes-Maries. Folco changed the name of the *mas* to L'Amarée, after a variety of plum-tree, the *prunier Sainte-Lucie* which is quite common in the neighbourhood. Some writers have described L'Amarée as a 'miserable *cabane*'; in fact it was a large two-storeyed house with a tiled roof and white-washed walls, with a clump of tamarisks and a *cabane* nearby, in a fine wild marshland setting. The interior of the house was well furnished, with pictures and rich

drapery and the room where Folco wrote was carpeted and had
an impressive ceiling of exposed beams. Folco had wished for a
son and dreamt of christening him Pierre, after the founder of
the Palais du Roure. Instead Henriette bore him three daughters,
the youngest of whom, Riquette, was born in March 1908.

Folco immersed himself in the world of the Camargue bulls
and *gardians*, acquired and perfected the many skills necessary to
a ranching life and adapted easily to the delta's hardships. His
young, sophisticated, town-bred wife, whose family fortune
derived partly from the Chateauneuf-des-Papes vineyards, did
not share his enthusiasm. Quite the reverse. In 1984, Riquette
Aubanel told me: 'My poor mother felt that she had sacrificed
herself to the Camargue and, indeed, for such a young girl with
her background, used to comfort and servants and society, the
early years at L'Amarée must have been hard and lonely. Papa
lived just like his *gardians*. He was away in the marshes from
daybreak until nightfall and, when he got home, he would spend
his evenings writing up L'Amarée's stock-records, or else
working on one of his books. My mother felt increasingly
isolated. If she often hankered after Paris and Avignon this was
surely understandable. Papa from time to time, had money
worries. Mama had not been accustomed to this. At L'Amarée,
she felt like a prisoner and this made her sad.' Photographs of
Henriette showed this sadness reflected in her eyes and her
sombre expression. The strains imposed by the life inevitably
affected her marriage and may have encouraged Folco to seek
solace and companionship elsewhere – notably in his friendship
with Jeanne de Flandreysy whose passion for the Camargue
matched his own.

The L'Amarée *manade* gradually prospered and its great
cocarde-bulls won an enviable reputation for their fierceness and
beauty. In 1905, Folco's herd comprised three *dompteurs* (master
bulls), sixteen *grands taureaux*, nineteen young bulls varying in
age from two to six years and fifty-six cows. Besides the bulls he
had some excellent horses, and the long silvery tail-hairs of one
stallion were used to string a bow belonging to a celebrated
concert-violinist in Paris. I find the idea of beautiful music

coming from the streaming tail of a Camargue horse thrilling and enchanting, a uniquely appropriate accompaniment to the poetry which Baroncelli-Javon created and pondered during his lonely rides across the windswept deserts of dry mud and *sansouires*.

In the autumn of 1931, at midnight in a storm of wind and driving rain, Baroncelli-Javon left the Mas de L'Amarée and brought his furniture and possessions in a cattle-waggon to Le Simbèu, the *mas* he had built near the shore. There he continued to live, almost until he died, between visits to the Roure where he ended his days.

Folco had been an inspiration to his contemporaries and was revered and respected even by those who considered him eccentric and perhaps a little fey. Among those who fell under the Marquis' spell were Henri Aubanel, who became his son-in-law, and Folco's distant cousin, the *manadier* and writer, Joseph D'Arbaud. Both men won literary distinction. Among the modern generation of Camargue authors, including older writers who are still alive, Aubanel's *Camarguaises: un gardian en hiver* remains an outstanding achievement. Although D'Arbaud's attainments as a *manadier* never equalled those of Baroncelli-Javon – in part due to D'Arbaud's lack of commitment and ill-health which dogged him for much of his life – as a poet and a novelist he was the greater. D'Arbaud's literary reputation rested mainly on two prose works, *La Bête du Vaccarès* (1926) and *La Sauvagine* published in 1929.

In *La Bête du Vaccarès*, D'Arbaud described the strange, symbolic encounter between a fifteenth-century *gardian* and the half-human beast he finds lurking in the depths of a primeval woodland, the Bois des Rièges, in the Etang de Vaccarès near Les Saintes-Maries. The world-weary creature tells the *gardian* of its search for peace, far from the domain of cruel men who dominated and destroyed the wilderness and its inhabitants. D'Arbaud's tale foretold with uncanny accuracy the fate which was destined to overshadow the Camargue of our own day and, indeed, countries much further afield where the wholesale destruction of rain-forests now poses a threat to the planet's very survival. The *Sauvagine* was a prose hymn which celebrated the Camargue's wild creatures. Both these works were written originally in Provençal and D'Arbaud was hailed as one of Mistral's greatest disciples, whose creative use of the language nearly matched the virtuoso performances of the master himself. In some ways, Joseph D'Arbaud's life was a sad one. Born at Méyrargues in 1874, he had followed Folco's example and set up as a bull-breeder, except that the bulls he raised were bred not for the Course but the *corrida*. D'Arbaud suffered from tuberculosis, a disease which forced him eventually to leave the damp Camargue climate for drier, healthier parts. He died in agony in March 1950, bed-ridden, unable to urinate. Even in his greatest moments of suffering, he could joke, saying, 'The man who can pass water doesn't know his good-luck!' And in a brief prayer he begged God to pity him, without resentment or loss of faith, asking only that his pain might be made a little easier to bear.

Riquette Aubanel loaned me several of her father's books, which I found again, here at the Palais du Roure. There was a novella, *Babali* (1890), the tale of a gipsy laundry maid, with a glowing preface by Mistral, illustrated by Ivan Pranishnikoff and Terissère de Valdrome; stories of papal Avignon, *Sous la tiaré d'Avignon* (1935); and a collection of Folco's poems and three songs, *Blad de luno* ('Moon-Wheat'), published in 1910, which he had dedicated to his fervent admirer, patron and *altesse*, Jeanne de Flandreysy, in the flowery troubadour language of the Félibrige: 'O Madame Jeanne! O exquisite pearl of goodness. . . . Sometimes you will see my verse dyed with blood: it is the image of the burning dream of my ancestors – even, alas! that of my heart, a pitiable field of carnage.'

These heady sentiments remind me of the tearful farewell speech delivered to an English lady, a confirmed spinster, by her cook when she left India. Handing her a bunch of roses he wailed: '*Memsahib*! Moon-faced pearl of chastity! In time these blooms will wither and die but you will smell forever!'

In Folco's case, the dedication might have been the epitaph for his clandestine, passionate affair with Jeanne de Flandreysy which his marriage nevertheless survived. Complex, intelligent and strikingly beautiful, Jeanne possessed an air of mystery and a passion for Provençal poetry and tradition which nearly equalled that of Mistral. She and Folco remained devoted companions and Jeanne was a frequent visitor at L'Amarée. She captivated everyone who knew her. Her background had been conventionally bourgeois and eminently respectable. Born at Valence on 11 July 1874, Jeanne was the elder daughter of Marie-Louise Ladreyt, an 'admirable, simple-hearted, loving' woman, and Etienne Mellier, *'un homme robuste'*, a mountaineer and amateur archaeologist who contributed articles to the *Journal de Valence*, the *Revue Dauphinoise* and the *Bulletin du Club Alpin*. Together, Etienne Mellier and Jeanne published a series of scholarly, yet very readable works between 1906 and 1917, among them studies of Marseille's artists, a book on Provençal costumes and the magnificent *Livre d'or de la Camargue*. It was with her father's help that Jeanne eventually bought the Palais du Roure for 110,000 francs and undertook its restoration.

Jeanne married twice, it appears: first in 1899 to a Scottish nobleman, who died aged thirty-eight soon after the wedding; and in 1936 to Emile Espérandieu, a distinguished member of the Institut de France, who was by then well up in years and died in 1939. Throughout her life Jeanne refused to divulge more than a few scant details about her first husband, which has led many people to believe that he never actually existed. According to Jeanne, he was Comte Aymar de Flandreysy, who owned a house called Les Glycines near the village of Oywesters, on the east coast of Scotland. That Jeanne had visited Scotland was proved by a letter which she wrote to her parents from Edinburgh in April 1899. But no one has managed to trace any records of her alleged husband or his family, or the Wysteria House, or the village whose name sounds like a variety of shellfish. I have consulted a number of genealogical directories without success, including the definitive 1,600-page *Titled Nobility of Europe* compiled in 1914 by the Marquis of Ruvigny. There is no record of a Papal title by that name; and it seems likely that the Count de Flandreysy and Jeanne's hasty marriage, were figments of her imagination.

She returned to France, a widow, alleging that her husband had drowned in a storm somewhere between the Firth of Forth and the French coast. She even went so far as to arrange a memorial service for him. But, when a priest demanded quite reasonably to be shown the Count's death certificate and at the same time asked whether he had been baptised, Jeanne retorted angrily: 'My poor husband has been baptised in the ocean! Surely that will satisfy you!'

Assuming she *did* simply invent Comte de Flandreysy as the evidence suggests, it is hard to explain why Jeanne should have gone to such extravagant lengths. Jeanne's parents seem to have taken her 'marriage' and its consequences in their stride. She continued to use her married name; and instead of causing a scandal, the story and its farcical postscript won Jeanne a measure of harmless notoriety. Perhaps after all, it had been the limelight she sought – that, and the fun of keeping her friends guessing. Besides, in Provence at the turn of the century, as a married woman or a widow, she gained a measure of independence and freedom. If indeed these were Jeanne's motives, the Scottish escapade was not entirely pointless.

Jeanne de Flandreysy's lifetime of dedicated labour establishing the Roure's collections of Dante, Petrarch and, above all, Mistral was recognized by the award of a Légion d'Honneur in 1953. She died on 15 May 1959 in her eighty-fifth year, an enigmatic figure to the end, and the mysteries surrounding aspects of her life, such as her first marriage and the intimate details of her affair with Folco de Baroncelli, died with her. These were touched upon, but never fully explained by her biographer, Christian Chabanis (Guy Chambelland) in his lengthy if somewhat ineffectual *Jeanne de Flandreysy: ou la passion de la gloire*, despite the promise of the book's apt and revealing title. A perceptive American traveller, Amy Oakley, who interviewed Jeanne in 1935, described her as a 'radiant lady . . . with enticing wiles' in a 'little black hat . . . pulled low on her forehead, shading strange unfathomable eyes'. Jeanne's beguiling charm still cast a spell, but even by then Mrs Oakley sensed that her youthful fire had begun to wane, for Jeanne had sighed and said 'I am world-weary, weary' as though her battles had been fought and she had little left worth living for.

A discreet doorway from the conservator's office led to the attic stairs through a large, shuttered room – like a rather splendid interior garage – containing the Graveson diligence. The beautiful old coach was very like one immortalized by Daudet's story, 'The Beaucaire Stage-Coach', in *Lettres de mon moulin* ('Letters from my Windmill'). It had been installed there by Jeanne de Flandreysy, hauled up from the courtyard by means of ropes and pulleys; and I believe that part of the Palais du Roure's roof had to be dismantled in the process.

In the low-ceilinged attic rooms which Baroncelli occupied between 1918 and 1943, I was shown the Marquis' little iron bedstead on which lay, neatly folded, the pale-blue silk shirt with its pleated front he had been wearing when he died on 15 December 1943. Earlier that year, he had worn the shirt 'in honour of the Virgin, at an *abrivado* at Uchaud'. Riquette Aubanel had presented the shirt to Madame Dibon, who in turn gave it to Jeanne de Flandreysy for safekeeping. Folco's riding saddle hung on a stout wooden frame, complete with its pouches, stirrups and his initials, 'F.B.', worked in round-headed pins behind the cantle. The basket-stirrups of wrought-iron barely fitted my heavy walking-shoes. What slender feet the Marquis had! – when you realize that he often wore the cumbersome wooden *sabots* attached to thigh-length leather waders which protected the *gardian*'s feet and legs when herding bulls in the marshes. His leather saddle-bag was embellished by designs of finely sewn beadwork: a horse's head and the head of a bull; a trident with its iron prongs shaped like a crescent-moon; the Baroncelli arms; the seven-pointed star of the Félibrige; and, below the star, the legendary mastless boat which it is said carried the Holy Marys to Les Saintes-Maries-de-la-Mer. I saw Folco's branding-iron, used at the *ferrades*, with the Baroncelli shield of a simple diagonal pattern. There was a rough horsehair *seden*, a *gardian*'s lazo plaited in strands of dark grey, cinnamon and white; and a collection of Red Indian beaded bangles, given to Folco by a Sioux chieftain, White Cloud, with flowers delicately woven in blue, white, green, orange, red and yellow. The Sioux named Folco Zind-Kala-Wasté, which translates as 'Faithful Bird'.

My patient, informative guide, Madame Barnicaud, led me past the large numbers of old photographs, oil-paintings and watercolours which lined the passages and filled the rooms. All these amounted to little more than a handful of the Roure's extraordinary treasures. In the chapel, preserved in urns, were the hearts of Folco de Baroncelli and the poet-priest, Louis Le Cardonnel; in the courtyard and around the staircase, some of Jeanne de Flandreysy's fascinating collection of 150 bells of all shapes and sizes, a few of which dated as far back as Dante; and, somewhat unexpected, John Stuart Mill's piano. John and Harriet Mill had visited Avignon together in 1858. After Harriet's sudden death, Mill continued to live here until 1873 when he, too, died and his superb collection of books unfortunately was sold later at the Librairie Roumanille. It seems strange that a man as meticulous as John Stuart Mill should have been remembered by his neighbours as 'untidy'; but I discovered that this was due to his mania for horticulture. His gardens at the Villa Stuart Mill (which, Mrs Oakley remarked, 'the French pronounce so funnily') became so overgrown by the exotic specimens he had planted that they were frowned upon by the Avignonais who condemned the wildly proliferating trees and shrubs as an eyesore.

That evening, after a light supper of fried meat, bread and coffee, I returned to my hotel where I slept badly. The hotel-keeper had assured me that my room was not only cheap but exceedingly 'quiet'. In fact, it was next-door to the boiler-house whose machinery roared into life at regular intervals, all night long. To make matters worse, the hotel's watchdog, a Great Dane, padded up and down the courtyard until well past midnight and his dismal howls, added to a security-light flashing at my window and the gurgling deluge of overhead plumbing, kept me awake until the small hours.

The hotel-keeper's idea of what constitutes quiet was perhaps better suited to the African jungle than a back-street *pension* at Avignon. Even at breakfast, it seemed, there was no respite and I ate my *demi-baguette* and regulation strawberry jam to a chorus of piercing whistles emitted by a pair of yellow canaries – *'jolis oiseaux'*, the waitress informed me, rather unnecessarily, *'qui ne parlent jamais, mais sifflent sans cesse'*.

The canaries were much admired by a couple at an adjoining table. They hailed from Aberdeenshire and had come to Avignon on a flying visit after a hectic week's sightseeing in Paris. Andrew, very tall, thin and soft-spoken, was a French teacher in his late forties. His wife, Ellen, in a fluffy grey-angora jumper and ski-slacks, did most of the talking. 'I was terrified just asking for directions in Paris,' said Ellen. 'You never knew who you might be talking to. We prefer Avignon. It's slower, more like it is at home, and here you find people who are – well, more like yourself.' Ellen shrank back in disbelief when I mentioned the drug-addicts I had seen at the railway station. But, not wishing to spoil her impression of what Baroncelli used to call 'delicious Avignon', I added hastily: 'In Petrarch's day, in the fourteenth century, Avignon really did have a bad reputation. The outskirts were infested by highwaymen and Petrarch called the city an "impious Babylon, a cesspool of vice, and the sewer of the earth".' This seemed a far cry from the Avignon of today and I did my best to reassure Ellen that, like most towns and cities in Provence, with the exception of Marseille, Avignon was comparatively free of serious crime.

Avignon's checkered past had been a weighty subject for the breakfast-table, however, and Andrew and Ellen seemed relieved when we were joined by a youngster in a green T-shirt, a trainee market-gardener from Toulon, whose hawkish nose and mop of black curly hair looked uncannily medieval. In a tunic and hose, with a falcon at his wrist, the lad easily might have passed for a contemporary of Petrarch.

He told us that he had been on a walking tour of the Southwest and he gave us some marvellous descriptions of the Roussillon's densely wooded valleys where he had tramped for a fortnight, living on a spartan diet of goat's cheese, peaches and bread. This choice of frugal fare made him a worthy disciple of a seventeenth-century provost of Digne cathedral, Pierre Gassendi, a precursor of the science of atomic physics, who wrote an essay entitled, '*L'homme est destiné à ne manger que du fruit*' (Man is destined to eat nothing but fruit!). Here was living proof of Gassendi's wisdom for, compared to the gaunt wretches I'd seen at the station cafeteria the previous day, the young market-gardener with his sunburned face and arms looked a picture of health.

After breakfast, I strolled down to the station, where I checked the train times for Arles and enquired about the Arles hotels. The girl at the desk was a language student and, at her request, to give her a little extra practice, I spoke in English. Much to my amusement, an American lady in an ankle-length musquash coat and sun-glasses, standing behind me in the queue, tapped my shoulder and gushingly complimented me on my 'English pronunciation'. Taken slightly by surprise, for a moment I wondered if she had mistaken me for an English-speaking Avignonais. But no – of course she hadn't. She beamed: 'In Texas, where I come from, you just never hear English spoken the way you do. My God, you sound exactly like Prince Charles! I just wanna say "hello" and shake you by the hand. And, believe me, I hope that you'll keep right on talking in that *delightful* old-world accent of yours!' I thought it better not to confuse the lady by telling her that I was a Scot, born and bred, and so I accepted her well-intentioned remarks without further comment.

By the time it occurred to me to look for a *charcuterie* where I might buy a slice or two of cold ham or sausage for lunch, most of the shops off the rue de la République had already closed. Even my faithful standby from previous visits, the Co-op near the place de l'Horloge, was *en travaux*, with its roller-shutters firmly bolted and a decorator's van parked by the door. However, a fresh-faced woman with flaming red hair and red rubber gloves from the florist's opposite the Co-op insisted on escorting me to an *épicerie*, which sounded hopeful but actually turned out to be an open-air foodstall thronged with university students buying wildly over-priced salad-filled *baguettes* and piping-hot *croque-monsieurs* spread with melted cheese.

I munched my expensive, rather tasteless snack-lunch in the place l'Horloge, sitting in a patch of warm sunshine near the gaily-painted Carousel. Then I meandered back to the Palais du Roure where I explored the courtyard's fountains, statuettes and inscriptions and after that pored over the poetry books in the library's grey-painted *armoires* until Madame Bosqui arrived, as usual punctually, at three.

Bustling, freckled and grinning broadly, wrapped in a fringed woollen shawl, with her age-defying auburn tresses swept up loosely into a bun, she exuded energy and enthusiasm. Madame Bosqui as usual wasted little time with small-talk. Her know-ledge of Frédéric Mistral, Folco de Baroncelli-Javon and the poets and writers of the Félibrige and the Camargue is almost unrivalled. After Mistral and Baroncelli perhaps her greatest favourite is Joseph D'Arbaud, who wrote such Camargue classics as *La Bête du Vaccarès* and *La Sauvagine*. She knows the Roure's collections by heart and now, even in semi-retirement, to her the Roure is like a second home. Riquette Aubanel put us in touch many years ago. I shall never forget, at the end of our first meeting, how Mireille Bosqui sang for me in her low-pitched husky voice, her eyes shining, snatches of Mistral's 'Coupo Santo', which is in effect the Provençal national anthem.

Madame Bosqui laughed when I reminded her of this. She clapped her hands and exclaimed: 'So, you have decided at last to write a book. This is wonderful! And if I've understood you correctly, it will be a journal of travels, a *chronique* as we say, in Mistral's Rhône landscapes and Baroncelli's Camargue. Of course, it's up to you to decide how you write about your experiences. We can't foresee what will happen along the way. But how to deal with the poets and artists is another matter.' Here Madame Bosqui, paused in contemplation, her hands folded on her lap. 'My suggestion would be: however much you may be tempted to follow paths which, to us, are facinating but really obscure, try to remember that only fragments of our poets' writing have been translated into English. The poets' names may not be familiar to English readers, let alone their poetry. Even the best French translations lose much of the beauty and the subtler nuances of the Provençal originals. Paintings like music in this sense do not require translation. Their language is international.'

Madame Bosqui smiled: 'You mustn't imagine that I am trying to dissuade you. The Rhôneland's writers and artists often led quite extraordinary lives. Jeanne de Flandreysy is a splendid example: a talented, deeply sensitive creature.' Madame Bosqui chuckled with impish delight: 'Yet Jeanne was the sort of woman who might be capable of strangling a hare with her bare hands!'

I listened as she sketched in a few sentences eloquent, perceptive word-portraits of Folco de Baroncelli and Frédéric Mistral. The Marquis' background, said Madame Bosqui, had been aristocratic and highly cultivated. Impractical, often short of money, a gifted poet and writer, Folco had lacked Mistral's staying power and his overmastering need to write. Baroncelli's turmoil of passion, acute depressions, anxiety and insatiable cravings for women's company had contrasted sharply with Mistral's 'harmonious' life at Maillane, which had been very orderly, intensely productive and free from financial cares.

Small-boned and slight of build, weatherbeaten and tremendously hardy, Baroncelli, with his Mediterranean charm and commanding Renaissance profile, had been sexually attractive to women. Mistral, on the other hand, won their admiration and affection. Mistral's placid temperament and controlled lifestyle were mirrored in his sensitive features, his statuesque bearing and his gentle manner. With his silk-bordered wideawake-hat tipped at a rakish angle and the white goatee beard and moustaches he affected in later life, Mistral bore a striking resemblance to Buffalo Bill Cody. A born leader with a natural talent for showmanship, Mistral allowed himself to be drawn, painted in oils and photographed; and his house at Maillane, between Avignon and Arles, had been filled with these portraits.

I reminded Madame Bosqui how, years ago, Riquette and

Henri Aubanel, somewhat to my surprise, had described Folco as 'charming, with an Italian temperament, and yet *un homme fermé*'.

She replied: 'I see that quite clearly, but I also suspect that you haven't grasped exactly what was meant. I don't believe that Baroncelli was in any way shy or even particularly secretive. He understood discretion, that goes without saying. And he was the sort of man who keeps his deepest feelings hidden. It's obvious from his poetry that he felt strong, sometimes overwhelming and painful emotions. But, like most poets, including Mistral, Baroncelli was absolutely sincere and he didn't wear his heart on his sleeve.'

Later on, in the evening, I accompanied Mireille Bosqui and her husband to a meeting of the Provençal Society held in the Roure, where Marcel Bosqui led the singing and afterwards gave an interesting talk about the region's winds and their Provençal names. Colourfully dressed in an open-neck vermilion shirt and a black leather jerkin, with drooping moustaches like Charlie Chan's, Marcel Bosqui and a companion played traditional Provençal airs on the flute and drum. Each of the players held the flute, or *galoubet*, in his left hand, and with his right hand, using a padded stick known as a *baguette*, beat the rhythm on a drum which was suspended from his shoulder by a cord. Monsieur Bosqui's partner had a small kettle-drum with a light, sharp *timbre*; while Monsieur Bosqui thumped away on a larger drum, the *tambourin*, which had a dark-walnut case, hooped with crimson bindings. I gathered from Madame Bosqui's whispered commentary that the red hoops were of medieval origin and represented the bloody streaks left by a drummer's fingers when he was fatally wounded in battle and his *tambourin* was torn from him by the enemy soldiers. The *tambourin* played by Marcel Bosqui was a very valuable instrument and had once belonged to Folco de Baroncelli.

The evening recital began with a lively jig, the *farandole*; and this was followed by some country music played in a rather plodding 'one-two-three' tempo. One of the tunes had a rhythm not unlike the samba. The wild fugitive strains of the flutes, the banging drums and the audience's lusty singing, the words of which I could not understand, together created a repetitious, hypnotic effect which after a while dulled my senses. It wasn't just the music: a lack of sleep, the change of air and the effort of concentrating on fairly difficult subjects such as Provençal poetry and literature discussed relentlessly for many hours in French, a language which I do not pretend to speak very fluently, had begun to catch up with me. But, just as I began to feel myself drifting away, the spell was broken by shouts of the 'Coupo Santo' which raised the roof; and then came a brisk, cheery song whose 'AAAHHH-OOOH-EEEH-OOOH!' chorus left the audience streaming-eyed with laughter. Second only to the 'Coupo Santo' on the Provençal hit-parade, this song was repeated immediately by popular request. This time I threw caution to the winds and joined in several loud choruses of 'AAHHH-OOOH-EEEH-OOOH!' to the merriment of my neighbours on either side, who congratulated me and said that I was, indeed, *un homme remarquable*.

During Marcel Bosqui's lecture on the Provençal winds, a theme which seemed very appropriate for a flute-player, I made some notes with the aid of Madame Bosqui. The North Wind was called the *vent tenan*; the West Wind was *lou granes*; the *levant*, logically enough, blew from the East, and from the South came the *marin*, also known as *lou gregar*. The most famous, or perhaps I should say notorious wind of all, the fierce *mistral*, or *mistrau*, was of course from the Northwest.

After the lecture, each member of the audience, except for myself, was asked to translate into French a sentence or two from Charles Galtier's story, 'Prince Charming'. Mireille and Marcel Bosqui tactfully steered some of the less confident readers through its trickier passages, a performance which demonstrated the couple's near-encyclopaedic knowledge of the Provençal tongue. But nevertheless a few of Galtier's expressions defeated everybody and these Marcel Bosqui officially pronounced as 'untranslatable'.

3

Settling in at Arles

The purpose of my journeys had been defined very accurately by Mireille Bosqui: any book that resulted should combine anecdotes and experiences of travel with my search for the writers and artists here in southwest Provence. I recalled John Elderfield's essay on Matisse's years in Morocco in which he wrote: 'Travel is an implicit quest for anomaly. . . . We travel in search of the strange and the wonderful and we try to remember the marvels we have seen.' For me, the challenge lay in writing a book which somehow managed to balance the episodic, free-wheeling diary of my travels with sketches of the writers' and painters' lives – and, without becoming too deeply involved with technical matters, in plain language too esoteric, try to weave a tapestry of travels and cameo-portraits which included images of Rhôneland Provence and the Camargue, past and present. While the life and work of Mistral, Baroncelli, Lelée, Pranishnikoff and others were a *fait accompli*, the product of my journeys was uncertain. but, instead of despair, this very uncertainty created an atmosphere of tense anticipation and excitement. Far from being a discouragement, the difficulties merely added to my determination. Now I felt impatient to get away from Avignon and into the heart of Mistral's country and, from there, to the Camargue.

★

After an early breakfast, I took my watercolours into the rue
Joseph Vernet and sketched the tall wrought-iron gateway I had
admired the day before. A haze of thin white cloud masked the
autumn sky and the air had a brisk, cutting edge to it. I made a
quick drawing and washed in the shadows with a grey tint
mixed from Ultramarine and Burnt Sienna; but my numbed
fingers made the pencil awkward to handle and the sketch failed
to capture the delicate scrolls of wrought-iron tracery which
were the gate's most striking feature.

I returned to the hotel, paid my bill and made my way to the
station where I caught a local train to Arles.

The train journey was a short one, a little more than twenty
minutes, and I had an entire carriage almost to myself except for
three American girls on a student vacation and an undergraduate
from Aix who was on his way home to Saint Martin-de-Crau. The
Aix undergraduate talked throughout the journey – mainly about
his passion for bull-games. The girls understood enough French to
follow the drift of the conversation and their grim expressions
registered strong disapproval as the young man warmed to his
theme. 'I enjoy the Course Camarguaise,' he said, 'but, even
though I do not care for it myself, I see no reason why the *corrida*
should be banned, as some people suggest. The *corrida* is not really
typical of Provence, but it has become part of the scene. I think it is
good to keep an open mind on such matters. I've started a scientific
training and a scientist should remain as objective as possible at all
times, don't you think? It is a bad mistake to permit the heart to
rule the mind. The *corrida* is an emotional subject. People allow
their feelings too much freedom, I fear. As a scientist, I cannot
afford the luxury of sentimentality. After all, where would this
lead to? No, *monsieur*! My preference for the Course while it may
be partly instinct, has been arrived at only after prolonged, careful
thought.'

While I admired the young man's sincerity, I found his
breathless ardour and his somewhat monotonous, penetrating
voice uncomfortably tedious. I felt relieved when we arrived at
Arles and went our separate ways.

I found Arles bathed in pale sunshine and patches of blue sky breaking through the cloud. I remembered that this was how Van Gogh had seen the town for the first time in February 1888 – the view of Arles from the station-yard, with the Rhône curving past the fishermen's quarter, La Roquette, on my right and the place Lamartine with its circular fountain at the bottom of the hill, with the porte de la Cavalerie and the decorative Fontaine Amedée-Pichot just beyond it. Despite Arles' impressive history as the fourth-century capital of imperial Rome's southern provinces, the Praefectura Galliarum which included Spain and Gaul, I have never found the monumental presence of Roman Arles intimidating. The first impression has always been that of a much smaller, much more intimate town than Avignon, with a more relaxed and, yes, a friendlier atmosphere.

Coming to Arles I have always felt the same. I like the narrow streets with their narrow pavements, the sense of enclosure the houses give (besides some protection from the *mistral*) and the intimate scale of the old town inside the walls. If the streets become too claustrophobic, you can walk along the river-bank as far as the Trinquetaille bridge and come back into the town-centre by the rue de la République which brings you to the main square and the church of Saint-Trophime. One of the charms of Arles is that everything is within easy walking-distance, from the Alyscamps – whose name means the Elysian Fields – with its leafy tombs to the modern suburbs of Trinquetaille and the Fourchon. But most of all, I like the maze of narrow cobbled streets and alleys at the town-centre and the cheerful, bustling life you find there. Arles is the opposite of larger towns and cities where passers-by 'look through you'. As I made my way along the rue du 4 Septembre to my hotel in the rue des Suisses, people would make a space for me to squeeze past with my suitcase; and at the same time they smiled and nodded a greeting, a muttered '*bonjour, monsieur*' and added some remark about the weather.

From Avignon I had booked a room at the Hôtel de la Muette, where my wife and I had stayed some years previously. The owner, Monsieur DePlanck, gave me a warm welcome. He led me upstairs to the second floor where I was installed in a small,

well-furnished bedroom overlooking a courtyard flanked by the crumbling walls of a neighbouring house which had geraniums at each of the windows and the remains of an old stone arch filled in by rough masonry.

Having settled in at La Muette, I strolled over to the place de la République, to the Tourist Office in the cloister of Saint-Trophime, where I found an old acquaintance, the Deputy-Director Alain Marion, in a scarlet pullover, drafting a long complicated letter at his desk which was piled high with papers. I waited until his letter was finished and then we went next-door to a cavernous dimly-lit room with bare stone walls and a refectory table; and there we sat for an hour while Monsieur Marion listened attentively, from time to time making notes, as I outlined my plans for the forthcoming weeks.

'You would be wise to make Arles your base,' said Monsieur Marion. 'The Pays d'Arles, as you say the Rhôneland, covers a lot of ground, but the distances are not great and from here everything is accessible. Arles is the natural centre for your work. You will find it easy to visit the Camargue – but, of course, you will wish to live there, too, for a while. From Arles, you can make all your trips to Maillane, Fontvieille, Saint-Rémy and Tarascon without difficulty. You will find Mistral's collections here in the Museon Arlaten and I can introduce you to many people who will answer your questions about our folklore and traditions. For example: an exhibition of Ivan Pranishnikoff's paintings has just opened at Fontvieille. I will arrange a meeting with Michel Gay who owns the gallery there. Gay has also written a book about Pranishnikoff, and another about Leo Lelée who painted the Arlésiennes. Michel Gay and his partner, Marcel Fouque, know the region's artists better than anyone. They will advise you. And, if you wish to discover more about the Arlésien costumes and hairstyles, you must talk to Madame Castanet and Madame Niel. The Director of the Museon Arlaten, Madame Serena, like your friends Madame Bosqui and Madame Barnicaud, is a great expert on Mistral. Let me assure you, none of this is any problem. Besides,' Monsieur Marion grinned, 'the people of Arles love to talk. They like nothing better – that is, apart from eating.' Monsieur Marion rubbed his hands with enthusiasm. 'Arles, *monsieur*, is like a nest of chirping birds!'

In the Camargue, where I had many friends, I could look after myself; but Alain Marion said that Madame Magali Dunant, the secretary of the *confrérie* of Camargue *gardians*, was often away from home. 'And,' he added, 'she may be very busy between times at the *mas* where the cattle are calving and she is giving life to the new beasts.'

He cupped his hands and smiled: 'In Arles, we are surrounded by so much antiquity, so many lovely buildings. . . . But also we keep up to date. Life here is constantly changing, though change is a slow process as a rule. Did you know there is a scheme afoot to dredge the Rhône and open it up for large vessels? Again our river may become the great highway that it was in Mistral's day. How history repeats itself! Of course, the Marseillais won't be pleased, but Arles will benefit enormously. We must, however, be careful not to sacrifice our town's character simply in order to progress. For, as you must be aware, the *vie tranquille* is also important.'

Alain Marion had been reading Peter Mayle's best-seller, *A Year in Provence*, which I gathered he found not only very amusing, but in many respects also very accurate. (The novelist and satirical journalist, Yvan Audouard, author of a splendid novel about bull-fighting, *Les Lions d'Arles*, has observed that, if Peter Mayle's book were translated he would have to make a run for it, so shrewd and penetratingly exact is its portrayal of Provençal character.) Alain Marion said: 'Monsieur Mayle really understands how things get done here in the South, or, should I say perhaps, how they don't get done! You must cultivate patience. How do you say this in English? Ah yes, you need to bend with the wind. In our country, the serious and the humorous walk very closely side by side. One moment there is acute frustration – everyone is bad-tempered or in a state of panic. The very next moment, their problems dissolve in laughter and nobody seems to have a care in the world! Am I right that you may become like our serious Peter Mayle?'

Well, that was one way of looking at it, I suppose.

I spent the rest of the afternoon wandering about in Arles and in the evening I went down to a little restaurant, Lou Gardian, where I had an excellent dinner off the 53-franc menu. The *potage-du-jour* had been freshly made from good beef-stock and was served from a big tureen with plenty of bread. At Avignon, I had had very little appetite but now I felt ravenously hungry. As a result, I rather overdid the soup and bread and left hardly enough room for the main course – the Taureau, a beef casserole, with rice from the Carmargue cooked in saffron and olive-oil – and after that, goat's cheese which had a thick, creamy texture and dark, piquant-flavoured rind. The pretty blonde waitress carried a chromium cork-screw like a pistol, hooked into the hip-pocket of her jeans. At the next table there was a big party of local farm-workers, two or three youngsters but the majority middle-aged men, in open-necked shirts and jerseys, who ate and drank heartily and carried on a mild flirtation with the waitress which she seemed to enjoy. They were a polite, boisterous crowd and the most daring behaviour consisted of pretending to dither over their choice of food. In the end, the joke wore thin and they settled down to eat, much as they would have done at home, speaking hardly at all until their plates were emptied.

Across from where I was sitting, an American woman of about forty was having a rather strained conversation with a bronzed young Australian three tables away. The situation caused a good deal of amusement among the farmers, as I gathered from one or two stray remarks. Neither the American woman nor the Australian spoke French. They were the only foreigners in the restaurant, apart from myself. The young Australian was clearly anxious for company; or perhaps he had his eye on something more than just idle chatter? At any rate, for a while the American did her best to keep him at arm's length. But eventually he got up and joined her and they finished off what was left of her carafe of red wine. The move set the farm-workers guessing as to the outcome. The odds seemed to be against the Australian, however, and they were right. After about ten minutes, the woman rose and left the young man, who now looked red-faced and sheepish, staring fixedly at the empty carafe. Evidently he'd made his pitch and lost. But the moment of pathos and even the crude symbolism of the empty carafe were seized upon by the farmers who made the most of them, exchanging winks and chuckling like schoolboys.

I made Lou Gardian my dining-room during most of my stay at Arles. The good, plain cooking suited me admirably and the atmosphere was cosy and cheerful. The little restaurant and my comfortable room at La Muette, where I lived for some weeks, made me feel completely at home.

When I returned to the hotel in the evening after dinner, I very often stopped for a chat with the night-porter, Alexandru Florescu, and sometimes we smoked a cigarette or two, propped on our elbows on either side of the reception desk. Monsieur Florescu was a Romanian, very well-educated and something of a philosopher. He was seventy years old, with a fine thick head of hair and a big moustache; friendly, but somewhat reserved – a mixture I found highly agreeable. After a few meetings I began to look forward to our nightly conversations, which covered every subject under the sun and almost always included politics (an unusual topic for me), in which Monsieur Florescu took a great interest.

At La Muette I usually slept like a log, for I was out and about every day and the days were usually busy. As a rule I got up at six, showered and dressed and wrote my diary or sometimes finished a drawing from the day before. Breakfast was served in the foyer, either by Monsieur Florescu or by Alain DePlanck, who arrived promptly at 7.30 am each morning. It was a simple meal – bread and jam, orange-juice and *café-au-lait* – and yet somehow it always tasted better than any other.

In the hotel foyer there was a large ornamental fish-tank, to which a water-recycling system was attached by a transparent-green plastic tube. To begin with, I found the continuous bubbling irritating, but after a while I scarcely noticed it. The tank was strewn with pebbles and sand and half-buried in the sand there were fragments of Roman tiles and tiny reproductions of classical columns and a temple façade set in a forest of slimy aquatic plants. The fish consisted mainly of rather listless pop-eyed Chinese carp, but I became intrigued by a slender little fish of a different species which swam in short spurts vertically up and down the sides of the tank, like a panic-stricken sardine, polishing the glass with its fins. This, I learned from Alain DePlanck, was the *nettoyeur de vitre*, the 'window-cleaner'. The *nettoyeur de vitre* certainly lived up to its name: when it had finished polishing the glass, it scurried about dusting the temples and columns and seemed particularly attracted to one which was meant to represent the Leaning Tower of Pisa.

Sometimes, when Monsieur Florescu was in charge – having had all night to ponder mighty matters of Life and Death, international affairs, religion or whatever took his fancy – he would launch into a deep discussion, poised with a coffee-pot in one hand and a bread-basket in the other. With my linguistic motor starting from cold, it demanded a certain effort of concentration to follow his frequently complex arguments and, moreover, provide the sort of replies he expected. One morning, for example, he announced: 'God isn't a person, in my view. That can't be possible! People tell you – Man is made in God's image. But, surely, that isn't possible either? Look at the sick, the deformed, the lame. Do you mean to tell me that God looks like them? Is he a man or a woman, for instance? Answer me that, if you will! I am a fervent, though not a consistently practising believer, *monsieur*. For me, God is visible everywhere: in the grass, in the trees – all around. He is a power, not an individual like you or me. The silence of the nave allows us to think peacefully about these great questions. This is reason enough for attending church regularly, but there again I find all the peace and quiet I need during the night, here at my reception-desk. In the night, I'm able to reflect on such things. That is, of course, if I haven't a crossword puzzle or a good detective-novel on the go. Ah yes, belief can be difficult, but then so is daily life. Inventing explanations and theorizing doesn't count for much. It's the *doing* that's the hard bit!'

Monsieur Florescu was not only extremely intelligent and well-read, fluent in five or six languages and himself the author of a history of Romania, but he was touchingly eager to please, solicitous and genuinely kind. He took his job as the hotel's night-porter very seriously and was much respected by the DePlancks, quite rightly; but, as you might expect, his mind was apt to range over such a wide field that occasionally the necessary trivia of day-to-day would be forgotten. He would go off and fetch a cup of coffee, thinking I looked tired or thirsty, and place it in front of me with several cubes of lump-sugar tastefully arranged round the saucer. I would sip it, only to discover that he'd forgotten to boil the kettle and the brown mixture was stone-cold; but I always drank it, for it seemed unthinkable to do otherwise.

But it was an entirely different matter when I asked Monsieur Florescu to fill my thermos with iced water from the refrigerator and found the contents bubbling out at near boiling point!

As Monsieur Florescu never tired of observing, tugging wistfully at his big Kaiser Bill moustaches, 'In this life, alas, one can't have everything.'

Florescu was a many-faceted personality and a true original.

He loved to talk about the *eeesms* which fascinated him: 'Commun-*eeesm*, patriot-*eeesm*, capital-*eeesm*, barbar-*eeesm*' and so on. The life of servitude under Commun-*eeesm*, he said, was one of grinding hardship – hard to eat, hard to live. But, to my surprise, he repeated again and again, there were compensations. The Romanian peasant life was meagre and uncertain, but it gave people time to think, time to reflect. When he came to live in France, he had found material life easier – incomparably so; but this, in turn, created pressures. Life in the Rhôneland was slow compared to the North, but even so it wasn't like the country life of Central and Eastern Europe. Perhaps capital-*eeesm* was merely another kind of servitude which put food in your mouth but gave less time to ponder? As he turned over these ideas like the small change in his coat-pocket, it occurred to me that he had made an important connection between the Rhôneland poets and the horsemen-poets of the Camargue. The poetry of the Camargue had been inspired by hardship and beauty. The *gardians* spurned material rewards – the constant struggle with the elements, the marshes and the beasts which they loved brought a sense of freedom and independence no amount of wealth or possessions could possibly match. They had no desire for these things; and what outsiders regarded as their struggle against heavy odds for little obvious return was to the Camarguais merely a way of life. But such a life! One which guaranteed their liberty, identity and self-respect, and, besides, was the stuff that dreams and poetry are made of.

The Camarguais, in this sense, were completely different to Monsieur Florescu's countrymen – indeed they differed to their own countrymen of the Rhôneland. In the Camargue, the *gardians* had actually chosen to live as they did. They had been bred to the life, it is true, and the choice, in many cases, had been made for them; but it was something they accepted without the wish for change.

Not all my conversations with Monsieur Florescu were as serious as this. He dabbled in astrology, and one day I found him pouring over an astral chart he had been asked to prepare for a friend, which he had made using biros of various colours.

'There's something more to this than meets the eye,' he said. 'I am a rational thinker. I don't have the *ésprit* to be a medium or a clairvoyant. Everything we do is affected by radiation. People and objects each have their own wavelengths and their power varies, as you'd expect. Switch on the radio and you get an emission of sound. If you turn the knob, the sound either fades or gets louder. Explode an atomic bomb and you have tremendous emissions flying about in all directions. These emissions, I believe, influence us. The medium needs to be *en face* to receive his subject's emissions properly. That's another affair altogether. I just stick to working out these little charts.' He brushed some grains of cigarette-ash off the sheet of paper onto the carpet and scuffed the carpet with his heel. 'Emissions are happening all the time,' he said. 'They continue happening whether we like it or not.'

Monsieur Florescu's talk reminded me of a remark I had heard at a dinner-party in London. Among the guests were a recently-married elderly couple, a novelist and his French wife. The lady had been an actress of the old school and even her merest whisper drowned the rest of the dinner-table conversation. I was rather taken aback when, *à propos* of nothing, she bellowed in my ear: 'It is high time that my husband had a rest. He has been having emissions almost every other night since our wedding!' I discovered that she meant the old gentleman appeared very frequently on radio and television programmes. Monsieur Florescu laughed heartily and asked if my story was a typical example of 'the British sense of humour'. '*C'est normal*, this playing with words,' he cackled, 'but I think maybe it is a very English game, like the *mots croisés* your nation is so fond of.'

Monsieur Florescu suggested that one evening, if I had nothing better to do, I might care to assist him in solving one of the crossword puzzles to which, he confessed smiling his enigmatic Ruritanian smile, he was addicted. 'It will be good for your French,' he said, 'and for both of us a little challenge.' Being a relative newcomer to Arles, where he had arrived only four years earlier, although a fluent French speaker, Monsieur Florescu's viewpoint on Provençal affairs was still that of an immigrant. Yet he had adapted naturally and easily to the Arlésien lifestyle and in some respects had become even more Provençal than the Provençaux themselves. The same might be said of Ivan Pranishnikoff, another settler from Eastern Europe, who was the first of Mistral's circle to settle permanently in the Camargue, over 100 years ago.

4

The Painter of the Gardians

As an artist, Ivan Pranishnikoff's imagination had been influenced by two distinct cultures: Russia, where he grew up; and southwest Provence, where he lived from middle-age until his death. I knew something about Ivan Pranishnikoff's paintings but very much less about his life, until Alain Marion introduced me to the art-historian and writer, Michel Gay, and his partner, Marcel Fouque, both of whom I met shortly after my arrival in Provence. Michel Gay's book about Pranishnikoff had been published to mark the 150th anniversary of the artist's birth at Kursk in Russia, in May 1841. Until then I knew nothing of Pranishnikoff's active military career, fighting alongside Garibaldi in Italy and later in Montenegro's war of independence. I did not realize that he had lived and worked in Canada, the United States and Mexico before settling finally in Provence. However, I was aware that his arrival at Les Saintes-Maries in the Camargue in 1881 had preceded that of Folco de Baroncelli-Javon, the most famous of the delta's pioneers, by a decade.

'You will remember this painting, I think,' said Michel Gay, pointing to a watercolour of bulls and *gardians*. I had seen it first ten years ago at the Baroncelli Museum in Les Saintes-Maries, from which it had been borrowed for Gay's exhibition, a vigorous little picture heightened with Chinese White, which bore the hand-written legend, '*Arrivée du taureaux de Course au village des Stes Maries en Provence pour la Fête Patronale*'. The painting on tinted paper showed a party of *gardians* and bulls careering along at full gallop, kicking up clouds of white dust, with a dog scampering at their heels. The picture had fired my interest in Pranishnikoff straight away. Tremendously lively, with all the fresh immediacy of a rapid sketch made from life, it showed the village as it appeared in Baroncelli's youth, unchanged since Mistral's description in *Mireille*, and the *gardians*' simple costumes before the introduction of black velvet jackets, patterned shirts and black-seamed moleskin trousers which were adopted only after the Nacioun Gardiano's foundation in 1904.

How perfectly Pranishnikoff captured the Camargue's mysterious atmosphere: a tiny watercolour of Les Saintes-Maries showing the church and some houses reflected in the lagoon; a lonely *cabane* near the sea sketched on a burning hot, windless day; a marsh landscape in winter – *cabanes* catching the dying rays of winter sun, the burnt, dry vegetation and a sky of such a piercing blue that looking at the picture you could almost feel the cold evening's approach.

'And here,' said Monsieur Gay, 'we have Daudet's little mill.' Another evening landscape, this superb oil-painting showed the mill against a background of golden sky, overshadowed by dark clouds, the dark colours of the foreground muted at dusk. The mill was one of Pranishnikoff's finest pictures. At least I thought so; and Michel Gay did not disagree. In fact he had used a reproduction of it for the cover of his book and the mill painting was featured on the exhibition's posters. Its atmosphere was restful, meditative and yet it expressed such yearning: forgetful-ness and the acceptance of things past evoked by evening shadows, and the dawn promise fleetingly captured in the sunset's afterglow. Michel Gay added: 'Of course this wasn't the actual *moulin de Daudet*. That was still a ruin. But the mill Pranishnikoff painted nevertheless symbolizes Daudet's world. See how the mill-sails are at rest, like the sails of old Cornille's mill in Daudet's story, which stopped turning when the old man died.'

I remembered the final sentence of 'Old Cornille's Secret' – which Pranishnikoff's painting seemed to echo: 'Everything comes to an end in this world, and we shall have to get used to the idea that the windmills are things of the past, like the boats pulled by horses up the Rhône, and our local courts of justice, and the long tail-coats with flowers embroidered on them that the men used to wear.'

Ivan Pranishnikoff's artistic skills were very diverse, like his interests which ranged over a wide field. He had been a journalist, reporter and soldier. In Provence, his work as an archaeologist and paleontologist led to the formation of a large fossil collection which he presented to the Museon Arlaten. A poet and writer, Pranishnikoff translated his friend Turgenev's stories into Provençal and Mistral's into Russian. He had worked as a war-artist under Tsar Alexander III and in the Camargue he became a co-founder and painter of the Nacioun Gardiano. A striking figure in old age, with a commanding profile, a flowing white beard and moustaches and the lanky

swaggering gait of a natural horseman, it was little wonder that he became known as the 'Patriarch' of Les Saintes-Maries.

Pranishnikoff was probably the first of the nineteenth-century artists and writers to settle in the Camargue, having come there in search of peace and inspiration. Many of the Rhôneland's poets and writers, including Mistral, Daudet and Jeanne de Flandreysy, wrote on Camargue themes. Pranishnikoff went further: like Baroncelli-Javon and Joseph D'Arbaud, he made the Camargue his home and embraced wholeheartedly the *gardian* life and its traditions, although he never became a *manadier* and instead lived with his wife, Josephine Héry, in a modest village house close to the church.

Over lunch at the Galérie Saint-Michel, Michel Gay told me: 'Pranishnikoff had a great influence on his contemporaries. He was the earliest of the Camargue's true *aficionados*. I've written in my book that "Ivan dreamed, like Alphonse Daudet, of finding a tranquil region where he might cast aside the artificial life and *fièvres de Paris* to rediscover between earth and sky a happy natural alliance of flora and fauna and a true source of inspiration." '

I remarked that, since Pranishnikoff was a poet and a translator, it seemed odd that none of his writing appears in the famous collection of Camargue verse, the *Flourilege de la Nacioun Gardiano*.

'Perhaps,' Gay replied, 'but such is life! Pranishnikoff had many talents, yet he is best remembered as a painter. Besides, his Camargue landscapes are full of poetry. The painting of a *gardian*'s hut near Les Saintes-Maries, for instance.' As he spoke, I pictured the work in my mind's eye: the dry, sun-scorched earth, the hut immersed in deep shadow, a track bordered by clumps of *sansouires*, the cloudless blue sky tinged with a yellowish haze. In his book, Monsieur Gay titled the painting *'Cabane de Gardian au bord de la route du "bout du monde"* ', and this, to me, expressed perfectly the stark beauty of the scene and the sense of finality it conveyed. A gardian's hut by the road to the world's end. 'The world's end' aptly described Les Saintes-Maries a century ago when the tiny village still remained

inaccessible and desolate. For 'Monsieur Ivan' it had been like
the rainbow's end where he had dug deep and found his pot of
gold – the Camargue's melancholy beauty – and peace of mind
which had been his heart's desire.

Ivan Pranishnikoff died in April 1909 and was buried at Les
Saintes-Maries. His widow received a host of tributes, among
them a long message from Léo Lelée, celebrating their friendship and praising Pranishnikoff's artistic vision and childlike
simplicity, *'cette jeunesse de coeur'* which had lent 'the colossus
with his immense white beard' such incomparable charm.
Marius Jouveau, the *capoulié* of the Félibrige, wrote that
Pranishnikoff had become 'a pure-blooded Provençal' – a
sentiment which Folco de Baroncelli-Javon repeated in a poem
composed in September 1912, which ended with an heroic
flourish, so typical of the writer:

> Moi je lève mon trident, aujourd'hui, sur ma tête,
> Trois fois, en ton honneur, en face des Gardians,
> Des Saintes, du Soleil, et de la Provence, Ivan!

(The original had been written in Provençal; literally translated,
it runs 'I raise my trident, today, above my head, / Three times,
in your honour, / before the Gardians, the Saints, the Sun and
Provence, Ivan!')

Michel Gay and Marcel Fouque, besides being extremely
hospitable, devoted much time and energy to discussions of the
Rhôneland's artists – apart from Pranishnikoff notably Lelée and
Yves Brayer – as well as introducing me to others whose work
was less familiar. Among the latter were Auguste Chabaud
(1882–1955), who had lived and worked in seclusion at the Mas
de Martin, near Graveson, and the Spanish-born painter, wood-
engraver and typographer, Louis Jou (1882–1968), a neglected
genius, sometimes called 'the Gutenberg of France', whose
atelier Michel Gay later arranged for me to visit at Les Baux.

Gay and Fouque helped me to explore the byways of
Tarascon, Aix-en-Provence and Fontvieille; and they accompanied me to Les Saintes-Maries during one of my spells in the

Camargue. But first and foremost I was anxious to revive my impressions of Mistral's Maillane and Saint-Rémy-de-Provence where Joseph Roumanille, Mistral's lifelong friend and mentor, had spent his youth.

5

Windswept Saint-Rémy

The weather had turned very wild and windy when I visited Saint-Rémy with my self-appointed, informative guide, Michel Gay. Monsieur Gay had led an eventful life before taking up Fine Art. He had been a major in the French Army, had served for years in Indo-China and was invalided out from Dien-Bien-Phu. Painting had always been his chief enthusiasm and, although he spoke very little about his wartime experiences, I sensed that art had been an antidote to the scenes of brutality, killing and distress which he had witnessed abroad, and which surfaced occasionally in our conversation. As a result of his war-experience in Indo-China, he had become a virtual insomniac; he observed with a grin, 'It is fortunate that I am *célibataire*, a bachelor, for I do most of my writing at night. Like Napoleon, I don't need much sleep.'

We approached Saint-Rémy across the Caieou, the fertile plain which gives the town its picturesque setting, couched in verdant, open countryside between two great rivers, the Rhône and the Durance, below the jagged blue ridges of the Alpilles. The plain has been rightly described as 'the garden of Provence' and has been famous for centuries for its garden produce, including vegetables, seeds and flowers of every imaginable colour and variety.

Saint-Rémy grew up in the Middle Ages on the site of the Roman town of Glanum which, in turn, had been built over the remains of an earlier Greek settlement.

A series of archaeological digs begun in 1921 are still in progress and they have revealed amazingly rich treasures, among them Greek inscriptions and beautiful mosaics. The houses, shrines, baths and temples of Glanum stand in a magnificent, wild scenery of wind-carved rocks and pines which sets them off to perfection. The House of Epona, dating from the second century BC, a triumphal arch and a cenotaph, the so-called Mausoleum of the Princes of Youth decorated with battle scenes in *bas-relief*, are some of Glanum's best-preserved, most imposing remains.

The Roman antiquities lie a kilometre or so south from the town-centre and it is these the visitor is generally most anxious to explore. But Saint-Rémy has other claims to fame, besides. The celebrated Jewish astrologer Michel de Notredame (1503– 1566), better known as Nostradamus, a friend of Catherine de Medici and physician of Charles IX, is said to have been born at a house aptly named Lou Planet, in the rue Hoche, which can be seen to this day. Certainly Nostradamus was alive when some of Frédéric Mistral's forebears came to Saint-Rémy from Tarascon via Maillane in the sixteenth century, and perhaps for this reason the poet's mother had wished him to be christened 'Nostradamus' after the prophet.

The famous 'Coupo Santo', the loving-cup of the Félibrige which commemorates the ancient links between Catalonia and Provence, was first used in 1867 at a banquet held in Saint-Rémy. Mistral replied in verse to a passionate address delivered by the Catalan poet, Victor Balaguer, which marked the occasion:

> Provençau, veici la coupo
> Que nous vèn di Catalan:
> A-de-rèng beguen en troupo
> Lou vin pur de noste plant!

Coupo santo,
E versanto,
Vuejo à plen bord
Vuejo abord
Lis estrambord
E l'enavans de fort!'

According to Richard Aldington's prose translation, this reads: 'Provençaux, here is the cup which comes to us from the Catalans. One by one let us drink from it the wine of our own growth. Sacred and plenteous cup, pour out abundantly, in waves, the enthusiasm and energy of the strong!'

Read in cold blood, these lines sound rather stilted. But they were meant after all to be declaimed before an audience, and they undoubtedly achieved a very dramatic effect at the time.

When Mistral and the other *félibres* visited the ruins of Glanum in 1888 they were drawn by the bell tolling from the nearby twelfth-century monastery of Saint Paul-de-Mausole. The monastery's atmosphere of Gothic gloom appealed to one of their number who wrote of the place 'hiding, so near to all that luminous poetry, such misery and such obscurity'.

The poet was referring of course to the lunatic asylum at Saint Paul-de-Mausole, the Asylum for the Alienated run by Dr Théophile Peyron, where Van Gogh spent almost exactly a year undergoing treatment, from 8 May 1889 to 6 May 1890. Van Gogh came there as a voluntary inmate 'suffering from acute mania with hallucinations of sight and hearing' – not mad, as it has been widely supposed, but a victim of severe attacks of epilepsy which were partly hereditary and were gradually worsened by the potent combination of heavy drinking, syphilis and meagre diet that characterized his life at Arles.

We may be sure that Van Gogh's experience of Saint Paul-de-Mausole differed enormously from the romantic, distanced view of the Félibrige poet captivated by its Italianate languor. Nevertheless he made many paintings of the garden from a room which Dr Peyron set aside for his own use, and also one of his finest self-portraits – the famous 'Self-portrait with a palette'.

It was neither the Roman remains, Nostradamus nor Van Gogh which interested me most, but instead Saint-Rémy's connections with Mistral's oldest colleague, the poet Joseph Roumanille. It struck me as very curious, especially here in Provence where poets and artists as a rule receive their proper share of recognition, that Roumanille's name was often omitted from guide-books to the region. When I tried to find directions to his birthplace, the Mas des Pommiers, no one could offer much help. Amy Oakley and her husband had found similar problems in 1935 when they came to Saint-Rémy in search of Roumanille's grave. The Oakleys were told: 'There are a hundred Roumanilles buried here,' and left to their own devices. And now, whenever I mentioned the Mas des Pommiers, people merely shrugged and remarked that this was a popular name and there were plenty of 'Appletree Farms' from which to choose.

Having made a number of detours and excursions along the way, we arrived at Saint-Rémy after midday, later than Monsieur Gay had intended, and after some difficulty managed to park his large-bodied estate car among some plane-trees just off the main street. By this time, my companion was ravenous, having eaten nothing, I gathered, since breakfast at six, and he suggested that we might lunch straight away at his favourite restaurant, the Bistrot des Alpilles in the boulevard Mirabeau where at the same time we could enquire about the Roumanille *mas*. It had started to rain, the sky was dark and overcast and the wind was bitterly cold. Much as I wanted to get on on this occasion, the prospect of a well-cooked hot meal in comfortable surroundings seemed attractive.

At the Bistrot des Alpilles, we found a pleasant table overlooking the street, in the corner of a glazed verandah which gave onto a room whose walls had been decorated with bull-fighting posters and paintings of Arlésien woman by Léopold Lelée. The restaurant was already very crowded and delicious smells wafted from the kitchen beyond, where I saw an immense fire of aromatic logs and the chef busy grilling *brochettes*, pieces of lean, tender pork, on steel skewers.

Instead of the meat, we chose instead a delicious *entrée* made of grilled sardines – the large Mediterranean variety – garnished with rosemary, with a fish-sauce mixed with tomatoes and olive-oil and great helpings of spaghetti, slightly *ardiente* – what they call in Provence 'Italian chips', *frites Italiennes*. For dessert there was vanilla ice cream, served in delicate, tall glasses shaped like a lily, with crisp wafer-rolls and flat slivers of dark chocolate stamped with an Arlésien motif – a woman's head and shoulders after an original design by Lelée – which also appeared on the covers of the menu. As an *apéritif*, Michel Gay had ordered Perrier flavoured with *menthe*, a refreshing green syrup which tasted as good as it looked.

A guide-book which Gay had brought with him, titled *Provence the Mysterious*, had been well named, for it gave no clues whatever as to the whereabouts of the Mas des Pommiers. Despite all the assurances I'd received, nor did our large-scale map, the Série Bleue 1:25000 which showed every *mas* between Saint-Rémy and Eyguières. The name, Mas des Pommiers, simply did not feature on the map which suggested among other possibilities that the name might have been changed sometime during the last hundred years. This seemed unlikely; and yet I remembered the *mas* where Frédéric Mistral grew up, the Mas du Juge, had been known formerly as the Mas de Clément. In Scotland I was brought up in the widely-held, if superstitious belief that changing the name of a house or a ship brought bad luck. Perhaps in Provence this was not so. The owner of the restaurant, whom we questioned closely, had never heard of the

Mas des Pommiers; and nor had any of the waiters, many of whom had been born and had lived all their lives at Saint-Rémy.

During lunch, we talked a good deal about Joseph Roumanille and we tried to imagine his early life at the Mas des Pommiers, the gaunt old building with its shuttered, twilight rooms, shaded by trees, a photograph of which I had seen in the 1907 English translation of Mistral's autobiography.

Joseph was born in 1818 and was the eldest of Jean-Denis and Pierette Roumanille's seven children. As a boy he had been frequently ill and, in Aldington's words, 'owed his life to his mother's devoted care, which he repaid by deep filial love'. His father had fought under Napoleon at Waterloo and was awarded the Croix-de-Guerre, although for some reason, much to his disgust, Jean-Denis never actually received the coveted decoration. He worked all his life as a market-gardener and seems always to have been poor, yet in spite of this, to his credit, Jean-Denis gave Joseph a good education, first at Saint-Rémy and later at Tarascon where he attended college.

Even as a youth, at Tarascon, Joseph achieved some celebrity for his Provençal translations of Virgil and Homer. He also wrote poetry of his own. At that period, the fine *langue d'oc* of the troubadours had long since degenerated until it became little better than a coarse public-house slang, shunned and despised by the literary establishment. The speaking and writing of Provençal was discouraged and actually punished in the region's schools and for this reason Joseph's early poems were written in French, which was to all intents and purposes a foreign language in the Roumanille household.

By encouraging his son's education, it may be fairly assumed that Jean-Denis had accepted that he would adopt the language of the bourgeoisie and the possibility that this and book-learning might gradually distance Joseph from the rest of his family. It appears that Pierette feared her son's estrangement even more, Joseph having been so close to her as a child. The story goes that, one day, he was reading some of his latest verses to friends at the Mas des Pommiers when he noticed his mother weeping quietly by the door. To his dismay he discovered the reason for her tears: she couldn't understand the words of his poem and she felt miserable and ashamed of her ignorance. Joseph was horrified. From that moment onwards, for Pierette's sake, he determined only to write his poetry in Provençal, and it was thus he began to appreciate the beauty and potential of his native tongue. His talent for poetry flourished from then on, as Mistral would write many years afterwards, like 'a blossoming of April flowers, harbingers of the Félibrige spring which filled me with delight'.

As it transpired, however, Joseph Roumanille's prose writing in the end eclipsed his poetry and his later fame rested mainly on this, his skill in organizing the Félibrige movement in its early days and his reputation as Mistral's poetry tutor, collaborator and friend.

As a young man Joseph had been handsome, with thick dark curly hair and large wistful eyes. His expression was reflective, but revealed more than a hint of self-willed determination. He was by nature sensitive and sympathetic, though in later years he was inclined to be dogmatic, somewhat narrow-minded and more than a shade prudish. These conflicting characteristics, one imagines, had been inherited equally from his parents; and, throughout his life, until his death in 1891, Joseph's devotion to Pierette and Jean-Denis never waned.

With a degree of patience and tenacity which put our feebler efforts to find the Mas des Pommiers to shame, Amy and Thorton Oakley finally discovered Joseph Roumanille's grave, aided by the keeper of Saint-Rémy's cemetery whose knowledge of his charges seems to have been vague in the extreme. In the green shade of the cypresses they found at last a headstone carved with flowers and fruit, on which the names of Joseph's parents were inscribed in Provençal:

Jan-Danis Roumanille
Gardener.
A man of worth and courage.
1791–1875.

Peireto de Piquet
His wife.

Good, pious and strong.
1793–1875.

They lived as Christians
and died in peace.

The stone was erected by Joseph in their memory and the Oakleys were told that here, too, his remains lay in an unmarked grave. There is something very touching, and also very appropriate, in the fact that Joseph Roumanille should have chosen to be buried in this way. Unlike Frédéric Mistral, who had his tomb constructed in some style as a reproduction of Queen Joanna's Pavilion, a design based on the original at Les Baux, Roumanille preferred obscurity.

Over lunch at the Bistrot des Alpilles, Michel Gay observed: 'Roumanille was, in a sense, the real founder of the Provençal renaissance. Mistral carried on his work and took the movement much farther. It was Mistral who later spearheaded the Félibrige, who brought the poets together and inspired them to write in good Provençal. He was beyond all doubt the finest of these poets and none, possibly excepting Théodore Aubanel, came anywhere near him. Think of Mistral's greatest works, *Mireille* and *Le Poème du Rhône*. They're quite outstanding. And then we must also remember his great Provençal lexicon, the *Trésor du Félibrige*, which brought together all the strands of dialect and standardized language. It's not surprising that the *Trésor* was singled out as well as *Mireille* by the committee of judges who awarded Mistral the Nobel Prize.'

Joseph Roumanille's influence on Mistral can never be underestimated, or the effect of Roumanille's first collection of poems, *Les Paquerettes*, printed by Sequin, the Avignon publisher for whom Joseph had worked as a reader. Roumanille was by no means alone at the time he began to write poetry in Provençal. There were others, such as Victor Gélu, a revolutionary poet from Marseille, and Jacques Boé – known as Jasmin – who kept a small barber's shop at Agen and sang to his customers. Like the best of Gélu and Jasmin the freshness of

Roumanille's poems is explained by the fact that he wrote simply and directly from the heart about everyday subjects, in sharp contrast to the eighteenth- and early nineteenth-century writers who modelled their work on classical themes, or sought to revive the lavish, fantastically detailed yet defunct troubadour traditions, neither of which had any bearing on contempory life.

And this was precisely the point of my companion's remarks. The revival brought about by Roumanille, Mistral and their friends was much more than a merely intellectual exercise. Just as Roumanille had written verses for his mother's delight, in a broader sense the poets aimed to re-awaken the people's interest in their native language and take a renewed pride in their traditions. This they hoped to achieve partly by reviving disused or forgotten customs and ceremonies, or, in some cases, such as the Festo Vierginenço where girls were encouraged to wear the traditional Arlésien dress, by inventing new ones, and partly by writing poetry which touched the daily lives and hearts of the common people, showing them that Provençal was not simply a coarse *patois* but a rich dialect capable of expressing a wealth of beautiful, noble sentiments and ideas.

Provençal had deteriorated steadily since the Troubadour age. In 1617, in his preface to *Le Ramlet Moundi*, Goudelin, a native of Toulouse, jeered at his fellow citizens who from ignorance scorned their region's dialect 'because they cannot enter into the understanding of its graces'.

Little or no serious effort was made to resurrect and improve the standard of Provençal for a further 200 years. In the late eighteenth century a few archaeologists and philologists, among them Lacurne de Sainte-Palaye and the Abbé Millot, began to study the troubadours' poetry and songs, fascinated by their dramatic power and picturesque realism. But it was the realism of a vanished era and the scholars' texts, scrupulously annotated in French, made no impact on the Rhôneland people who were neither able to read their books, nor for that matter afford to buy them. In the countryside stories and legends which formed the basis of popular Rhôneland tradition were still largely handed

down from generation to generation by word of mouth. And
so, in spite of the enthusiam shown by Sainte-Palaye, Millot and
other scholars, the quality of this living oral tradition continued
to degenerate and weaken, as Provençal itself grew more
poverty-stricken and debased, until by Roumanille's day the
writer, Louis D'Astros, felt obliged to warn the Provençal
Academy at Aix: 'The Provençal language is dying.'

D'Astros realized only too clearly that the élitist meanderings
of the Abbé Millot and other *savants* through the remote,
impassioned love-sick world of the troubadours – fascinating
though it might be – offered no sound prescription for the ailing
langue d'oc. Even D'Astros's own writings and his contemporary, Jean Dioulofet's splendid translations of La Fontaine's
fables into Provençal, had had little effect. These were admirable
enough in their way, but they failed to set the peoples' hearts
afire. While a shelf of expensively-bound translations might
dignify a scholar's library, such works remained beyond the
reach of ordinary folk and did nothing to inspire or unify them in
a common awareness of their decaying culture.

The situation might have been less serious had not the
Provençal language been broken down and divided into such a
wide diversity of local forms. Each of the districts spoke its own
distinctive *patois* and defended its right to do so with fierce pride.
The effect of this on Provençal as a whole was disastrous and the
work of regional writers of the early nineteenth century still
tended to be idiosyncratic and unfocussed. Until Roumanille
and Mistral, little appeared in print that touched the Rhôneland
spirit, as such, by appealing to a wider audience regardless of
their political beliefs, social background or locality. This was the
genesis of the revival sometimes called the Provençal
Renaissance, which Roumanille fathered, largely by inspiring
Mistral to write. Though it was really Mistral's poem *Mireille*
which struck the spark, halted the decline and created a popular
market for the Félibrige poets and their revolutionary creed.
Mistral, guided and inspired by Roumanille, strove for the
development of a new kind of literature. This, in turn, called for
nothing less than a rebirth of the Rhôneland people's self-

awareness and the rekindling of their self-respect. In other words, a revived sense of their ancient Provençal identity. And Mistral sought to achieve his lofty aims chiefly through a fundamental re-appraisal, re-working and ultimately the reformation of the *langue d'oc* – the Provençal language – itself by restoring it to its purest form.

Like Roumanille and Mistral, Gélu and Jasmin had believed fervently that their poetry, written in good Provençal, should not only derive from the people of the Midi, but must be made widely available to them by being recited and cheaply printed.

A hard, uncompromising realist, Gélu's writing penetrated to the very core of Marseille's poverty and corruption. He became the sworn enemy of all forms of literary conceit and artistic affectation. Instead of prancing fawns and pretty shepherdesses, Gélu drew his inspiration from Provence's dark side, the pitiless world of the Marseille slums, a gutter-world of vice, ugliness and deprivation which found no counterpart in the 'gentler' poverty of the countryside and its villages like Mistral's Maillane.

Gélu's fiery energy and abrasive candour, which alienated the critics and offended his bourgeois readers, was admired by Jasmin. Yet, in contrast to Gélu, Jasmin had been gentle, humble and sensitive to abuse. Over a period of twelve years, Jasmin wrote five long poems totalling some 2,400 lines; in its way, a *tour de force* the equivalent of the *Trésor du Félibrige* which took Mistral twenty years to complete.

In his poetry, Jasmin never forgot his lifelong debt to the Church which had rescued him as a child from poverty and starvation. In his *Introduction to Mistral*, Richard Aldington has given a touching example of Jasmin's loyalty and gratitude by telling how, in 1843, Jasmin raised, single-handed, the money needed to restore a ruined church by tramping the countryside, singing and reciting to the villagers and townspeople in exchange for their donations.

Aldington wrote: 'Among the songs was one in which he imaginatively foresaw the church rebuilt: "And I shall say it to myself: 'I was naked and I remembered that when I was a little

child the Church clothed me. Now I am a man, and there is a
naked church, and I want to clothe it. Give all of you, oh give,
and let me taste the sweetness once of doing for Her what She so
often did for me.' '' ' Aldington continued: 'And, moved to
tears, the humble people of the Midi dropped their pence in the
curé's hat, so generously that soon the church was rebuilt by a
poet's songs.'

Before he met Roumanille, Jasmin had been one of only a
handful of Provençal poets read by the youthful Mistral.
Mistral's attitude to Gélu in later years would prove to be
magnanimous, even though Gélu wrote disparagingly of
Mireille when it appeared in 1859, stating that there were not as
many as fifty good lines in the poem! It is easy to see, on the
other hand, that Mistral as a boy would have been attracted by
Jasmin's poetry and deeply moved by its humility and sweet
nature. He went so far as to send Jasmin a fan-letter, set out as a
poem, but received no reply. As an old man, writing in *Mes
Origines: mémoires et récits* in 1906, Mistral finally confessed how
much Jasmin's snub had hurt him. In any case, Jasmin's
behaviour, which does seem a little unreasonable, contributed to
the habit Mistral formed in later life of replying promptly and
without fail to his vast correspondence from admirers all over
the world, regardless of how busy he might have been with his
poetry or his other affairs.

Mistral's meeting with Roumanille at Avignon was in many
ways fortunate for them both. Although Roumanille came from
a more modest background, his country origins were essentially
the same as Mistral's. Roumanille was twelve years older than
Frédéric and his poetic wings, so to speak, had already been
tested and proved. It was natural that Mistral looked up to him
and bestowed on Roumanille something like a schoolboy's
hero-worship. Their families lived withing a few kilometres of
one another and worked on the land. Roumanille's landscapes
were familiar; the two found themselves to be neighbours; and,
above all, they shared a passion for the Provençal language and
wrote poetry.

Roumanille was the first poet Mistral met and befriended. For

Mistral, perhaps even more than Roumanille, the meeting marked a watershed in his career. Mistral wrote in *Mes Origines* that, guided by Roumanille, 'I, trembling with joy (entered) the sanctuary of my dreams; and thus, as sons of the same God, we were united in the bonds of friendship under so happy a star that for half a century we walked together, devoted to the same patriotic cause, without our affection or our zeal ever knowing diminution.'

Though a believer and in many ways 'a good Christian', Mistral in fact, much to the priest's dismay, attended church very seldom at Maillane. It may be that Mistral's reply to the question, 'Whether I believe in God?' would have echoed that of Matisse, who wrote in *Jazz* (1947), 'Yes, when I work.'

6

Mistral's Country

When my wife and I visited Maillane for the first time some years ago, we found the village and its surroundings, much as Mistral had described them, basking in the warm sunshine under a cloudless blue September sky.

Today, however, the countryside looked dank and drab, the sky heavy and leaden and the trees – except for the pines and some bushy evergreens – stripped of their summer foliage by a *mistral* wind which swept the plain. To my relief, the worst of the rain had blown over, and the windscreen-wipers of Michel Gay's Citroën were at last switched off and silent as we drove to Maillane from Saint-Rémy along a winding back-road.

Just off the road, to our left, about 2 kilometres from Maillane, I recognized Mistral's birthplace, the Mas du Juge, a stark, unprepossessing farmhouse two storeys high, standing in the fields at the end of a short driveway which was thickly carpetted with leaves. The house seemed closer to the road than I remembered. Hemmed in by bare trees which gave little shelter from the wind, the grey, shuttered house looked derelict and dismal.

The Mas du Juge, where Mistral was brought up, had been bought by the poet's father, François and his brother, in 1804. Until 1811, the brothers worked the land together; after that,

François purchased his brother's share, married and fathered a son, Louis, who eventually inherited the *mas*. In 1825, François's wife, Françoise Laville, died and three years later François married again. He was then already fifty-seven. His second wife, Adélaïde Marguerite, known as Délaïde, was a lovely young woman of twenty-five, a younger daughter of Etienne Poullinet, a staunch Republican, who had been at one time the mayor of Maillane.

The Poullinets, like the Mistrals, came of highly respected, landowning peasant stock; but, as individuals, Etienne and François could hardly have been more different. They were contemporaries: François was serious-minded, hard-working and thrifty; and he took a great pride in being able to trace his ancestors back to the fifteenth century, to Barthélemy Mistral who in 1471 came from Tarascon and settled first at Maillane, then at Saint-Rémy. Etienne, in contrast, had been a *bon viveur* and a drunkard who wasted the remains of his fortune in the taverns round Maillane. The Poullinet *mas*, in consequence, was mortgaged to the hilt; and as for his family of eight children, including six daughters, Etienne dismissed their future propects with airy unconcern

In *Mes Origines*, Frédéric Mistral related the romantic circum-stances of his parents' first meeting, no doubt embellishing the facts and creating an idealized picture.

The story goes that, one hot summer day about the time of the Feast of Saint John in June 1828, François to his astonishment saw Délaïde in a freshly-harvested field near the Mas du Juge, gleaning her share of the stubble alongside Maillane's paupers who yearly claimed this ancient right. Délaïde explained that she and her sisters had to earn whatever money they needed to buy clothes and any little extras, since their spendthrift father had refused to provide them. François Mistral was struck by Délaïde's beauty as much as he felt distressed and angered by her plight. He took pity on her, courted her for six months and on 26 November brought her to the Mas du Juge as his bride.

The couple's only child, Joseph Etienne Frédéric, was born on the Feast of Our Lady, 8 September 1830. Instead of christening the baby Nostradamus as Délaïde wished – a name which even in the early nineteenth century, must have sounded antiquated and absurdly affected – the name Frédéri or Frédéric was chosen, since it reminded François and Délaïde of a little boy who had carried messages between them during their engagement.

An upstairs bedroom at the *mas*, where Frédéric was born and where François died, had been simply, yet comfortably furnished. It had white plastered walls and a floor of square red tiles, with a strip of carpet by the bed which, like my grandmother's bed in Scotland, occupied a niche curtained off from the main room. There was a gilt-framed mirror above the fireplace, a small chest of drawers on top of which stood a crucifix and jars containing dried herbs or wild flowers, a few pictures and two or three hard-backed chairs with woven rush-matting seats of the type you will find anywhere to this day throughout Provence.

The bedroom scene which Mistral arranged at the Museon Arlaten was more elaborate, but no doubt – if it had really been inspired by his own birth at the Mas du Juge – Mistral had wished to show his mother's *accouchement* in the flattering surroundings he considered most appropriate for the occasion. Besides, the Museon exhibit had been mainly designed to show the traditional ceremony following a birth, and also furnishings and clothes which were typical of any reasonably affluent Rhôneland household of the period.

If you compare the Mas du Juge of today with a photograph taken 100 years ago, which can be found in Mireille Bosqui's lavishly-illustrated book, *Mistral par l'image* (1986), it becomes clear how the building has changed since Mistral's lifetime. The exterior of the house was altered and refurbished in 1890 and tall trees nowadays screen what had once been an uninterrupted view across open pastures to La Montagnette.

Frédéric's childhood at the *mas* seems to have been blissfully happy and provided not only a vital source of inspiration for his later poetry, but the key to his 'harmonious', long life at Maillane. Recalling these halcyon days when he played in the fields and listened, entranced, to the Provençal legends and stories told by his mother, he wrote: 'The Mas du Juge, at that time, was a place of pure poetry, biblical and idyllic.'

As the son of a well-to-do *ménager*, a landowning husband-man, Frédéric had ample leisure and freedom to romp about in the countryside without ever having to toil, as his father's labourers or their children toiled, in a blazing sun and freezing cold, to earn a crust. His parents had spared him that. Even so, François' employees were probably better fed and cared-for than most. Frédéric grew up shielded from hardship in a region where even the poorest villagers lived well above starvation-level. He would never experience at first-hand, like Victor Gélu, the sordid poverty of the cities, or the hunger, degradation or violence of the city slums.

Frédéric worshipped Délaïde and idolized François, through him extolling the virtues of the *ménager* class, who bridged the gap between peasant-farmers and the town-bred bourgeoisie for whom he had scant regard. He wrote: 'If the peasant, living in the village, cultivates his little plot by the sweat of his brow, using the spade or grubbing-hoe, the *ménager*, a grander sort of husbandman in the farms of the Camargue, the Crau or elsewhere, works upright, singing his song, guiding his plough.'

As I strolled about Maillane with Michel Gay, I could not help wondering what might have happened had François Mistral married Délaïde first instead of Françoise Laville and Frédéric, the poet, been his first-born instead of Louis. As it turned out,

Frédéric's elder stepbrother had been content to follow in their father's footsteps, while François saw it as his duty to educate Frédéric for a career other than farming, for which he showed little real aptitude or enthusiasm. From the beginning, it seems that Frédéric's life and Louis' ran on completely different tracks. Louis had farming in his blood, while Frédéric had been a dreamer who spent much of his time alone, watching the harvesters in their smocks and wide-brimmed straw-hats at the reaping, or gathering wild-flowers, or reading under a shady tree.

It is nevertheless curious that Louis hardly featured in *Mes Origines* which gave such intimate, vivid portraits of Frédéric's parents, the household servants, farm-workers, villagers and friends he made at school and as an undergraduate at the University of Aix-en-Provence. All these he described with warmth and affection, though in a style which is perhaps a little too sweet, serene and uncritically romantic to suit the harsher demands of modern literature.

In *Mes Origines* Mistral loved to dwell on his boyhood adventures which were usually fairly mild. He tells how one day while attempting to gather water-lilies for his mother he fell into a stream three times and needed three changes of clothing. Having been accustomed to so much freedom, when he was sent eventually to the village school he played truant again and again; or, as the expression goes, *faisait l'école buissonière*, which means literally that he 'retired to the bushes'. Mistral the mature writer, recalled such episodes using the traditional devices of story-telling and fantasy: how he set off, glowing with joyful anticipation; his conversations with insects and lizards by the wayside; how he encountered a thieving band of gipsies; his terrifying, imaginary escape from a hungry wolf; and finally the warm welcome he received at the *mas* after the day's adventures were over.

From time to time, as a child, Frédéric was given little tasks, for example carrying out baskets of food to the harvesters in summer. His recollections of the work have preserved images of a lifestyle that has vanished for ever and yet are not so very far removed, even from my own childhood memories of Scotland in days when the harvest was still largely gathered in by hand.

The method of harvesting in nineteenth-century Rhôneland differed, however, since the men broke off every few hours to eat and drink and took all their meals, except for the midday dinner and supper, in the open. In the tremendous heat of the Rhôneland summers, in days when the wheat had to be scythed, it was absolutely essential for the men to rest frequently to avoid the risk of sun-stroke. To recoup their energy, they often ate as many as six light snacks, well-salted, and drank a mouthful of wine or wine mixed with water.

I was already familiar with this custom, having read Aldington's description in his *Introduction to Mistral* (1956) which, incidentally, after more than thirty years remains the best general account of Mistral's life and his poetry. There was also Frédéric's peom 'The Harvests', written in his seventeenth year but never published and his article 'The Harvesters' Six Meals' for the *Armana Provençau* in 1888, which Aldington condensed as follows. Asked by an incredulous townsman how they could stomach so much food, the harvesters' foreman, or *baïle*, proceeds to teach his enquirer a lesson. Aldington wrote:

> The mens' *baïle* . . . picks up two clods of earth, puts one in his trouser pocket and tells the bourgeois to do the same. The *baïle* then cuts a swathe with his scythe right across the wheat-field, while the bourgeois with his cane strolls after. At the end of the swathe the *baïle* asks the bourgeois for his clod, which he produces intact. The *baïle* then pulls a handful of dust from his pocket and says: '*Moussu, vacqui coume, en brandussant la daio – frin! fran! – li segaire fasèn la digestioun!*' – 'Monsieur, as the reapers keep moving their scythes – swish! swash! – that's what makes them digest!'

While his father reaped alongside his labourers, Frédéric's mother would have helped to prepare their food-baskets in the *mas* kitchen. The men's 7 o'clock breakfast consistened of bread soaked in oil and vinegar, with anchovy and raw onion, washed down by a glass of wine. At 10, they stopped for a hard-boiled egg, cheese and some watered wine. At 1 o'clock, the reapers returned to the *mas* for their dinner of soup and vegetables. A snack of garlic-bread was carried out to them at 4 pm, and they came back to the *mas* for the evening meal, a supper of mutton, pork or an omelette which François Mistral shared. There might have been one or two extra breaks during the day, but the routine generally was strict. Before supper could begin, each of the reapers had to stand and recite to François how much he had achieved that day.

As a boy, Frédéric Mistral carefully observed the details of farming life and committed them to memory. Mistral would draw on these recollections later for his long, narrative poems such as *Mireille*, whose chief characters and setting were based partly on his father, the farm-workers and surroundings of the Mas du Juge. *Mireille* was begun in 1852, while Mistral was still living at the *mas*, although it took seven years to complete before it was published in 1859.

Until he was a grown man, in his mid-twenties, the Mas du Juge remained the focus of Mistral's life and his major source of inspiration.

As a youngster, after a brief spell at the Maillane village school, he was sent as a boarder to another, so-called 'progressive' school run by a Monsieur Donnat and his elderly parents at the abandoned Benedictine abbey of Saint Michel-de-Frigolet. The abbey's name derives from *férigoulet*, the Provençal word for wild thyme, which covers the slopes of La Montagnette. Here the children played in spring and summer. In winter, they ran about in the church and its ruined cloister, playing macabre games of hide-and-seek in the tombs of the monks whose skeletons lay exposed 'to the four winds of Heaven'.

To Frédéric, the abbey school must have seemed like a home from home, except that food – and, for that matter, any formal education – were always in short supply. The abbey lay almost within sight of the Mas du Juge, in those days a journey of about two hours, and so François was able to keep an eye on the boy's progress. Once, after Frédéric had written to his parents asking for various odds and ends he needed, the old man arrived at the school, riding his favourite mule, 'Babacho', with a bag stuffed with quills, bottles of ink and an immense quantity of paper.

The less well-to-do pupils' fees were often paid in kind. But it appears to have been a minor scandal, caused by the school's cook getting one of the maids pregnant, rather than the lack of money for wages and provisions, which eventually closed Monsieur Donnat's *laissez-faire* establishment for good.

A plaque at Saint Michel-de-Frigolet proudly records Mistral's time there. It reads, translated from Provençal:

> In memory of the time that
> FREDERIC MISTRAL
> Passed at Saint-Michel-de-Frigolet
> For the beginning of his studies
> 1839–1841.

The abbey was afterwards refurbished and taken over by the Prémontré canons who, as the Oakleys discovered, kept a better table than Monsieur Donnat had a century before. The priests and nuns in 1935 kept a hundred rabbits in hutches, as well as beehives. When the Oakleys arrived it was a fast day, but they lunched on a good *pot-au-feu*, white beans flavoured with garlic, omelettes, thyme-honey, bread and black coffee. Mrs Oakley was allowed a mere glimpse of Mistral's old school-room. Her guide, a young monk, explained quite straight-faced: 'To enter would risk purgatory, madame.'

The remainder of Mistral's education has been described at some length by Aldington and, of course, by the poet himself in his autobiographical fragment, *Mes Origines*. I will merely add that, after Saint Michel-de-Frigolet, he spent several years in Avignon: first, at Monsieur Millet's school from which he ran away, homesick and bored with the school menu which, it appears, consisted chiefly of boiled carrots; and later at the Collège Royal, where the poet Charles Dupuy was headmaster and where Frédéric met Joseph Roumanille and struck up a friendship that was destined to shape his future.

When he met Roumanille, Frédéric was then fourteen years of

age, and sang well enough to have been among the Collège
Royal's pupils who formed part of the choir at the Église des
Carmes. Roumanille, whose duty it was to supervise the
choristers, noticed Frédéric one Sunday evening at Vespers,
scribbling on a piece of paper. He confiscated the paper which,
to his astonishment, contained Frédéric's beautiful translation
into Provençal of the penitential psalm which begins: 'Purge me
with hyssop, and I shall be clean: wash me, and I shall be whiter
than snow'.

What followed Roumanille's discovery is a matter of history.
After the service, he took Frédéric aside and questioned him
about his interest in writing, and in the Provençal language; and
he then read to the boy some of his own poems, such as 'The
Poor Man' and 'Little Joseph', which were scarcely masterpieces
but nevertheless impressed young Mistral greatly at the time.

In the summer of 1847, Mistral took his *baccalauréat*, a series of
written and oral examinations which were roughly the
equivalent of modern 'A' Levels here in Britain, at 'the ancient
and pleasant town of Nîmes'. Being highly intelligent, and in his
later teens a hard worker, he passed with flying colours. His
father then allowed him a year's sabbatical at home, during
which Frédéric took his share in the lighter farm-work but spent
most of his time either reading or writing, or gathering
information for his poems from journeymen and other visitors
to the Mas du Juge.

This leisurely interlude was followed by three years at the
University of Aix, where, aged twenty-one, he took his degree
in Law. Aldington has observed that not much detail of these
university years was recorded by Mistral. There had been a
platonic love-affair with a girl named Louise, which seems to
have been an affair of the mind and was conducted mainly
through letters. And at Aix, Mistral renewed his friendship with
Anselme Mathieu whom he had met at the Collège Royal, a
love-lorn eccentric poet who later became one of the seven
founder-members of the Félibrige.

By then François Mistral was eighty-two and going blind.
Throughout his life he had worked hard and his reading, in

contrast to Frédéric's, had been limited to three books: the Bible, *The Imitation of Christ* and *Don Quixote*. It is certain his life reflected each of these in some part. François' pride in his son's achievements was both humble and very touching. He told him: 'Now my boy, I've done my duty. You know more than I was ever taught. You must choose your own way of life – I leave you free to choose.'

These words launched Frédéric on his poetic career and the moment was captured in a sensitive sketch made by Jules Bonaventure Laurens, a gifted artist from Carpentras, on 18 July 1852, which shows him in determined profile, at the time he began to write *Mireille*.

7

Images of Maillane

However bleak and forbidding the Mas du Juge appeared today, lashed by a bitter wind and framed by the dark sky and rainsoaked hills, I could not forget that in Mistral's eyes his life here had been near-perfect. As a result he neither sought nor wished for any other which might have been remotely comparable. When his father died in 1855, Frédéric's stepbrother, Louis, who was by then married and had children of his own, took charge of the Mas du Juge. Thereafter, the poet's break with his boyhood years was almost complete.

Though he inherited another farm nearby, the Mas de Belle-Vue, Mistral never lived there. Instead, he went with his mother to live at the Maison du Lézard, on the outskirts of Maillane and here Mistral remained until 1876 when he married and moved to another house he had built just across the lane, which he occupied until his death on 25 March 1914.

Although most of his life was spent at Maillane, within easy walking distance of the Mas du Juge, he seldom visited it again – no more than eight or ten times between 1870 and 1908, according to the recollection of an old farm-labourer.

The fields round Maillane are cultivated with wheat, vines and sunflowers; and the crops and apple-orchards are fairly well protected against the mistral's blast by plane-trees, poplars and immense hedges of cypress which a local writer has described rather tongue-in-cheek, as 'sombre but not funereal'.

Various roads through the village lead to Graveson, Chateaurenard, Eyragues and Avignon, and these carry a certain amount of heavy traffic, such as container lorries and trucks, as well as cars, which inevitably disturbs the peaceful atmosphere. Even so, Maillane has somehow contrived to remain a quiet backwater. This is due largely to the fact that it has no hotels and few attractions for tourists apart from the pleasant scenery and Mistral's house, which in 1943 was turned into a museum. The village church, where Mistral was christened, has a fine hexagonal spire, balustrades of delicate, pierced masonry and a neo-classical façade which cannot be seen from the square, but jars somewhat with the building's medieval, rustic character.

I found the church's quaint mixture of period details far less confused than the adornments of Mistral's surprisingly grandiose tomb in the cemetery which, as I have said already, was reproduced from Joanna de Quiqueran (Queen Joanna's) Pavilion at Les Baux. The construction of Mistral's tomb is perhaps lighter and if anything more graceful. Like the Queen's Pavilion, it consists of open arches, the keystones carved with the heads of two Arlésiennes and the seven-pointed star of the Félibrige which perhaps stand for Mistral's heroine, Mireille, and mark his lifelong task of restoring and reviving the Provençal language. Two of Mistral's favourite dogs, Jan-Toutouro and Barbocho, which he called '*mes chiens magiques*' also figure on the tomb, curious, superstitious emblems which openly conflict with the cross set at the apex of the roof. And there are numerous inscriptions: lines of the 'Coupo Santo'; the device etched on a wall of the Maison du Lézard (his mother's house) which reads '*Lou soulèu me fait canta*' ('the sun makes me sing'); and, most striking of all for being in Latin rather than in Provençal, the text:

NON NOBIS, DOMINE, NON NOBIS,
SED DOMINI TUO
ET PROVINCIAE NOSTRAE
DA GLORIAM

which may be translated as, 'Not unto us, O Lord, not unto us, but to Thy Name, and our Provence, the Glory'.

The square at Maillane is fairly typical of many Provençal villages and the scene you will find here is not very different from others elsewhere in the region, or indeed other parts of France. There is a *boulangerie* and one or two cafés; and in fine weather you will see men of all ages, in checked-cloth caps and black berets, seated at tables in the shade, drinking *pastis* and cold beer, while they – and the women grouped at the *boulangerie* door – discuss subjects of importance only to themselves.

'*Bon! alors!* my companion shivered, as he pulled down the brim of his black *gardian* wideawake and buttoned the collar of his long green trenchcoat against the bitter wind. 'Tell me, what do you think of Mistral's little village?'

I had hardly begun to reply when an enormous articulated lorry, fifteen metres long and broad as a Brighton bungalow, loomed at the road-junction where we were standing near Gay's car. The roar of the diesel-engine drowned my voice completely, as the lorry executed a slow, lurching turn, mounted the pavement and, brushing aside an overhanging tree, lumbered away in the direction of Chateaurenard. The huge juggernaut overwhelmed its surroundings as it rumbled by the Maison du Lézard. Seeing the vehicle suddenly juxtaposed against a house where Mistral had lived without ever hearing the noise of an engine, where his timeless masterpiece, *Mireille*, had been composed, shocked my senses.

I noticed Gay glaring at the lorry and I realized that, had we come across somebody perched on the steps of Mistral's tomb, playing loud pop-music on a transistor radio, the feeling of desecration could hardly have been greater.

The Maison du Lézard, where Mistral and his mother came to

live in September 1855, is a plain, substantial house on three floors which stands between the crossroads and a narrow *cul-de-sac*. The house flanks the avenue Lamartine, and it was bought back by Jeanne de Flandreysy who presented it to the Commune of Maillane two years before her death, on 18 July 1957. The Maison du Lézard is now the municipal library. Through the windows by the entrance, I saw bays of metal shelves, the commonplace DIY type on adjustable framing, lined with paperbacks and boxes of correspondence.

The house's interior had been robbed of its original character and it required some effort to imagine Mistral living there, cared for by Délaïde and writing the great narrative epic poems of his youth and middle-age, *Mireille* and *Calendal*, or the collection of colourful lyrical verses which made the *Iles d'or*.

Above the door, I saw the famous sun-dial and the lines engraved there which read:

> Gai lesert, béu toun soulèu,
> L'ouro passo que trop lèu,
> E, deman, ploura, belèu.

Translated from Provençal, this is roughly: 'Beautiful lizard, drink the sunlight, / time passes only too quickly, / Tomorrow perhaps it will rain.' The usually meticulous Richard Aldington for some reason gave a slightly different version – why I am not sure since he had presumably visited the Maison du Lézard. But whatever the niceties, as Aldington pointed out, 'What matters is the sentiment.'

The double-storeyed villa opposite, which Mistral built for himself and his young wife, Marie-Louise Rivière, at the time they were married in 1876, fronts a large garden and faces towards the Mas du Juge and the blue Alpilles which the poet loved and contemplated almost daily. Mr Gay and I found the building was closed for renovations which, we were told, had been long overdue. Our luck had been well and truly out that day! But it did not greatly matter since I had visited the house before and had a clear recollection of the rooms and what they contained.

Some of the best furniture was removed to the Museon Arlaten after the death of Mistral's widow. But even allowing for the fact that it has been preserved as a museum-piece, the house feels, if not quite 'lived-in', at least homely, especially the little study off the spacious, tiled entrance-hall, where Mistral wrote at his desk near a window overlooking the terrace.

The study walls are lined with glass-fronted bookcases which contain editions of Mistral's poetry; and hanging above his desk, there is a large photograph of Mistral and his friend, Alphonse Daudet, in a rather ridiculous pose, facing one another, seated on fireside chairs in what appears to be the middle of a field! At this desk, which had been a gift from Mistral's early sponsor, Lamartine, the later poems were written: among them, *Nerte*, *La Reine Jeanne*, *Le Poème du Rhône* and *Les Olivades*. Here also, Mistral compiled his lexicon of Provençal, the *Trésor du Félibrige*, which many believe to have been his greatest contribution to Rhôneland literature, apart from *Mireille* and, some say, the Rhône Poem.

The salon across the hall has been arranged more for display purposes than anything else. It has a fine gilded mirror and many photographs, plaques, and small paintings which nobody ever bothers to straighten after they've been dusted; and the room is dominated by a large portrait of Mistral carrying his cloak, cane and familiar sombrero, against a sunlit landscape of hills. In the hall, busts of the composer, Charles Gounod, and Lamartine stand at the foot of a simple winding staircase leading to the upper floor. The busts add a formal touch. And they remind us of Gounod's successful opera based on *Mireille*, which enhanced this already popular work; while Lamartine's approval of the poem had brought Mistral to the attention of the Paris critics and gave him a wider audience beyond the Rhôneland as a young man.

The dining-room at the back, apart from a lavishly decorated frieze above the fireplace, is plainly furnished with a small table, a sideboard, a wall-mounted bread-box of the traditional sort, copper pots and pans and other memorabilia including a flintlock gun and Camargue trident. Judging by old photographs, it remains very much as it was in Mistral's day.

But the house seems to have been more comfortable and less austere than the Maison du Lézard where, according to Daudet, Mistral slept in 'a modest peasant's room, with two large beds. The walls had no paper on them; on the ceiling the rafters remained exposed.' When *Mireille* was awarded the Montoyon Prize worth 3,000 gold francs by the Académie-Française in 1861, Mistral's mother begged him to spend something on redecorations, but Mistral flatly refused saying this 'poet's money' was sacrosanct and not for personal use. So too, thirty years later when he invested 10,000 francs from the Prix Jean-Reynaud in the journal *L'Aiöli* which Folco de Baroncelli-Javon helped Mistral edit and publish at the Palais du Roure. And again, the 100,000 francs – his share of the 1904 Nobel Prize – which was used to establish the Museon Arlaten. True, the legacy left by his father had ensured Mistral's financial independence for life, but like his father he was also thrifty and, besides, a man of high principle for whom wealth and its trappings meant nothing compared to the pursuit of a dream. This attitude of Mistral's I found wholly admirable and refreshing.

The garden with its dusty evergreen shrubs, palms and gravel walks, where a tall solitary pine stands by the wrought-iron gates let into the garden's high wall, remains an island of calm. Here Mistral composed his poetry, or else walked arm-in-arm with his wife every evening before supper in the quiet country lanes near Maillane.

Like his father before him, Mistral had married a young bride. At the time of their wedding, Marie-Louise Rivière, from Dijon, was a girl of nineteen. To Mistral, she had been the living image of his heroine, Mireille. Indeed there was a saying in Maillane, '*sèmblo la bello Mirèio, mis amore*' ('like the beautiful Mireille, my love') which it is believed inspired his heroine's name, just as it perfectly described Marie-Louise. The couple were looked after by a faithful maidservant, known as 'Marie-du-Poète', who became like one of the family and sometimes entertained visitors such as Amy and Thorton Oakley, who called on Madame Mistral during their 1935 tour of Provence.

Mistral's widow by then was seventy-eight. Amy Oakley portrayed her as 'a cordial gentlewoman emanating quiet dignity'. In Marie-Louise, Mistral had found an ideal soulmate whose delight had been creating and maintaining the tranquil atmosphere necessary for his art. The couple had no children and it may be their marriage had been based on companionship and mutual interests more than passion. To most of the poet's friends it seemed a perfect match. The only exception perhaps was Mistral's admirer, Jeanne de Flandreysy. A temperamental, possessive *prima donna*, who bitterly resented competition in any form, Jeanne it is said, in a jealous rage, hacked Marie-Louise's face with scissors from a group photograph in which the two women were posed on either side of Mistral.

When I explored Mistral's house with my wife, we found the garden rather bare and neglected, unlike the Oakleys who noted that it was well tended, with Mistral's favourite yellow irises in bloom. To the eager Americans the garden appeared like a shrine, for which Maillane and the Alpilles made a perfect setting. Like the Oakleys, we had imagined Mistral there, lost in thought, absorbed with the landscapes or the characters of some new poem. As Amy Oakley wrote: 'How often the Master must have sat upon this terrace on which the distant Lion of Arles looks down, we thought. What peace, what stillness!'

And so, what were these poems which Mistral contemplated and refined at leisure in his quiet village garden?

The early works, *Mireille* and *Calendal*, had been written and published years before Mistral built his house and married Marie-Louise Rivière. In 1876, *Les Iles d'or* was published – a brilliant miscellany of shorter poems composed after 1853, while other longer works and the task of gathering material for his lexicon, the *Trésor du Félibrige*, were still in progress.

Mireille was begun at the Mas du Juge in 1852 and completed in 1859 at the Maison du Lézard. It is the story of a Provençal Romeo and Juliet. The poem tells how Mireille rejects the three suitors approved by her parents: Alari, a shepherd; Ourrias, a Camargue *gardian*; and Veran, a horse-breeder. Instead she falls hopelessly in love with Vincent, a poor wanderer. The story reaches its climax with Mireille's distraught journey to Les Saintes-Maries in the Camargue, where she seeks the help of the Holy Marys and eventually dies.

Mireille allowed Mistral to write in detail and at considerable length about the Rhôneland life he had seen and experienced; and quite naturally the poem's background and characters were based to a large extent on the Mas du Juge, as well as the Camargue, which Mistral visited for the first time in 1855. In this sense, *Mireille* is really a poem about Rhôneland Provence, a magnificent treasury of Rhôneland customs, religious belief, superstitions, myths and legends recounted in a wealth of meticulously observed detail. Roy Campbell succeeded in capturing the flavour of Mistral's description of galloping Camargue horses in *Mireille* by writing a separate poem of his own, *Horses on the Camargue*, which interpreted Mistral's lines far better than any literal translation.

Mistral's next major poem, *Calendal*, was composed entirely at the Maison du Lézard. *Calendal*, too, is a Provençal story. Its hero, a fisherman from Cassis, has to win the hand of a princess, Esterelle – based on Countess Alix of Les Baux – by accomplishing a series of heroic tasks. Thus Calendal uses a record catch of tunny to buy jewels for Esterelle; and, to prove his strength, he fells the larches on Mont Ventoux. Apart from the fact that Mistral chose to set this poem outside the borders of Rhôneland Provence, in a coastal village east of Marseille, where there now stands a monument to his fisherman hero, *Calendal*'s content had a less widespread appeal and showed how, inevitably, Mistral had begun to drift – however slightly and unintentionally – away from his peasant origins. This drift is hardly surprising: what is extraordinary was Mistral's ability to expand as a writer and a man of culture while continuing to identify closely with the unlettered country-folk with whom he had grown up and among whom his life was spent. Truly, in Aldington's words, this made Mistral an 'extremely rare person'.

The swing away from strictly 'popular' themes continued

with *Nerte* (1884) and *La Reine Jeanne* (1890). At Maillane, besides, Mistral completed the mighty *Trésor*, a work of 2,400 pages and his Provençal translation of Genesis, which appeared first in serial form in the *Armana Prouvençau* between 1878 and 1908. In 1906, he published his autobiographical fragment, *Mes Origines: memoires et récits*.

Amy Oakley's rapturous image of Mistral, seated peacefully on his terrace and gazing towards the Alpilles – although accurate enough in its way – gave no impression whatever of the immense quantity of work the poet achieved there. And, of course, the brief resumé I've made here concerns only a handful of Mistral's literary works. It does not include his increasing number of public duties throughout the Rhôneland; or his vast daily correspondence which totalled over 60,000 letters; or his fifteen years' hard work in establishing and arranging the contents of the Museon Arlaten.

8

The Félibrige: The Magnificent Seven

The Mas du Juge saw the birth of two important events in Mistral's early career: the beginning of his great poem, *Mireille*, in 1852 and the foundation of a loosely knit, but enduring association of Provençal poets and writers, the Félibrige, two years later, in 1854.

In 1852 and 1853, Joseph Roumanille organized congresses of the Provençal poets at Arles and Aix-en-Provence, whose aim was to standardize the dialects forming the *langue d'oc* – at the same time, by popular consent, endeavour to raise the tone and improve the quality of the written language. Mistral approved strongly; but in spite of his enthusiasm for Roumanille's efforts, by 1853 he was forced to admit that the congresses had failed. The poets being by nature individualists, and in many cases also rather 'precious', resented the idea that their work should be governed by a set of rules, or conform to standards imposed by others – its intrinsic excellence, presumably, being the only 'standard' they chose to recognize. A few, notably Jasmin and Gélu, treated Roumanille's proposals with open contempt.

This reaction was a set-back, but on the other hand, it was only to be expected from such a diverse, widespread group – men like Jasmin and Gélu who angrily rejected any attempts by

Roumanille and his followers to modify the variants of Provençal in which their verses were written.

In the end, it fell to Mistral, Roumanille and a few like-minded companions to organize a movement of their own: this they did. On 21 May 1854, Saint-Florentin's day, some of the poets met at the Château of Font-Ségugne, near Avignon, a fine country house which had formerly belonged to the Dukes of Gadagne, but had since passed into the hands of an Avignon lawyer, Paul Giéra, and his brother. As a result of this meeting, the Félibrige was established – tradition has it, by a group of seven poets. These included Mistral, Roumanille and Paul Giéra; the other founder-members being Théodore Aubanel, Alphonse Tavan, Jean Brunet and Mistral's friend of his school and undergraduate days, Anselme Mathieu. The concept of the Félibrige was vital to the Provençal renaissance of language, literature, arts, traditions and festivals. It has been invariably linked with Frédéric Mistral and it tells us more about his development as a poet and a unifying influence in Provence, as well as some of his personal quirks and often strange idio-syncrasies even as a young man of twenty-three.

First, the Félibrige would preserve for the future the Provençal language, the *langue d'oc* – its colour, its freedom to develop and prosper, its regional and intellectual status. Second, the Félibrige was to be a joyful brotherhood, dedicated to simplicity and freedom of expression: its wine should be Beauty; its bread, Goodness; and its path, Truthfulness. The sun would be its fire, it would cherish the ways of Love and put its trust in God. With the lesson of the earlier congresses before them, the *félibres* stressed that provided poetry was written in good Provençal the association's members should be free to write as and how they saw fit on whatever themes appealed to them.

Having settled a code of practice, so to speak, Mistral and his colleagues reached two further important decisions: the move-ment's name, which Mistral proposed as the Félibrige; and the publication of an almanac aimed at the widest possible reader-ship throughout the Rhôneland, the *Armana Prouvençau*. Richard Aldington observed that, while the *Armana Prouvençau* contained 'highbrow' as well as more generally popular material, its object was to 'instruct by amusing' its readers and 'to kindle in them that love of Provence which was the motive of the Félibrige'. The almanac's popularity was proved by its growing circulation over the years, which increased from 500 copies in 1855 (the year it was first issued) to 10,000 by the turn of the century. Those who were unable to read the almanac for themselves, had it read to them 'aloud on winter nights' all over the region 'in cottages and lonely farm-houses'. By writing about subjects which they had experienced and understood, Mistral and his companions at last began to produce poetry which touched the people's hearts. This to an extent perhaps paved the way for the success of Mistral's *Mireille*.

While other nineteenth-century poetry groups vanished without trace, the Félibrige, despite its small, even obscure beginnings, flourished. It thrives in Provence to this day and its membership is now world-wide. Mistral's choice of the name alone had been a master-stroke. Nobody really knew for certain what the word Félibrige had been intended to mean and Mistral's explanations remained tantalizingly vague. The inevitable controversy over its meaning kept the Félibrige (both the term and the movement itself) alive in people's minds and thus strengthened popular awareness of Mistral's aims. It was a splendid example of shrewd public relations, whether or not Mistral had actually foreseen this possibility at the time. According to some, the name derived from the Latin *felibris*, or *fellare* – meaning to suckle, hence a suckling child: by extension, this could be taken to mean *nourrisson* – a 'nourishing' infant, or a student *novice*. In Spanish, an equivalent word *feligres* means a follower – another apt translation. While other scholars, conscious of the early Greek influence in Provence, preferred the Greek *philebraios* – a lover of beautiful things. Aldington has written: 'A Teutonic origin has been suggested, and somebody (possibly Bonaparte Wyse) suggested that it was Irish.' This was William Bonaparte-Wyse, the son of a British Minister at Athens and the daughter of Lucien Bonaparte. Bonaparte-Wyse became an enthusiast of the Félibrige cause after reading *Mireille*

which he bought at the Librairie Roumanille in 1860. An 'odd mixture of Irishman and Corsican', Wyse was befriended by Mistral, learned to speak and write fluently in Provençal and published a collection of Provençal verse, *Li Parpaioun blu* ('The Blue Butterflies') before his death at Cannes in 1892.

When, in May 1854, at Font-Ségugne, Mistral proposed the name, Félibrige, he quoted then in support of his choice the Biblical *sept félibres de la Loi* – the seven *félibres* of the Law. And when Paul Giéra, the notary, demanded to know 'which Law?' Mistral immediately undertook to provide it. The 'Law', a dictionary which Mistral researched and compiled over the next twenty years, was finally published at his own expense as the *Trésor du Félibrige*, the ultimate Provençal lexicon, in 1878. The seven *félibres* were, of course, the seven doctors of law with whom the Virgin Mary found the boy Jesus deep in discussion at the temple in Jerusalem.

One of Mistral's lifelong idiosyncrasies was his superstitious attachment to the number seven. Take the Félibrige: based on the seven doctors of the Jewish Law, it was founded by a group of seven poets (a number Mistral arrived at after some trouble, as I will demonstrate presently); a symbol of the Félibrige was the seven-pointed star of Saint-Estelle – and Saint-Estelle was chosen as the movement's patron saint, even though 21 May had been the feast of Saint-Florentin. The date of the first meeting, 21 May, was divisible by seven; and at Avignon near Font-Ségugne there were seven churches, seven gates, seven hospitals, seven colleges – and over a period of seventy years, seven Popes had reigned there. (As a matter of interest, although I believe there was never any connection with the Félibrige idea, a sixteenth-century literary group with somewhat similar aims, had been called the Pléiädes after the constellation of seven stars). There are numerous other examples of Mistral's obsession: his poems, *Mireille* and *Calendal*, each took seven years to write; and the poet's wedding-day in 1876 was the 27th of September – as Aldington pointed out, the seventh month (ie sept-embre) in the old Roman calendar.

At the inaugural meeting in May 1854, it seems that only *four* of the seven founder-members were actually present: Mistral, Roumanille, Aubanel and Giéra. Apart from Mistral, Roumanille and Aubanel, the others were poets of little consequence. Jean Brunet replaced Eugène Garcin, who had been accused of betraying the Félibrige's ideals. Brunet wrote little poetry, but gathered an astonishing collection of 14,000 Provençal proverbs! Alphonse Tavan, a railway-worker, wrote sad poems inspired by the deaths of his wife and daughter. Anselme Mathieu, 'a fantasist and amorist' contributed inconsequential, charming trifles – he was one of Mistral's favourites and a good companion. Paul Giéra and his brother, Jules, provided the romantic stage-setting for the inauguration ceremony and later hosted many Félibrige gatherings, when the poets met at the Château of Font-Ségugne and there feasted, drank and declaimed their latest verses to each other and to the pretty girls – the *damisello graciouso* – who accompanied them on such occasions.

To Mistral, even the name Font-Ségugne seemed propitious: it combined *font*, like *fontaine*, meaning a spring of pure water; and Segugne, or *seguido* in Provençal, meant continuous – hence, the continuously-flowing spring of the *félibres'* inspiration and perhaps also the pure spring of the *langue d'oc*.

It is interesting that Mistral and Roumanille, both sons of the *mas*, chose to launch the new poetry movement in such elegant, aristocratic surroundings. Mistral must surely have considered other possibilities – the Mas du Juge for example – but he evidently concluded that the Château of Font-Ségugne, like the ancient Troubadour castles, better matched the character, mood and importance of the occasion. His careful selection of Brunet and Tavan, men of humble origin, also implied that the Félibrige was a democratic association and in contrast to Paris's literary 'schools', its doors were open to poets and Provençal loyalists from all walks of life.

The first issues of the *Armana Prouvençau* were managed by Aubanel, a member of the long-established, renowned Avignon publishing family, whose business still flourishes there in the place Saint-Pierre; but after 1858, the task fell to Roumanille who later published works by Mistral and many other *félibres*.

Mistral's choice of the founder-members shows that he possessed shrewd organizing skills. We must not forget that, like Giéra, he too had had legal training at Aix. But, according to Marcel Bonnet, Mistral did not *add* three poets to the Font-Ségugne group of four to achieve his mystical seven – this number was arrived at by *reducing by four* the original company of eleven, all of whom had contributed to the first issue of the *Armana Prouvençau* in 1855. Of the remaining four, therefore: Garcin, I have said already, was replaced by Brunet; Denis Cassan and J-B Martin both resigned; while Dr Toussaint Poussel died in 1859. By natural wastage and some tactful manipulation, Mistral achieved his company of seven *félibres*; but only after some time and not, as has been generally accepted, at the moment the Félibrige was actually founded.

Some critics maintained that it became little more than Mistral's 'fan-club' which broadcast and perpetuated his achievements. It would have been difficult to avoid this effect, since Mistral's genius set him far above the other poets, much of whose work was mediocre. What was more to the point, however, a widespread public interest in things Provençal had been created and this, as much as poetry, prose-writing and art, made the Provençal renaissance a genuine reality.

The Félibrige's members eventually included all the great Camargue writers and artists – Folco de Baroncelli-Javon, Joseph D'Arbaud, Marius Jouveau, Ivan Pranishnikoff, Jeanne de Flandreysy and – nearer our own day – André Chamson, Henri Aubanel and Marie Mauron. Their work gained recognition outside the Rhôneland and Provence; some including André Chamson and Michel-Droit were members of the Académie-Française and were awarded important literary prizes.

I spent many hours in the dimly-lit, large white-washed room at the Museon Arlaten dedicated to the Félibrige relics, where the movement's history unfolds through a fascinating collection of old photographs, paintings, books and mementos. The windows are kept shuttered, as a rule, to prevent the many rare documents and pictures from being damaged by exposure to sunlight. Wonderful as it is, the Félibrige room has a charmingly informal atmosphere, as though it were simply a larger arrangement of memorabilia gathered by anyone of literary tastes over the years for his own pleasure – and indeed this was how it originated. Mistral himself refused the offer of the Académie-Française's membership, 'preferring to serve Provence in his own way' as the bard of Maillane. And it is this attitude one finds reflected here at the Museon Arlaten. Simplicity and humility, his parents' legacy, lay at the heart of Mistral's outlook. Simplicity had been written into the Félibrige's code in 1854 and it became a byword of its early supporters and the aim of later generations of Mistral's disciples. Younger *félibres*, poets and romantics such as Baroncelli-Javon and D'Arbaud, towards the end of the nineteenth century carried their search for a simple life made of poetry and hard labour into the Camargue marshes where they lived and wrote. In Baroncelli's case, his pursuit of tranquillity and peace of mind had been literally blessed and encouraged by Mistral's words: '*Je te confie la Camargue, Folco. Tu la connais mieux que moi. Défends-la!*' (I entrust the Camargue to you, Folco. You know it better than I do. Safeguard it!)

Even the fine silver-gilt star, the Etoile Dorée worn by the *capoulié* or head of the Félibrige, had at its centre as a constant reminder of the simple way the humble wayside flower, the *pervenche* or periwinkle, a symbol of purity and faith.

9

Daudet's Mill

The scenery round Fontvieille is quite lovely; a closely woven tapestry of fields and woodland, but also very natural and wild. I came there from Arles one fine morning in mid-October and left the road a little to the south of the village and walked up through an olive-grove to a patch of high ground, where I sat on an outcrop of warm, white rocks to admire the view.

Nearby were the remains of a Roman aqueduct, dating from the first century AD, great piles of white and orange stone, which for five hundred years had carried a supply of fresh water to the plain from the springs and the rain-fed streams of the Alpilles.

From the edge of a steep precipice, the countryside unrolled at my feet like a huge relief-map: streams and meadows shimmered in the strong sunlight, with Mont Ventoux and the outstretched, slumbering mass of the Corde, in various shades of blue, touched with pink and amber, at the horizon. I saw houses with red roofs and smudges of dull-green garden shrubbery; the metallic-green olives, silvered, dusty like the aromatic thyme which carpetted the dry hillsides; and the blue-green pines, which cast slender shadows of a deeper blue or made little pools of shade like ink-blots on the brown sunbaked earth.

A tiny brown lizard, startled by my shadow, scuttled away and vanished in a wisp of withered grass.

Somewhere below me, hidden in the woods, lay the eighteenth-century Château of Montauban where the novelist Alphonse Daudet came year after year from Paris; the great house which he had made his headquarters while he gathered material for the stories later to be published in 1866 as *Lettres de mon moulin* ('Letters from my Windmill').

And there, less than two kilometres away, was Daudet's mill itself! The squat little building, shaped like a salt-cellar, with its sails and its conical roof, capped by a bull-shaped weather-vane, which had once thrived like others in the neighbourhood and, in its heyday, produced five kilos of finely-ground flour every hour.

In his preface to *Lettres de mon moulin*, Daudet described the Château of Montauban in the 'visual and musical' prose for which he became justly famous; his 'eye-music', as Walter de la Mare called it, made of delicate, precise images which Daudet selected as a painter selects his colours. He drew romantic beautiful pictures of Montauban's Italianate colonnades, its vines, peacock-perches, 'sheds glittering with harrows and ploughshares', the fig-tree entwined round an iron well-head, and the sheepfold which stood near a field of almond-trees, the lush grass strewn with their pink blossom torn and scattered by the mistral. The once formal gardens of the Château had long since reverted to a wilderness of rocks and pines and 'its tangled, overgrown paths,' Daudet wrote, were 'slippery with dry pine-needles'. The old farmhouse kitchen tacked onto the main building, with its rough plastered walls and earthen floor, made a homely contrast to the Château's cool, paved, twilit galleries, the wide stately staircase, the draughty corridors and the elegant salons, furnished with sofas and cane-bottomed Louis XIV armchairs.

Daudet always lived in the main house, which his cousins, the Ambroys, owned. But he loved to spend his evenings after dinner in the kitchen where the taciturn old shepherd, Dominique the coachman, the gamekeeper Mitifio, nicknamed

'Pistolet', and others gathered to gossip and sing by the fire of olive-roots that burned in the immense stone hearth overhung by a brass lantern.

From here Daudet made frequent excursions to the ruined mill which was in those days little more than 'a crumbling pile of stones and old wooden beams which had not turned in the wind for many years and which stood there helpless, as useless as a poet'. (I wonder what Mistral and the Félibrige made of this remark!) The mill became a friendly refuge. Daudet wrote: 'Between ourselves and things strange affinities exist. From the first day I saw it, this abandoned outcast of a windmill had been dear to me: I loved it for its distressed condition, for its path lost under the herbs . . . for its crumbling platform where it was good to idle the hours away sheltered from the wind.'

The stories collected as *Lettres de mon moulin* were written in Paris and, unlike the Félibrige's works, they were written in French. All through his life, Daudet's love-hate relationship with Paris continued to haunt him. In Paris, he wearied for the thyme-scented hills of Fontvieille; and at Fontvieille, by the ruins of the mill, he mused, 'it seems to me, as I lie in the grass, aching with the pain of my memories, that I am seeing . . . all my Paris passing between the pines.'

The younger son of a silk-manufacturer, Alphonse Daudet was born at Nîmes in Provence, on 13 May 1840, and educated first at Bezouce and afterwards at the Lycée Ampère in Lyons. Still in his teens, he abandoned his studies to become an usher, a junior master in a college at Alais in the Cévennes – a post similar to that held by Roumanille at the Collège Royal. In November 1857, Alphonse joined his brother, Ernest, in Paris where he worked as a reporter for the *Spectateur* and found a publisher for the poems he had written at Lyons and Alais. The privately-printed collection, *Les Amoureuses*, was highly successful and led to Daudet's appointment as a secretary to the Duke of Morny, the Emperor Napoleon III's half-brother, who was President of the Legislative Council. While in Paris, Daudet contracted syphilis, a disease which gradually worsened and caused his agonizing, early death in 1897.

Daudet's years of intense suffering were compensated for by a happy married life with Julia Allard, whom he wed in 1867 as a girl of twenty, and who outlived him by more than forty years. As a novelist, he achieved celebrity and wealth. By 1890, according to his translator, Frederick Davies, Daudet's income had been the equivalent of about £40,000 a year (I might add that Mr Davies was writing in 1978). And it had been the success of these later novels such as *Le Petit Chose* (1868), *Tartarin of Tarascon* (1872), *Le Nabab* (1877) and, arguably his finest, *Nouma Roumestan* (1881), that eventually created a market for *Lettres de mon moulin*.

It is interesting that the *Lettres*, when first published in book form in 1869, sold fewer than 2,000 copies.

While he became a close friend of Mistral, whom he met in 1859 soon after *Mireille* appeared, Daudet was never really associated with the Félibrige or the Provençal renaissance as such. Yet it was largely Daudet's writing (in Mistral's words, '*ce délicieux parfum de la Provence*') which gave English readers their image of life in nineteenth-century Rhôneland, through translations of *Tartarin* and *Lettres de mon moulin*.

Daudet stayed for the first time at Fontvieille in the summer of 1860 with his cousin, Timoleon Ambroy, at Montauban. His poor health, which necessitated long periods of convalescence at Fontvieille, led indirectly to his *Lettres* being written. Daudet toyed with the idea of buying his beloved windmill, but he never did so. Appropriately, the mill remained a place of fantasy and inspiration – like the *querencia* of the arena, a corner to which the exhausted bull returns again and again, the mill afforded Daudet a safe retreat, and solace in times of distress.

The hills round Fontvieille were ideally suited to windmills and the corn-grinder's trade. The wind blows, it is said, from no less than thirty-two different points of the compass, and for more than 300 days of the year. By the wind, I do not mean only the mistral. Already I had learned from Marcel Bosqui's talk at the Palais du Roure that, here in the Rhôneland, many other winds coming from the West, South, East and points between, like the northerly mistral, were widely known and each had its name in Provençal.

At Daudet's Mill I found the names of the winds inscribed around the wall-head timbers of the grinding-chamber. Even in Provençal some of them had a familiar ring: the Tremountano (tramontane) for example, and of course the Mistraou (*mistral*). I saw the mistral's relative, the all-devouring Mango Fango, though from the wind-diagram, this appeared to mean a wind other than the *mistral*, a wind blowing from a more westerly quarter; or else it may be a variant-name for the *mistral*, I am not quite certain.

Among the less familiar north winds are the Temps Dre, Mountagnero, Ventouresco and Aguieloun; those from the east include the Gisampo, Auro Rousso and Eissero; from the south, the Vent de Souleu, Marin and Vent Laro; and from the west, the Poumentau and the Vent de Damo. This is a fairly random selection, but at least it gives some idea of the winds' numbers and variety of names in the lyrical *bas-latine* tongue of the Rhôneland.

The mill, known as the 'Moulin de Daudet', is one of several which still exist near Fontvieille. It was built in 1804 and was known formerly as the Moulin Ribet or the Moulin Saint Pierre, after the village's patron saint. Apart from this, the only working example today is the Moulin de Bédarrides, which has been adapted to electricity and is used for manufacturing the excellent quality olive-oil for which Fontvieille is renowned. Others such as the Moulin Tissot (sometimes called the Avon), east of Fontvieille, and the Moulin Sourdon to the west, are merely roofless shells. Michel Gay, is his splendidly illustrated history of Fontvieille, published in 1990 to mark the bicentenary of the village, has observed: 'The mill has always been the sacred fetish, the soul of the village. If one breaks down, or ceases to function, everybody is upset: flour is bread and bread is life. And when the Fontvieille folk want to celebrate, they dance a *farandole* for the mills.'

Daudet's mill is approached by a steep path, flanked by umbrella-pines, and from its hilltop site there is a magnificent panoramic view of the Rhône valley and the Alpilles. The small museum beside the mill has been designed to show Daudet's life by means of photographs, copies of his novels and objects connected with him, including his writing-desk which has a silver plate bearing Madame Daudet's engraved signature.

Here I discovered something I had never realized before: the fact that the entire mill-roof could be rotated (and indeed *must be*) so that changes of wind blowing from different directions kept the sails turning at maximum speed. This device was essential to maintain the mill at full production. The roof and the horizontal beam to which the sails are attached are seated just inside the wall-head and they revolved on a ratchet-mechanism operated by a wooden pole which acted as a lever. This must have been a back-breaking task, for many of the moving parts were made entirely of wood, oak and chestnut mainly. To re-align the mill-sails, it required a crew of three strong men, hauling on the lever-pole, like sailors at the rigging of a yacht.

The massive grinding-stones were about a metre in diameter and a good handspan in depth. They had been worn as smooth as glass by years of constant use and were hewn from a durable, hard, grey stone quite unlike the creamy-white porous stone from the quarries near Fontvieille. All these details were explained to me by the mill's caretaker who, with his thick curly black hair, drooping black moustaches and gaunt features, reminded me somewhat of Daudet in middle-age. The caretaker smoked incessantly, Gitanes Maïs cigarettes rolled in yellow paper. He chain-smoked from habit, I imagine, but perhaps also to discourage the midges which hovered in clouds all round the mill. I got badly bitten on my scalp, face and neck and the itching caused by the swellings, which looked like a chain of tiny red volcanoes, continued to irritate me for the better part of a week. However, the midge-bites seemed a small price to pay for the enjoyment of such beautiful scenery and the charm of Fontvieille and its surroundings.

Much of Fontvieille's old-world character has been preserved, in spite of its popularity as a tourist-centre. Apart from its fine public buildings, such as the Town Hall, and the church in the place de la République, there are lanes and byways with pretty terraced cottages, whose old-fashioned gardens and pergolas are festooned with roses, bougainvillea and jasmine. These were the quarry-labourers' dwellings. Along many of the garden walls grapes ripened in the sunshine in luscious dark ruby-red clusters, which the villagers reached for and casually sampled as they strolled by.

I had been invited to lunch at the Galerie Saint-Michel by Michel Gay and Marcel Fouque. A discreet private entrance at the rear led through a wild little vegetable-garden where strawberries, raspberries and courgettes sprawled on beds of cracked, unwatered soil. The walled garden beyond was a mass of brightly-coloured flowers and rank vegetation: great bunches of greenery, curling tendrils and heavy blossom covered the roofs, walls, trellises and footpaths in profuse, romantic disarray.

It had been an exceptionally dry summer but vegetables and flowers nevertheless had flourished: the courgettes I saw had attained truly heroic proportions; and spires of the sinister *datura*, the poisonous narcotic shrub used in *vodoun* ceremonies in Haiti, with its sickly whitish petals, rose to a height of nearly three metres.

Lunch began with a delicious rabbit *mousse*, garnished with wild fennel (a herb which, I was told, relieves flatulence) and sliced mushrooms; and after that came roast chicken *à la Provençale*, served with spaghetti and lightly-boiled vegetables which included wafer-thin courgettes of less intimidating size than those I had seen in the garden. Five cheeses were produced, among them the bitter-tasting *gardian* cheese from the Camargue, made of ewe's milk, and a fine mature Brie. Then came a generous dessert salad to round off, a mixture of kiwi fruit and pineapple, spread on a layer of sweet home-made ice-cream. Needless to say, as usual the bread was first-class, freshly baked that morning at a *boulangerie* in the village. Marcel Fouque who, like Michel Gay, is an acknowledged expert on the Rhôneland artists, is also a very accomplished chef. He apologized politely but quite unnecessarily, saying that lunch had been a rather pot-luck affair, cobbled together rather hurriedly after a busy morning. This I put down to an excess of modesty, but afterwards on several occasions when I ate lunches and dinners which he had prepared – as he said, 'with proper care' – I realized that he meant it, for some of these were really superb creations.

Over lunch, we talked at some length about Daudet and Fontvieille and Michel Gay explained how the Société des Amis des Moulins de Daudet had been founded in 1932. As I understand it, the Société had nominated the Moulin Ribet, owned by Hyacinthe Bellon, Fontvieille's Mayor, to represent Daudet's Mill. The commitee refurbished the delapidated building which had been a working mill until 1915, and they converted the nearby *bluterie* as the museum.

The opening ceremonies held at the Mill between 29 June and 2 July 1935 were typically flamboyant and colourful. They included folk-dances, music, speeches and feasting on a grand scale. An audience of 5,000 gathered on the hillside for a performance of the *Arlésienne*, Daudet's play written in 1872. Baroncelli-Javon led a procession of Camargue horsemen, members of the Nacioun Gardiano, who were joined by the ancient Confrérie des Gardians. Folklorist groups attended from all over the Rhôneland and fanfares were sounded by trumpeters from the gaily-uniformed Spahis d'Orange.

The four days of festival ended with a pilgrimage to Daudet's birthplace, the Maison Sabran, and sprays of flowers were laid at his statue in the place de la Couronne, in Nîmes. At Fontvieille, the celebrations concluded with a grand ball, held at the Château of Montauban, with a galaxy of distinguished guests including women dressed in Arlésien lace and shawls. As Gay observed, it was perhaps the most glittering pageant that Montauban had ever witnessed.

Like so many other Rhôneland towns and villages, Fontvieille also has its rue Frédéric Mistral. Here I was introduced to the owner of Fontvieille's famous hotel, the Auberge La Régalido. According to their brochure, *régalido* means 'the re-awakened flare of the fire, stirred up with a handful of twigs to welcome a late visitor'. The Régalido was originally an oil-mill and it has been tastefully restored, with a spacious vaulted dining-room and comfortable bedrooms which overlook an attractive rose garden.

The owner, who doubles as the Régalido's chef, was dressed in smart country casuals, a tartan shirt and an open-fronted shooting coat. Proudly he told me how, on 17 May 1972, he had prepared a special lunch for the Queen and Prince Charles when they visited Fontvieille and he gave me a photocopy of the menu. He said: 'Her Majesty likes simple traditional dishes. One of her Aides came the day before and we discussed the meal. He told me Her Majesty would not drink any wine, but that I must be sure to have a good supply of mineral water. At lunch, however, the Queen said that she would like some wine after all! Fortunately we had plenty of good wine from the Baux district and that saved the day.'

The Queen had an excellent lunch: *Brouillade aux truffles*, followed by *Grenadin de veau aux morilles* and artichokes with asparagus-tips. The cheese board was simpler than Marcel Fouque had provided, just a good plain *Fromage de chèvre*; and for dessert the Royal party were given strawberries.

Mr Gay remarked that the Queen Mother used to stay every year with friends near Fontvieille and she was very popular with the local shopkeepers. 'Such a generous lady!' said Gay. 'Once she visited a souvenir shop here in the village and bought nearly everything they had in the basement. The old man who runs the shop said he'd never sold as much rubbish in his life to a customer, and he used to pray every night for the Queen Mother to come back soon!'

At the Town Hall, I was shown some magnificent paintings by Léo Lelée which hung in the main reception room. These were large works carried out in watercolours heightened with gouache and they were fine examples of Lelée's mature technique and the subjects for which the artist is best known. A pair of landscape-format pictures showed Arlésiennes in their flowing white dresses dancing a *farandole* on the beach against a background of bright-blue sea and sky. Another showed the horsemen of the Nacioun Gardiano with their captain, Folco de

Baroncelli-Javon, holding the Gardiano's maroon and gold banner, on the hill near Daudet's Mill.

For years I had been a great admirer of Lelée's work. Lelée lived at Fontvieille after spending some years at Arles and his prolific output included drawings of his house which is now a clothes shop, the Course Libre with *razeteurs* and a bull in a makeshift arena encircled by farm-waggons, and studies of Daudet's Mill. The painting of the Mill at the Town Hall was very fine, but I like even better Lelée's looser, spontaneous sketches: one which shows a winding procession of mules carrying up the heavy sacks of corn; and another of the 1935 celebrations which gives a remarkable impression of the crowds gathered on the hillside, the *gardians* on horseback with their wives and daughters riding 'pillion' and the Arlésiennes shaded by parasols, all of which Lelée suggested in a vivid shorthand washed-in with luminous colours.

Lelée succeeded in capturing Fontvieille's atmosphere and the strong southern light in a way that even Van Gogh failed to achieve when he came and drew at Fontvieille in 1888. Van Gogh's drawings of the countryside and its mills, in particular his oil-on-canvas study of the 'Paysage à Fontvieille', depicted a kind of scenery that seems more typical of Holland than Provence. It is possible that he was still uncertain how to deal with the powerful sunlight. Van Gogh's sketch of Daudet's Mill, with the undulations of country emphasized by clusters of short, thick strokes of the pen, produced an effect which was both restless and sombre. The drawings he made at Les Saintes-Maries-de-la-Mer using the same technique, were far more successful; but the frenzied rushes of his broad-nibbed pen seemed to burden the airy landscapes of Fontvielle which, in turn, responded to Lelée's sensitive brush like flowers to a shower of rain.

This north Rhôneland countryside is a wonderful place for children to grow up in. It has always been so. Mistral's recollections of his Maillane childhood were idyllic, as we know; and Lelée's daughter, Yvonne, told me that here at Fontvieille her upbringing had been wonderfully carefree. In his autobiography *Fantômes et vivants* Daudet's son Léon (1867–1942) recalled the magic of his boyhood years at Fontvieille, writing: 'As a child, then as a young man, I enjoyed a limitless freedom there, drinking in the air and the light, aware of the past history that quivered all round me. . . . These southern landscapes teach us the meaning of spiritual harmony and serenity.'

In her book, *The Heart of Provence* (1936), Amy Oakley recorded her conversations with Baroncelli-Javon, Léopold Lelée, Marie-Louise Mistral and Jeanne de Flandreysy, in a discursive rambling style which brought the Oakleys' experiences to life with great immediacy and preserved many unique and delightful anecdotes which otherwise might have been lost for ever.

Whenever I read Amy Oakley's descriptions of the Rhôneland of pre-war days, the more I envied the couple's good fortune having arrived there in time to meet these fascinating men and women who had been deeply and personally involved with Mistral's revival of Provençal traditions and the region's language, literature and art.

In July 1935 the Oakleys reached Fontvieille too late for the ceremonies at Daudet's Mill, but they heard about them from Lelée himself some weeks afterwards. Lelée reckoned that at least 18,000 visitors had passed through the village. He told how the hordes of sightseers had cheated the gate-keeper: 'Families of five pushed in with three tickets. . . . Many scurried past . . . hugging a cane or umbrella to their bosoms and murmuring the magic word "Musician"!' To Lelée, who had been to Athens in 1930, the 'Arlésiennes supple and flexible in their shawls' seemed 'like a Greek frieze come to life' as they danced the *farandole*.

That year, even by Rhôneland standards, the mid-summer heat was overpowering and the people swore that figs had ripened overnight. Somebody from Arles, evidently a forerunner of the modern tourist-trade, set up a book-stall displaying quantities of Daudet's novels and stories. 'And did he sell any?' Mrs Oakley wrote. 'Not he. The only things he sold that day were four hundred kilos of peaches and barrels of cool beer – not to mention *pastis*.'

Later on, when the American couple visited Tarascon, they managed to track down the owner of the Villa Tartarin, a Parisian lady named Madame Plèche, who showed them over the elegant house and gardens which dated from 1763. Hidden among lush palms and Barbary figs, the Villa Tartarin had previously belonged to an eccentric, retired colonial officer who, it was said, inspired many of the absurdly comical adventures of Daudet's most famous character, Tartarin. To paraphrase Daudet: 'All Frenchmen have in them a touch of Tarascon.' And, one might add, of Tartarin also. Perhaps the most attractive edition of *Les Aventures prodigieuses de Tartarin de Tarascon* was published in 1937, illustrated by seventy superb lithographs from drawings by Raoul Dufy made over six years from 1931.

Daudet has been criticized, usually by outsiders, for poking fun at the Rhôneland; as Aldington wrote, 'exploiting the Midi for the amusement of the Parisiens', while being 'very careful always to keep on the right side of his public'. A similar criticism has been made of Marcel Pagnol who, according to François Cali, followed 'the same path' as Daudet. But surely this is being a little over-sensitive. As an elderly acquaintance observed when I put this to him: '*Cher ami*! We Tarasconais are perfectly capable of enjoying a joke at our own expense. Besides, we've actually profited from *Tartarin*, for there is no doubting the fact Daudet's novels helped to put Tarascon on the map.'

The Rhôneland folk are a bit like Yorkshiremen: they are far too practical to look a gift-horse in the mouth; and, being also blessed with a sense of humour, they would no more dream of denouncing the author of *Tartarin* than the Spaniards of La Mancha would think of disowning Cervantes.

10

Tarasques and Razeteurs

Like Avignon and Arles, Tarascon has a magnificent situation on the banks of the Rhône. It is linked to Beaucaire on the west shore by a fine motor-bridge and the views of the surrounding country from vantage points such as the castle towers, are good enough to justify a visit by themselves. Tarascon was founded originally by the Greeks, who built a trading-post, supplied from Marseille, on the island of Jernica in the Rhône. Centuries of alluvial sediment widened the island until eventually it was joined to the east bank of the river. After the Romans captured Jernica, they changed its name to Tarusco after the Tarasque, a ferocious dragon-monster with a lion's head, spiked backbone and a long serpent tail, which the legend states devoured countless human victims and terrorized the district from its marshy lair, deep in the woodlands of Nerluc.

According to the legend, Saint Martha, the sister of Saint Mary Magdalene, confronted the fearsome beast in its lair, pacified it with her crucifix and led it on a leash made from her girdle, three times round the walls of Tarascon. Different versions of the story tell how the Tarasque was then locked away in a dungeon, where the twelfth-century castle now stands, or stoned to death by the mob, or else drowned in the Rhône.

In 1474, 'Good King René' founded the Jeux de la Tarasque which marked the occasion, as an amusing diversion for his second wife, Jeanne de Laval and, at the same time, created the Order of the Knights of the Tarasque. A rowdy procession held on the second Sunday after Pentecost, featured a Tarasque belching smoke from its nostrils, a sprawling pantomime affair rather like a Chinese dragon, which shuffled along supported by sixteen volunteers. On 29 July, Saint Martha's Day, a smaller replica of the Tarasque in tamer mood was led through the streets by a girl dressed to represent the saint.

The Tarasque I had seen at the Museon Arlaten seemed to me a rather pathetic, harmless-looking creature. This has a face like a cartoon-cat with red-rimmed, soulful eyes, sharp-pointed teeth and a little scrubby mane of coarse bristles, rather like a Punk's 'Mohican' haircut. Its fat, round body, made of stretched cloth and paper painted with green and yellow scales, is dome-shaped like a Christmas pudding. The saw-toothed ridge along its spine and its armour of cardboard spikes are painted dark-green to match the rest of its body. Including its wooden tail, this Tarasque measures 3½ metres long and it stands roughly 1½ metres in height.

A further version of the Tarasque's timely demise records that 'so repentant was the beast upon hearing the name of Jesus that she threw herself into the Rhône'. The Tarasque's eleventh-hour baptism, however, appears to have won over the minds and hearts of the terror-sticken, pagan Tarasconais for immediately afterwards Saint Martha succeeded in converting them to Christianity. This being so, the affair ended happily, if not for the Tarasque, for the people of Tarascon and it may be, after all, that this has been the real point of the legend.

Besides its famous connections with Tartarin and the Tarasque, Tarascon is the centre of the Course Camarguaise and the ceremonies associated with it. The contestants who take part in the Course are judged annually, and prizes are awarded in order of merit. On 26 October I visited Tarascon at the invitation of the Mayor, Madame Thérèse Aillaud, for a reception held in honour of the season's three best *razeteurs*.

The *razeteurs* are young men who face the Camargue bulls in the lively and often dangerous sport, the Course, which is Provence's equivalent of the Spanish *corrida*. Unlike the *mise-à-mort* bull-fights of Spain, the bulls which take part in the Course are never killed in the arena. In Provence the Course is regarded as a sport and, as such, comparable with football or lawn tennis. So, too, is the *mise-à-mort* style of fighting; except that, whereas nowadays opinion is apt to be divided over the killing of bulls, the bloodless thrills provided by the Course have an almost universal appeal.

The Course Camarguaise – also known as the Course à la Cocarde or the Course Libre – began towards the end of the nineteenth century, although the origins of such bull-games are very ancient and may date as far back as 5000 BC. According to local experts, the risks taken by the *razeteurs*, while they are not great by comparison with other dangerous sports (motor-racing and mountaineering for example) are significant enough: between 1924 and 1965, no fewer than eight *razeteurs* were killed; and many more have been injured besides, some of them seriously. With a vigorous five-year-old bull in the arena, it is actually surprising that far more serious accidents don't occur. This is due partly to the amazing agility and acrobatic skills of the *razeteurs*, and partly perhaps to the younger bulls' lack of experience or killer-instinct.

The bulls used for the Course are actually much more dangerous than those of the *corrida*. The Spanish bulls, like the Spanish-Camargue cross-strains in Provence, face the matador only once during their fifteen or twenty minutes in the arena which ends in death. A good *cocarde*-bull returns again and again to the arena and over the years, being also very intelligent, learns the ropes and the technique of the best *razeteurs*. The bull actually recognizes its tormentors and it will launch its attack at them, ignoring the others. For the *razeteurs*, such an animal is a worthy opponent and one which may cost him his life.

The modern *razeteurs* wear long white trousers, short-sleeved white shirts and white trainers which have replaced the rubber-soled tennis-shoes, or 'sand-shoes' of days gone by.

The object of the sport is to lift or 'tweak' off the *cocarde, ficelles* and *glands* attached to the bull's horns, in a graceful sweeping movement made by the *razeteur* as he dashes across in front of the charging animal. The *cocarde* is a red ribbon, 30mm long, strung between the bull's horns with the *ficelles*, or strings, and the *glands*, strands of wool, are fastened to the base of its horns with elastic bands. A larger *cocarde*, the *garrot*, may be attached to the bull's back. Should the *razeteurs* fail to dislodge the *cocarde*, the prize-money allotted to the bull is raised in subsequent contests.

In his hand the *razeteur* clutches a comb, or *crochet*, 100mm × 120mm, which he uses to cut free the *cocarde*. The comb has four metal teeth welded to a tubular grip, and each of the teeth is indented by four more sharp little teeth which help to tear away the ribbon. The old-fashioned comb which had jagged serrations between the main teeth, has been replaced by one with smooth interstices, so as to avoid unnecessary injury to the bull. The comb can sometimes damage the bull's eye, or else the animal may be injured when it tries to jump over the barricades, having been provoked or frightened by the noise of the spectators.

The play of rippling muscles and sinews, as the bull makes a sudden swift lunge with its head, narrowly missing the *razeteur*'s legs or tossing high into the air the red-painted boards of the barricade, is very striking and gives a tremendous sense of the creature's power and strength. Again and again I have watched breathless with excitement as a bull jumped the barricades, sometimes actually touching the *razeteur*'s heels as he made a flying leap for the wall, where he clung panting, hanging by his finger-tips like a great white bat, as the bull rushed past beneath him, wild-eyed, its muzzle clotted with saliva, its nostrils steamy and dripping. One can only admire the courage, skill and grace of these white-clad youngsters who pit their wits, reflexes and fleetness of foot against the sharper reactions and speed of the bull.

Most *razeteurs* are amateurs; but the prize-money can amount to quite large sums, £1,000 or more, and the best men who take part in the Course throughout the season, between March and November, including the Cocarde d'Or at Arles, and the Palme d'Or which attract audiences of several thousands, are effectively professionals. In the Rhôneland and southwestern Provence, the most famous arenas are those of Arles, Les Saintes-Maries, Saint-Rémy, Fontvieille, Beaucaire, Vauvert, Lunel, Sommières, Maurguio, Saint-Gilles near Aigues-Mortes and, of course, Nîmes.

The names of the great *razeteurs* of the past include Benoit, Ray, Cartier, Soler, Pascal, César and Gineste. The great bulls, the *cocardiers*, like Lou Paré, Le Sanglier and Vovo, which have distinguished themselves over many decades, have been glorified to a degree which supersedes, if not actually eclipses the fame of the *razeteurs*.

One of the most famous *cocarde*-bulls, Le Sanglier (the wild boar of the Camargue marshes) lived for sixteen years, 1916–1933, and routed many a fine *razeteur* in his day. This extraordinary animal was bred by the *manade* Granon-Combet and his remains lie buried under a handsome stone monument surmounted by tridents in the form of a cross, near the village of Le Cailar, northwest of Les Saintes-Maries.

Here at Tarascon, the day began with an *abrivado* staged by horsemen and bulls from the *manade* L'Amista. At a formal ceremony in the Salle des Fêtes du Panoramique near Saint Martha's Church, the three *razeteurs*, Archet, Ferrand and Mourade, were each presented with a bronze medallion; and after that a *buffet campagnard* had been provided for the 200-or-so guests, followed by dancing to the music of a brass band.

The morning had begun cloudy with a light westerly breeze which from time to time scattered the clouds to reveal patches of blue; but before noon it started to drizzle and after that came heavy rain which lasted for the remainder of the day.

The Town Hall near the Cloître des Cordeliers, where I went first by mistake, was deserted. For a moment I wondered if I had got the date wrong, but a woman carrying a big straw-basket solved the problem.

'You're for the *razeteurs*' party, *monsieur*? That's easy. Keep going until you find Saint Martha's Church and then head for the river. You'll see the ring they've set up for the *abrivado*. And there will be lots of people standing about. You can't miss it.'

I soon found the place. A crowd of perhaps a hundred had gathered on a patch of open ground near the castle. Among them were *gardians* in black hats and black velvet jackets, a handful of women and girls in Arlésien costume, local dignitaries including the Mayor of Graveson and the Senator-Mayor of Arles and, as usual, children of all ages – each turned out in their Saturday best. An arena had been laid out at one end: sections of high metal railing forming a wide horse-shoe arc, with an opening wide enough for the horsemen and bulls of the *abrivado* to pass through. On the opposite side a smaller gap in the railings was filled by a cattle-truck and its tailgate projected into the arena forming a ramp up which the bulls would eventually be driven. The *abrivado*, which simply means 'the arrival', is the first stage of the Course when bulls are driven by the *gardians* through the streets of a village or a town to the arena where the bull-games take place. Today, when there was no Course, the *abrivado's* bulls and riders merely added a dramatic flourish to the presentation ceremony.

Several of the crowd I recognized instantly. The Queen of the Arlésiennes, Carole Bressy, a tall young woman with a smooth, ivory complexion, in a splendid costume of red and green silk plaid; and her seventeen-year-old Maid of Honour, Catherine Aubert. The girls gave me a cheerful greeting and seemed quite oblivious to the dismal weather. Nearby stood an open carriage in which the Queen and her Maid of Honour presently drove away, clutching their rain-spattered parasols, applauded by the onlookers. The brass band in soft green jerkins and straw-boaters sat in a little waggonette, drawn by horses with long fringes of mane over their eyes, and played 'The March of the Toreadors' more or less in tune.

The Mayor of Graveson, Raoul Bonjean, introduced me to a

heavily-built man in *gardian* constume, whose grizzled white beard and wide grin seemed familiar though I could not place him right away. This was Jean Lavalle, one of Provence's famous character actors. I remembered several of his films and, having failed to recognize him, felt somewhat foolish. Lavalle brushed aside my apologies and asked whether I knew the work of the British director, Ken Loach. When I replied that I greatly admired *Kes*, Loach's beautiful, sad film about a boy and his pet falcon, Lavalle beamed: 'A wonderful director!' he exclaimed. 'One of your finest! I've worked with some good people in my time, but Loach is in a class by himself. *Kes* is a masterpiece!'

Jean Lavalle had barely finished speaking when a loud explosion shook the ground at our feet and sent a flock of pigeons clattering high into the air from the roof of Saint Martha's Church. The cannon-shot signalled the start of the *abrivado*. I joined the rush for the fenced enclosure and reached it just as L'Amista's *gardians* came galloping into the ring, driving some bulls ahead of them. Wild-eyed, snorting and prancing, the bulls charged straight at the barrier. The *gardians* manoeuvred them very skilfully, surrounding them on the flanks and from behind in a tight semi-circle. The riders kept this close formation until they were well inside the ring, and then they drove the bulls up the ramp of the lorry only a few metres from where I was standing. The heavy lorry shuddered and groaned as the bulls scrambled on board. A second rush of bulls followed immediately. The horses now became very restive, getting the scent of the bulls as they careered madly along, buck-jumping or trying suddenly to break back the way they had come.

As bulls go, the Camargue variety are not particularly large animals; but, seen from ground-level and almost within touching-distance, they appeared gigantic.

The bulls' sour-sweet cattle-odour hung in the damp air, mingled with the tangy smell of the horses, the pungent reek of manure, cigarette-smoke, various potent brands of after-shave and women's perfume. After a while the horsemen trotted away, followed by the lorry. I could hear the bulls lowing and stamping their hooves as the lorry went by: their blood was hot, the adrenalin was still pumping hard in their veins and their sudden confinement had left the bulls tensed by their immense charge of pent-up, frustrated energy.

From the arena we made our way through the rain to the Salle des Fêtes, where the remainder of Madame Aillaud's guests were already assembled in a reception room at the head of a 1930s marble staircase.

Madame Aillaud's opening speech concentrated mainly on the importance of the bull and bull-games in the region. The theme was taken up and expanded at some length by other officials in the platform party: the President of the Regional Council, the Senator-Mayor of Arles, the Mayors of Beaucaire and Nîmes and the Presidents of the Camargue Bull-Breeders and the Federation of the Course Camarguaise. In the Rhôneland, speech-making on these occasions tends to be somewhat overdone; but this is a country where the people love to talk, where conversation is still regarded as an art-form and elaborate, long-winded orations are normal, and indeed expected. Here, the speeches lasted for about an hour-and-a-half, but this also included the presentation of the *razeteurs*' medals.

The Regional President, Jean-Claude Gaudin, gave an excellent, well-informed address calculated to please his audience and (as I overheard some of my neighbours remark) win him extra votes in the forthcoming election. However much Gaudin's speech had been politically-orientated, the crux of his message was nevertheless sound: the Camargue's future depended on preserving the *manadiers*' way of life and the breeding of bulls and horses which, in turn, helped to preserve the Camargue's wetlands and their rich and varied wildlife. Like the sly old Mayor in one of Mistral's stories, the Regional President knew the value of 'soft-soaping' his listeners. His speech received hearty applause, even though the audience had heard it all many times before.

Each of the *razeteurs* had his own sponsor who sang his praises and gave an impassioned account of his achievements over the years. The sponsors rose to the occasion: even the dry catalogue of dates and names of past contests was delivered with dramatic gestures in a torrent of flowery rhetoric. It was all too much for young Mourade, a French-Moroccan, who wept for joy. I heard someone say: 'What a pleasant sight it makes to see courage rewarded – and a brave man's tears!' And so it was. Ferrand and Archet gave the impression of being more self-contained, but only just.

Ferrand, in jeans and a tweed jacket, lanky and awkward, muttered his shy thanks, finding the words with great difficulty, obviously relieved when it was over. Archet was from Tarascon, pale-faced, nervous, a popular winner who spoke in halting, spasmodic phrases and managed a few self-deprecating remarks which earned him an ovation. When I met Archet later on, the *manadier* who introduced me said that I would spread the news of his trumph in Britain. The *manadier* might as well have said, in Mongolia, for all the effect it had. Archet grinned and shook my hand warmly, but he seemed too overwhelmed and too bewildered by the morning's events to be concerned. After all, why should he have been? Having been honoured on his home-ground by his own countrymen was what really mattered to him.

An enormous buffet lunch had been laid out on tressle-tables along one side of the room: quantities of the famous Arlésien sausage and various other spiced meats; a selection of *pâtés* and salamis, meat-filled pastries, vegetable quiches, fruit tarts and cheeses, including goat's cheese and Brie. Other tables had wine, *pastis*, brandy, sparkling orangeade and *eau naturelle* which the waitresses poured out in generous measures in disposable plastic tumblers. The *pièce de résistance*, a huge trifle topped with whipped cream, 'hundreds and thousands' and chocolate, was greeted by wild applause and cries of 'Bravo!' The trifle arrived on a platter at least two metres long and half as much in width, heralded by a fanfare of trumpets, and needed two strong men to carry it.

The brass band meanwhile had regrouped on the platform and their loud music added to the uproar of voices and laughter.

Strains of Spanish flamenco were followed by a blast of jazz and swing. A chorus of 'Ain't she sweet?' got the dancing off to a brisk start and after that came the rumba and the samba. The rumba performed by mildly inebriated *gardians* and buxom Arlésiennes stuffed with chocolate trifle was truly something to behold! Actually most of them were excellent dancers, surprisingly light on their feet, and they had a wonderfully elegant sense of rhythm.

Had the tone of the ceremony been more formal, I dare say they might instead have danced a *farandole*, accompanied by the *galoubet* and the *tambourin*; yet the Latin-American tunes played on trumpets and saxophones sounded appropriate enough.

Even more than the rumba, the foxtrot 'Ain't she sweet?' had a nostalgic air which suited the oldly recherché atmosphere of the occasion. Only the sombre seventeenth-century portraits hanging in the Salle des Fêtes seemed a little out of step with the proceedings. Their disdainful, frowning expressions reminded me of the strait-laced old diehards we have all encountered at one time or another, bemoaning the strange antics of young people on the dance-floor.

11

The Museum of Life

During the month or so I spent in Arles, I visited the Museon Arlaten almost daily. It ranks among Mistral's most remarkable creations and, according to Marcel Brion, rivals the Alyscamps 'as one of the most impressive places in Arles'.

At the time the Museon was founded, Mistral was already in his late sixties; still busy writing poetry – verses which would be gathered in his last collection, *Les Olivades*, in 1912 – translating the Book of Genesis into Provençal and, over and above, dealing with his massive correspondence, besides a host of public duties. His creative energy and physical stamina, for a man of his advanced years, seemed astonishing.

The Museon Arlaten had been a project dear to his heart, which he described in *L'Aiöli* as early as 1896 as the '*musée de la vie vivante et de la race d'Arles*' – the museum of contemporary life and the people of Arles. The town's Musée Reattu and Musée Lapidaire represented a vanished way of life of the past, displayed in paintings, sculpture and architectural antiquities. This was just the opposite of what Mistral hoped to achieve. He foresaw the Museon Arlaten as a celebration of daily life in the Rhôneland, its many facets reflected in exhibitions of furniture, clothing, household utensils, farming implements and so on, at a period when the region's traditional lifestyle appeared increasingly threatened by the effects of the Industrial Revolution. With a degree of foresight which does him much credit, Mistral realized that the gathering momentum of social and economic change, leading to what Richard Aldington defines as an excess of 'machine-worship', would in time make relics of beautiful artifacts until then in daily use, which also expressed the region's spirit and character.

The original collections were assembled with the help and encouragement of the ethnologist, Dr Marignan, who became the Museon's first conservator. Mistral once confided to a friend that the task of arranging, researching and labelling the vast trove had occupied him, almost literally, day and night. Despite old age, Mistral's pace never slackened. He continued to visit the Museon every Thursday, for the best part of fifteen years, travelling from his home at Maillane to Arles by omnibus and train. He never owned a horse and trap and even after the turn of the century, when cars became more widely used, he flatly refused to buy one. This did not mean that Mistral had been either penny-pinching or poor; he was in fact generous and fairly comfortably off. But instead he chose to keep faith with his lifelong philosophy, repeated in a letter to the Chancellor of the Félibrige, Paul Mariéton: 'We have always walked side by side with the poor. We must remain with them.'

The Museon's collections were first set up in 1897, in rooms allotted to them in a building which today houses the Chamber of Commerce. However, the public response had been so generous that in a few years, Mistral and his committee were obliged to seek larger, permanent accommodation. Fortunately Mistral's share of the 1904 Nobel Prize, approximately 100,000 gold francs, enabled him to buy outright the spacious Palais de Castellane-Laval which had been divided between the Laval family and a Jesuit College. After some delays, the Museon was finally established in the rue de la République in this fine building with its handsome eighteenth-century façade, spread over thirty-two rooms surrounding a courtyard where excavations had uncovered a miniature Roman forum.

For Mistral in particular, the early years of the century

brought a wave of renewed fame and recognition largely due to the international publicity he received following the Nobel Prize. The prize coincided with the fiftieth anniversary of the Félibrige, a happy occasion, and yet one marred to an extent by the fact that Mistral was by then the sole survivor of the original group of poets. He mourned them, writing: 'The singers are dead, but their voices re-echo; the builders are dead, but the temple is built.'

The success of the Félibrige movement had far exceeded even Mistral's wildest dreams. Its membership rapidly expanded and in the years that followed, something like five thousand new works in Provençal were published. Even if much of the writing was mediocre compared to Mistral's, at least the Félibrige's spirit survived.

The Museon Arlaten's opening ceremony at the Palais de Castellane-Laval, held on 29 May 1909, formed an important part of the fiftieth anniversary celebrations which marked the publication in 1859 of Mistral's outstanding narrative poem, *Mireille*. A life-size bronze statue of the poet, by the sculptor Charles Roux, caused him some misgivings. Mistral told Roux: 'I shan't dare to walk about Arles any more. People will say: "Hello, here's the bronze come off its pedestal!" '

The Museon Arlaten became, as Mistral intended, a celebration of the common people, rather than Art. His influence was apparent everywhere; not least of all in the time-consuming work of classifying the exhibits, thousands of which he labelled with meticulous care in his own handwriting. While he had intended to represent the Rhôneland life as widely as possible, Mistral's involvement, and the fact that he had grown old, inevitably led to facets of his own past being mirrored in the Museon's collections. This may have been partly deliberate. Two major tableaux arranged behind plate-glass screens – the ceremony following a birth, and Christmas Eve preparations in a *mas* kitchen – recalled events which he had undoubtedly witnessed as a youngster.

One of the Museon Arlaten's assistants, Madame Germaine Dibon, explained their significance. She began with the *Visite à la couchée*, in which life-size wax models represent Arlésiennes who have come to visit the mother who lies in bed, rather formally dressed, holding her newborn child. In a corner, we see an old nurse busy with her sewing. The bedroom is well furnished and the floor is partly covered by a black calf-skin rug, rough side uppermost, with the tiny horns still attached to it.

Madame Dibon (whose late husband, I learned, had been a cousin of Folco de Baroncelli's biographer) told me: 'Each of the Arlésiennes has brought with her a traditional offering of an egg, bread, salt and a matchstick. The egg (*lou iòu*) is offered so that a boy-child may grow up to be sturdy, a girl well-rounded and fertile; the bread (*lou pan*) represents goodness; the girl with salt (*la sau*) prays the child may be wise; and the matchstick symbolizes honesty – may he or she be *dre coume uno broqueto*, in Provençal, that is to say, "as straight as a match".'

This simple ceremony was not exclusive to the Rhôneland, and it had already fallen into disuse by the time the Museon Arlaten was established. The young woman in bed with her baby was almost certainly meant to represent Mistral's mother; and he meant to honour her memory further by the carefully selected furnishings, clothes and the added touch of formality they brought to an otherwise everyday, homely scene.

Mistral's father is represented in a Christmas Eve tableau next to the *Visite à la couchée*. Here we find the kitchen of a Camargue *mas*, with the members of the household and their servants assembled standing round the kitchen table which has been laid for the Christmas feast. Mistral's father is said to be the old *manadier* who sits by the hearth, dripping wine on the yule log cut from an olive-tree. Madame Dibon pointed out the dress styles representing different periods and activities: there were Charles X costumes worn by the elderly grandparents; the proprietor's wife in Arlésien dress with her Louis Philippe hairstyle and long ribbon; the long cloak and working-smock of the shepherds; and the housemaid in her plain dress and her white-linen cap known as a *cornet*.

The kitchen table was laid with three white cloths, one on top of the other, and three candlesticks, which signified the Holy

Trinity. On the table there were dishes of *cardes* – coarse greens – and fish. There was bread, green olives and snails; and a small pottery jar containing wooden sticks used for opening the snail-shells. Another little vase of wheat in water symbolized the family's hopes for a good harvest in the year ahead.

I was fascinated by the collection of Provençal musical instruments I discovered in another room. Here I found the *galoubets* I had heard played at the Palais du Roure well represented – no fewer that twenty-nine examples made of ebony, ivory, and a pale straw-coloured wood like the *galoubet* played by Marcel Bosqui. There were drumsticks of various sizes and *tambourins*, and I noticed that here at the Museon Arlaten the *tambourins* had been stored 'tensed' (that is, the cords round the body of the drum had not been slackened), a detail which surprised Monsieur Bosqui when I mentioned it later on. One called a Bachas was a *tambour à quatre timbres*, a four-toned drum.

Some weird-looking trumpets had been made to resemble various reptiles. The Serpent, painted black, had five snake-like coils; while the brass Buccin, dating from about 1800, had very realistic, gaping jaws painted red inside and a pair of staring eyes. The Rhôneland bagpipe, the Carlamuso, had drones and a chanter sprouting from a pouch of red velvet and appeared to be a smaller version of the traditional Scottish pipes. Other instruments were less exotic than the Serpent and the Buccin and included a mandolin, a violin, a four-stringed zither and a shepherd's horn which was little more than a hollow wooden cylinder roughly fashioned by the player himself.

Until I met the Museon's Director, Madame Serena, who was among other things a musicologist, I had not realized the depth or refinement of Mistral's musical interest. We met and talked in Madame Serena's office, a magnificent stone-vaulted room to the right of the main entrance, with an immense writing-desk, carved Provençal *armoires*, glass-fronted bookshelves, table-lamps, huge decorative glass jars and cardboard files and papers scattered or heaped up on every available surface. Madame Serena was sallow-skinned and dark-eyed, with cropped dark hair. She had a biting intellect and said that she enjoyed nothing better than an intense, well-matched debate.

'People think of Mistral only as a poet and a philosopher,' said Madame Serena. 'He is the portly old man in a frock-coat and a big hat who wrote *Mireille* and compiled the *Trésor du Félibrige*.'

'Mistral had many other gifts besides poetry,' she continued. 'His musical knowledge was astonishing. He had no training but he had a great *feeling* for music and of course his poems have a marked lyrical quality don't you agree? We have many documents here at the Museon which prove Mistral's talent as a musicologist. Many will dispute what I'm about to say, but I think Mistral championed things which were already defunct, even in his day. His songs are the songs of a dying world. And the later *félibres*, many of them, did little more than blow over the ashes of Mistral's fire.'

Madame Serena's eyes flashed. She leaned forward in her chair. 'I don't wish to denigrate the Félibrige or its members, but it must be obvious that not all the *félibres* were geniuses or even moderately gifted. With a membership numbering thousands, that would be too much to expect! Instead, we have a handful of really fine writers and artists. Even so, Mistral stands out from this gifted minority. When Mistral wrote *Mireille*, the life he described there was typical of our country, and yet the world outside was changing. We find change always knocking at our door, isn't that so? Mistral's *Poème du Rhône* is also about change, the old river life passing away for ever. As a young man, he could see how the Provençal language was dying. He tried to save it by establishing the Félibrige and compiling the *Trésor*. *Mireille* and other great poems not only celebrated the life of our region, but they showed what power and beauty the language was capable of. There's no doubt Mistral re-awakened a general interest and respect for our speech and traditions, but even he couldn't stem the tide of progress or hold back change. Besides, that wouldn't be quite right either. The *Trésor* gathered together our language. The poems sang it. And the Museon Arlaten has preserved the artifacts. The fact that Mistral *saw the need* for these things proves my argument that, even in his day, the old life was being gradually replaced by the new.'

We discussed Mistral's links with the Camargue, where his influence can be seen to this day. Madame Serena continued: 'Before Baroncelli, the *gardians* were effectively "shepherds on horseback". They wore rough-hewn wooden clogs and shirts made from fabric produced in Alsace. The black felt sombrero was generally unknown. In this sense, Folco appropriated ideas of dress and style from elsewhere. The "cloth of the Indies" with its now typical *gardian* designs, began to appear. Maybe the soft felt hat was adapted from hats worn by other eighteenth- and nineteenth-century *petit-bourgeois*. The same applies to the velvet jacket and trousers. You might say that Baroncelli invented his own private world of *gardianage*. The Nacioun Gardiano gave the *gardians* a refurbished image and identity. Many of its members wrote poetry and belonged to the Félibrige. Not everyone was able to write poetry, but even the humblest shepherds sometimes expressed their feelings about the country in beautiful simple things.'

Madame Serena led me into another room, adjacent to her office, where she showed me a collection of horns, delicately carved, which told the rustic life of yesteryear – the contemplative shepherd life which gave the carvers a wealth of time for reflection. Some of the horns had been used as gunpowder flasks; others as drinking-vessels. The carvings recorded the shepherds' observations and imaginings: sailing boats, horses, dogs, flying birds; mermaids in wide-brimmed straw hats like lampshades. Some of the work was childlike, some revealed a real talent for figures and animals. The sail-boats on the Rhône had their canvas puffed out in the wind. One of the boats had the name 'The London' etched at the prow and '1851', the year of the Great Exhibition. Some of the carved figures had been shaded with finely judged slanting knife-cuts, fluid and yet precise enough to have satisfied even the critical demands of Ruskin who, I have been told, paid particular attention to the pencil-shading of architectural drawings.

'Wonderful work!' enthused Madame Serena. 'The poetry

made by simple solitary men who couldn't read and who spoke little. You might call it the poetry of silence.'

12

Bull-games

The owner of the Hôtel Lamartine near the porte de la Cavalerie,
Julian Panichi, was a jolly soul, merry and serious by turns like
everyone here in Arles – and he was a great enthusiast of the
Course Camarguaise. I usually found him not over-employed,
tousle-haired, shaved hit-and-miss fashion, grinning and eager
for someone to talk to. He had mixed feelings about the *mise-à-
mort* Spanish *corrida*, for he was really a gentle-natured sort.
However, the *corrida* has long since become a part of the
Rhôneland scene and he accepted it unapprovingly. Start him off
on the subject of bulls and you were in for a long session.
Sometimes an hour or two. It all depended.

Panichi's father came to the Camargue in 1924 and worked in
the salt-pans at Salin-de-Giraud. It was a poor living, but his
family were well fed and had a little house in the Trinquetaille
suburb, across the river from the fishermen's and gipsies'
quarter, La Roquette. Julian Panichi got his first real experience
of the bulls at an *abrivado* when he was still a small boy. He was
then only six or seven years old.

He remembered the event as though it were yesterday:
'Somebody, my father I think, carried me on his shoulders right
up to the bulls which were being driven down a narrow street.
This was here, in Arles. The street was like a ravine – houses

crowding in on either side and packed with people. The bulls
coming straight for us looked like the prow of a ship. When they
got really close, everyone started to run. My father had put me
down for a moment. I can't think why. Anyhow, I got pushed
aside by the crowd running past and for a few seconds I seemed
to be all on my own.

'I suppose things might have turned nasty. The bulls were
right on top of me by then. I flattened myself against the wall as
the nearest of the bulls went by and I felt the hot breath from its
muzzle. I don't remember being frightened, it all happened too
quickly for that. Thank God I'd enough sense to keep still, or
maybe I was too scared to move. I don't know. If I'd made any
sudden movement or cried out, one of the bulls might have
taken a swipe at me.' At this, Panichi got up from the table,
lowered his head and shook it, keeping his hands up, in a very
realistic imitation of a lunging bull. He chuckled: 'I'd have been
skewered like a piece of meat on a kebab-stick! Anyhow that
didn't happen. After the bulls had passed, I tried to run away and
fell flat on my face. I found my father eventually. A pretty sight I
made, I can tell you, covered with mud and manure from the
bulls. My father was worried, as you can imagine. But I wasn't
hurt and so everybody was happy.'

Panichi sat down again, his hands cupped round his rough red
cheeks, elbows resting on the table. With the merest hint of quiet
pride, the faintest drooping of an eyelid that might have been
meant for a wink, he added: 'You know, I really wasn't afraid.
Just a bit shaken. When I appeared looking as if I'd just stepped
out of a farmyard midden, everyone cheered. I think my father
got quite a kick out of that.'

He told me that his favourite among the old-time *razeteurs*
was André Soler, a wonderful man, brave and stylish. 'The
good *razeteurs*, like Soler, actually *advance* towards the oncom-
ing bull and make a fast swoop for the *cocarde* which is strung
between the horns. This is exciting to watch and very graceful. I
once saw an extraordinary thing, Soler holding off the bull,
quite literally at arm's length. He kept his arm straight – like this
– and he was forcing the bull's head down all the time. The bull

got very nervous and angry and dashed its muzzle on the ground, snorting and snuffling *en colère* – it was really mad. That was a sight, I can tell you.'

He loved the bulls. His descriptions of them in the arena were vivid and real, accompanied by gestures – heaving shoulders, rolling eyes and hand-movements – which added to the dramatic effect and made the picture more intense and very lively. He told me how he had seen the bulls in the Camargue, grazing up to their necks in water, thrusting their heads deep into the thick clumps of rushes so as to get at the tenderest, succulent green shoots. He showed me how they forced themselves at great speed through the deepest water, flailing his arms to represent the bulls' forelegs, demonstrating their terrific power and stamina, becoming for a while like a bull himself. The display was utterly convincing, for Panichi is thick-set and heavily muscled, the sort of man who knows his own strength and is gentle in consequence but who could lay you out flat merely by tapping your nose as he might tap at your front door.

How he loves the Camargue and the windswept plains of the

Crau! These places are heaven on earth for Mr Panichi. He extolled the virtues of the Crau's grassland, where there is a covering of fine alluvial soil, mixed with pebbles which make for good drainage. The sun, he told me, 'draws the grass and herbage up from the soil' and it is full of goodness and provides excellent pasture which produces strong, lively bulls with plenty of 'go'.

'I wish you'd come with me one day when I visit Crau,' said Panichi. 'It's a paradise! When you get right out into the middle of the plain everything is peaceful and quiet. The air is sweet-smelling and pure. Depending where you are, you can some-times see cars in the distance, but they're so far away you can't hear them. There's nothing to disturb you. It's just the wind noise, or else the sound of your own breathing. The sunlight glinting on the stones and the blades of grass and all around you the plain and the blue sky above it. If that isn't a glimpse of heaven, I'd like somebody to tell me what is.'

Panichi's eyes shone as he spoke. 'And then of course there's the Camargue. Really and truly, *monsieur*, I cannot tell you which of these places I'm more fond of. They're both magnifi-cent! Even if I were blind – well, let's not go too far, let's say blindfolded – I could recognize the fresh air of the Camargue immediately. I go there to shoot wildfowl mostly, but as often as not I come home empty-handed. The truth is, I enjoy the scenery and I don't mind if I don't kill a bird, for you see shooting isn't important. Mind you, I'm not denying that I enjoy eating a fine, fat duck or a goose. My wife, Nelly, is a wonderful cook and her roasts and casseroles are enough to turn a man's head. But I love the smell of the sea-breeze and being at peace among the birds and animals in the *marais*.

'Some men get drunk on *pastis* or brandy. Me, I get drunk on the ozone! As a matter of fact, I can't stomach *pastis*. When I was a youngster, my mother used to make me drink aniseed as a purgative and, would you believe it, ever since the wretched stuff has had the same effect!'

Panichi admitted that he found the English terribly stand-offish and haughty. I hope not entirely for my benefit, he said that he liked the few Scots he had met. They were quiet people, like his English guests, but at least they weren't patronizing. He added: 'Provence is maybe a bit like Scotland, after all. Here in the Rhôneland it takes time for us to know people well. We don't invite strangers into our homes right away. That's for later on.'

Leaving the Hôtel Lamartine, I had hardly gone fifty paces when I found myself surrounded by a big party of schoolgirls. They were from a convent-school in the southwest of Ireland and their teachers had brought them on a day-trip to Arles from Tarascon where they were staying. One of the girls thrust a compact camera into my hands and begged me to photograph them, bunched tightly together in a group by the Fontaine Amédée Pichot with its *faience* medallion by Paul Balze representing the Muse of Poetry.

All the while the girls chattered away like parakeets, bombarding me with questions. Was I here on holiday? What was I doing? Writing a book! Was I famous then? Did I like football? The eldest might have been about seventeen, but fourteen or fifteen was the average age, as far as I could gather. They gathered round and told me their names and I can still put a face to several of them.

The girls had been turned loose for an hour by their teachers who had retired to a nearby restaurant where, Sally remarked disapprovingly, they were 'most likely gettin' into a state of drink'. Sally smiled and fluttered her eyelashes. 'Would you mind if we walk along with you? Just to the top of the street?'

And so off we went. I felt like the Pied Piper of Hamelin, with the children trailing merrily at my heels. Jenny said they had been to mass that morning at Saint Martha's in Tarascon: 'It went on for an hour-and-a-half!' she exclaimed. 'Jaysus! Would you believe that now? And only the French language spoken!'

Our numbers were being constantly added to, as more children emerged from the cafés where they had bought their snack-lunches of pizzas and sandwiches.

As we made our way along the rue 4 Septembre, groups of

lounging teenage boys, Algerians as well as French, some of them rough-looking characters, tracked the girls with their idle, predatory gaze. Sounding more avuncular than I'd intended, I cautioned the girls: 'You lot must try and keep together if you can.' And I added: 'What would you do if these boys made a pass at you?' 'Oh, that's dead easy,' said Rachel without a moment's hesitation, 'we'd kick the bastards straight in the goolies!' 'Sure thing!' piped up Sally of the angelic smile. 'In France they're all balls and no brains anyhow!'

Foolishly I had at first taken these Irish youngsters for helpless 'innocents abroad'. Abroad, they were; helpless innocents, they were certainly not. The *macho* youth of Arles wouldn't have known what had hit them, had this Celtic St Trinian's mob been obliged to fight its way out of a corner.

In the afternoon a *corrida mixte* (with old and young bulls) was held at the Arles' arena. I went along as a guest of the arena's director, Hubert Yonnet, whose family has been long renowned for the fine Spanish-Camargue cross-bred bulls raised at their *manade*, La Beluge near Salin de Giraud.

I presented my blue guest-ticket at the gate and two attendants, women dressed from head to toe in black, led me to my seat in the Tribune, close to the barricade. From here I had an excellent view of the enclosure, in the centre of which the symbol of the Club Taurin, an inverted 'Y', had been marked on the sand with powdered chalk.

It had rained heavily the night before and today again the sky was completely overcast. Being so late in the season, the attendance was poor – I should have guessed well under a thousand – but the prospect of more rain also might have been responsible for this.

The arena attendants in their crow-black costumes appeared with a stout middle-aged woman, who came and sat next to me. A Spaniard from Barcelona, she told me that she and her husband were friends of Hubert Yonnet and that she also knew one of the matadors, a Venezuelan, who styled himself 'El Yazucuy'. The lady smoothed her voluminous pleated skirts and arranged a black chiffon shawl very carefully about her shoulders. Having established that I was 'Eengleeth' she beamed at me reassuringly and patted my arm.

'The bull eeth very *malo*, yes?' she confided, giving me another pat. 'MALO – you know M-A-L-O-! Theeth mean that he eeth VERY BAD! How you say in Eengleeth? VERY MUCH DANGEROUS! But you don' have to worry at all. My frien' the matador, he eeth MUY VALIENTE!'

She glared at the heavy clouds massed directly overhead and clutched her flimsy shawl. 'Today he eeth altho very MALO, eh? I think we have much wet and maybe thunder!'

The arena clock showed almost three. El Yazucuy's name went up on a board. Centre-right, high in the terracing, the little band in their smart red uniforms began tuning up, while the conductor practised a few self-important flourishes of his baton.

As the tension mounted, the crowd noise resembled exactly the rustling crescendo of hot milk coming to the boil.

On the stroke of three, a fanfare followed by 'The March of

the Toreadors' in quick tempo announced the arrival of the arena-party led by a brace of horsemen dressed in black with red and blue cockades in their hats, riding dark chestnut mares. Three matadors strutted after the horsemen in their tight-fitting, heavily embroidered, beaded suits of crimson, green and gold. The matadors' assistants followed in their flat black hats and pink stockings. Then the burly picadors, costumed in bright daffodil-yellow, their horses' flanks protected by heavy padded mattresses covered with yellow fabric. The little horse-drawn tumbril, painted a dark blood-red, brought up the rear, its winch and rattling drag-chains a grim reminder of the afternoon's business.

The procession turned and left the arena to a perfunctory clatter of applause. The gates of the barricade crashed behind them and the music faded away. For a few moments there was silence.

It started to rain – a pattering of big tepid droplets followed by a sudden deluge – and my Spanish neighbour scowled, muttering '*Madre de Dios!*' and made an imploring gesture at the sky.

At the far end of the arena the door marked TORIL swung open and out rushed a heavy bull, bellowing and snorting, pawing the wet sand. The bull careered this way and that, then attacked the secondary barricades one after another where the matador and his assistants had taken up their positions. The assistants, then El Yazucuy himself, taunted the bull with their peony-red capes; but after making a few short rushes the bull cantered away, then stood motionless facing its tormentors. The crowd became restless, whistling and jeering. The picadors came lumbering forward, each with a lance tucked well in at the armpit, the horses in their red blindfolds high-stepping, nervously twitching as they smelled the hot scent of the bull.

The bull charged, giving one of the horses a terrific head-butt. the picador managed to hold the bull at bay with his lance, driving the thick blade in hard between its shoulders, turning the blade in its flesh and making the blood run. Blood, dark wine-coloured gobbets of it, splashed down the animal's neck and

forelegs. The bull backed away, moaning. Already it looked weary. The *bandarillas* planted by El Yazucuy provoked some half-hearted rushes which the matador deflected by means of a simple *véronique*. Then a fanfare sounded. The *epée* was handed over the barrier. The bull attacked again, hooked away the cape and trampled it. El Yazucuy retrieved the cape and an untidy scuffle near the barricade followed. The first thrust of the *epée* failed to penetrate. El Yazucuy tried again – another failure. Each time the point struck bone or muscle and each time I saw the rainbow-arc of the blade as it flexed. A third strike: the blade jammed halfway. The bull faced El Yazucuy, trembling, bleeding, thoroughly beaten. Perhaps as a last token of defiance, the bull refused to lower its head for the *coup de grâce* to be delivered using the blocked sword. Impatient, the matador made several bungled attempts to locate the animal's brain. Eventually he succeeded and the bull collapsed and rolled over on its side, its legs jerking convulsively. One of El Yazucuy's helpers gave the bull a few savage thrusts with a broad-bladed dagger, just behind the horns. The crowd booed and whistled as the tumbril bore away the carcass.

By now it was raining heavily. My Spanish neighbour wailed and drew her shawl over her head. She appeared to ignore the matador's blunders, greeting every move with clucks and whimpers, alternating loud cries of 'Bravo!' with angry ejaculations of '*Toros Malos*!' Several times during the miserable performance she had turned to me, exclaiming 'MUY VALIENTE!' it seemed with precious little justification, but I assumed that she was merely keeping El Yazucuy's end up.

The next bull and another matador, El Millonario, provided the crowd with a good deal of excitement. The bull thundered in full of rage and menace, head well up, its forefeet splayed in tremendous straight-legged bounds. The odour of blood made it nervous. Its tongue protruded white and slavering. A terrific smashing blow against a picador's horse actually lifted the wretched animal clear of the ground, the bull grunting angrily, getting its horns low under the mattress dangerously close to the horse's belly. The man twisted in the saddle, driving home his lance in a fountain of blood. The picador exerted all his strength, using the lance to push the bull away.

Blood from the lance-thrusts spouted from the bull's back with each pounding heartbeat, spilling down in great quantities and puddling the sand at its feet. By now the bull was in a murderous temper, hurting from the lance and mad with fear. It attacked the second picador. Then it turned again on the first, a terrible battering onslaught which brought the horse down on its haunches, almost unseating its rider. A great gasp rose from the spectators. Incredibly the picador kept his balance and the horse regained its feet, helped to some extent by the fact that the bull's rush had forced it hard against the barricade which steadied it. The arena sand by now was waterlogged and very slippery. El Millonario skipped away and fell flat on his back, dropping the cape, as the bull made another determined charge. A powerful swipe of its horns missed the matador's outstretched body by a hand's breadth and brought the crowds to their feet with a roar as the assistant-matadors circled round, flapping their capes to divert the bull's attention. The bull's speed and tenacity were truly astonishing. The *epée* found its mark, slicing between the bull's shoulders like a hot knife through butter. El Millonario stepped forward and using the *croisée* sword plucked out the *epée* which angled away, red to the hilt with blood. El Millonario retrieved the *epée* and cleaned the blade with a few strokes on the bull's forehead.

In a supplicating tone, the matador urged the beast to lower its head for the final thrust. The bull hesitated, then did so. The *croisée* entered killing it instantly. Above the fanfares and applause I heard the cries of food-and-drink sellers as they moved to and fro along the terracing in the rain.

The floodlights were switched on for the third contest. The eighteen-year-old matador, Gilles Raoux from Beziers, proved to be easily the best of the three. Slim, supple and handsome, Raoux's movements were smooth, graceful and executed with faultless precision. He appeared to comprehend the workings of the bull's mind, to anticipate its temper. More than that, he showed a marked respect, even affection, for the mighty creature he had come to kill. Raoux's bull had as much energy and fiery madness as El Millonario's. It was also much faster. The surface of the arena had become glassy and very unsafe. The matador and bull alike found difficulty keeping their balance. In went the *bandarillas*, their feathery red tufts alighting (it seemed to me) in pairs, in perfect sequence. Down plunged the *epée* in a shining curve, straight to the hilt. I heard Raoux's barely audible '*Toro! Toro!*' as the bull, rocking from side to side, lowered its head and moaned. I saw the *croisée* flash and it was all over. The downpour continued. By now I was soaked to the skin. Many of the spectators had already gone home, my neighbour from Barcelona among them. She missed nothing. El Yazucuy fought again, but his second performance was even worse than the other – a real shambles.

I am not certain of the exact date when the Spanish *mise-à-mort* style bull-fights were first introduced into France. It was probably more than 150 years ago, since in 1873 the Ministry of the Interior endeavoured to ban both the *corrida* and the Course Camarguaise, which earlier petitions raised in the seventeenth century during the reign of Louis XIV had failed to abolish.

While he personally disliked the *corrida*, Mistral saw no reason why it should be discontinued and he went so far as to attend what was then an illegal bull-fight at the Nîmes' arena, on 14 October 1894, which was staged before a crowd of 20,000 including the Mayor of Nîmes and various local members of Parliament. The poet's arrival was greeted by a tremendous roar of 'Mistral!' followed by a standing ovation. His reception had been all the warmer since the people knew that, in private, Mistral not only disapproved of the *corrida* but also the introduction of Spanish bulls into the Rhôneland's *manades*.

Of course Mistral's name was added to the summons for illegal bull-fighting. Aldington tell us the fine was sixteen francs, but the Nîmes' *corrida* that day made a clear profit of 50,000 gold francs and so the fine was 'no serious injury'.

In Rhôneland Provence, the *corrida* attracts a large, en- thusiastic following although I believe that the great majority of people who profess to enjoy 'bull-games' much prefer the generally bloodless spectacle of the Course Camarguaise. I can readily appreciate why they are revolted by the sight of a bull being subjected to the *corrida's* bloody ritual.

Roy Campbell made an eloquent and impassioned defence of the *corrida* in *Taurine Provence*. I must admit that I find some of his arguments thought-provoking, if in the end not entirely convincing. Campbell became a genuine expert in such matters and, for this reason alone, *Taurine Provence* makes fascinating reading. The work is also by now slightly dated. Campbell rightly demanded to know why Englishmen and women who ate slaughtered meat and either condoned, participated in or ignored blood-sports such as big-game hunting, grouse-shooting and stag-hunting with dogs, should be so violently opposed to bull-fighting? If one of the objections was killing the bull in an enclosed space, from which it couldn't escape, as Campbell pointed out, even wild prey such as African antelope and English game-birds had been 'enclosed' – or, to put it another way, had their 'free space' determined by the range of the sportsman's rifle or shotgun. Nowadays, of course, these arguments carry less weight since only a minority of people still indulge in hunting big-game. As a pastime big-game hunting is now generally disapproved of, while there is such a widespread opposition to stag-hunting and fox-hunting that in all likelihood these will be eventually banned.

Campbell observed that the bulls raised for the *corrida* and the Course Camarguaise have a temper quite unlike that of the 'domesticated' bull, the Hereford or the Aberdeen Angus, for instance. The Spanish and Camargue bulls are born fighters and if they do not die (like *corrida* bulls) in the arena, or (as *cocarde* bulls) from injury or old age, they sometimes kill each other. In this sense, I suppose, the *corrida* bulls, compared to the English farm bull, are like grouse or pheasants compared to poultry. Campbell's opinion, that animal-lovers (and by implication animal-rights' activists) were frequently rabid haters of humanity must have raised eyebrows in 1932; and no doubt it would today, were *Taurine Provence* to be republished. In support of his argument, Campbell gave as an example the morbid interest ordinary people (animal–lovers included) often express in warfare and murder. There is something in what he says: nevertheless I am inclined to believe that it isn't so much the ritual killing of bulls in the *corrida* people find abhorrent, but the cruelty all too frequently inflicted on the beast in the process.

If I were asked point-blank: Do you approve of bull-fighting or not? I should find it impossible to give a cut-and-dried answer. There can be no denying the excitement of a really first-rate *corrida* with lively-tempered bulls and skilled matadors, where the absorbing interest lies in the working of the bull. As in hunting, the death-blow comes as an anti-climax. However, the sort of bloody shambles involving much unnecessary wounding, to me, is sickening and degrading. It is displays like these which cause me to question seriously the ethics of the *corrida*. Roy Campbell tended to write as though such disgusting butchery never occurred; as if the *corrida* should be judged solely by the matadors' finest performances.

If only this were true! The circumstances of the *corrida* vary as much as any other sport. At Arles, as I have described, the matadors were greatly hampered by bad weather. Besides it is probably fair to state that at best mediocre (and occasionally some downright inept) exhibitions of the taurine art outnumber the rest.

While I do not agree that in Britain we have the automatic right to interfere with the traditions of countries such as Rhôneland Provence, Spain or Mexico, where the *corrida* is still practised, the Taurine Associations in these countries might be encouraged to regulate with greater care the activities of all those involved with staged contests in which bulls are killed as a public spectacle.

I much prefer the Course Camarguaise which is sufficiently intricate and provides all the thrills and excitement anyone could possibly wish for. There can be no question that the Course Camarguaise is also by far the more humane. In the Course, any injuries are sustained, ninety-nine times out of a hundred, accidentally. Futhermore, the balance is usally weighted in favour of the bulls.

The Course Camarguaise and the *corrida* both provide colour and action and a variety of costume-ritual which have appealed to painters and sculptors from earliest times to the present day. The early artists whose work we find represented in the sculpture and pottery of Crete and mainland Greece, were anonymous. So too were those who sculpted the Assyrian bulls and likewise the artists of the Roman Empire. The artists of the Classical Period have been represented in the great works of tauromachy, including *Le Taureau Camargue*, a magnificently-illustrated, authoritative study by Jeanne de Flandreysy and G. Bouzanquet published in Paris in 1925. Dufy's representation of the bull in Apollinaire's *Le Bestiaire ou cortège d'Orphée* (1911) evoked 'both the winged bulls of Mesopotamia and the angel of paradise celebrated in the Bible'.

In a scarce catalogue, *La Civilisation du Taureau*, which I was shown by Madame Delpy at the Relais Culturel in Les Saintes-Maries-de-la-Mer, the authority on bull-games, Fabré de Santen, gives a list of more than twenty artists, English as well as French, who have to a greater or lesser extent specialized in Camargue scenes and bull-games. The English artists included William Lake Price (1810–1891), who aged forty-two published an account of his journeys in Spain and Portugal, *Tauromachia, or the Bullfights of Spain* (1852) illustrated with a collection of twenty-six plates which were criticized for being 'occasionally inaccurate'. And there was Felicity Katherine Sarah Askew, born in London in 1899 who painted in the Camargue and died there sometime after the Second World War.

Excellent studies of Camargue bulls were painted by Paul Vayson and Ivan Pranishnikoff; while one of the liveliest pictures I have seen showing the *ferrade* (the branding cere-mony), dated 29 May 1904, was the work of H. Daniel, a house-painter from Lunel, in the Hérault!

At Les Saintes-Maries, on the sea-front surrounded by a small plantation of tamarisks, there is an obelisk of cream-coloured sandstone dedicated to Folco de Baroncelli-Javon, which has the carved heads of a bull and a horse as a capping, on either side of the seven-pointed star of the Félibrige. The animals have been stylized in a way which reminds me of Eric Gill's sculptures, particularly the treatment of the bull's horns and the horse's mane. On the wall of the arena, near the entrance, a stone bas relief, dated 1986, commemorating the great *cocarde*-bull, Vovo, shows him in close pursuit of a *razeteur* as he vaults the barrier. The craftsmanship is good, although as an action-study the work seemed to me rather stodgy and lifeless. The inscription reads: 'vovo/ Aubanel-Baroncelli de Gyptis/FAMIHO DOU PROVENCO/ 1944–1959'.

13

Food and Fetishes

In Arles there was always something going on, always something worth looking at. Between my regular visits to the Museon Arlaten and the trips I made into the country, I wandered about the town. In London, this aimless beating about the streets would have bored me. Here it was just the opposite. It wasn't a case of familiarity that bred contempt. The variety one found in London somehow had got out of hand: it was almost too diverse, too fragmented. The big city atmosphere lacked personality and intimacy – at least, for me. In Arles, the balance seemed about right. I found that I got to know the town reasonably well after a few weeks and this added to my enjoyment of it. The pleasure of discovering new surroundings was increased by recognition, the little scraps of knowledge I picked up every day and the sense of becoming gradually a part of the scene. I would recognize the same people in the streets and they, in turn, recognized me. As often as not, they would stop and chat. Bit by bit, I was admitted into their lives – here a word or two about their families, there a snippet of gossip. Nothing much, I grant you, but just enough to make me feel accepted. At Avignon, where I never lived for any length of time and where I knew only a handful of locals, I always felt like a bird of passage – always a stranger. Avignon is twice the size of Arles and it has an entirely different character. Had I lived longer at Avignon I might have changed my mind, but somehow I doubted that. The cosy atmosphere at Arles suited my country-bred idea of life.

The pace of Arles was definitely leisurely. Even the beggars seemed to lack the urge to beg and lived in a grubby, sedentary world of their own. It struck me one day when I was strolling towards the place de la République on my way to the market, that the beggars' perspective was like that of small children. I don't just mean that they depended on others for the where-withal to live; but more simply, they viewed their surroundings from a child's angle, quite literally. The beggars sat either singly or in small groups on the pavement, backs to the wall, with a shallow cardboard box or an upturned cap or an old greasy hat beside them in which a few coins had been scattered as an encouragement to passers-by. They greeted you very civilly whether you added to their collection or not. They never followed you about, and only occasionally did I ever see them the worse for drink. The gipsy women at Les Saintes-Maries, and some of the gipsy men, could be very troublesome. They were beggars of a different type – often very aggressive, always persistent – and when their demands were refused, they showed their displeasure in no uncertain terms, muttering imprecations which were intended to be overheard, or even spitting at one's feet. The beggars at Arles merely existed and they appeared content to do so. A coin or two dropped into a cap was acknowledged by a nod and a grumbled *merci*. Otherwise they remained impassive and about as intrusive as a row of parking-meters. When they did look at you, they looked up.

Come to think of it, the act of looking upwards, like a child, was enough to tweak the strings of one's conscience and this was maybe the trick, after all.

One group of four beggars drifted between the streets near my hotel and the small square off the boulevard des Lices near the luxury Hôtel Jules-César. Another favourite spot was the steps of Saint-Trophime's church. Needless to say, the church steps were much frequented by beggars on Sunday mornings and they probably did quite well from visitors going to and from mass. This was 'good psychology' but, of course, it didn't cut much ice with the Arlésiens themselves. As much as anything, the beggars' movements seemed to be dictated by the weather. The sun seldom penetrated the narrow lanes. 'Trade' and sunlight were more reliable in the main squares and the boulevard and so, naturally enough, they tended to be favoured by the mendicants and their dogs. Once there was a big gipsy wedding at the Town Hall and the guests arrived in flashily painted, beaten-up old cars which had pink and white gauze ribbons tied to the bonnets, bumpers and radio aerials. After that, for a week the beggars' dogs trotted about with ribbons round their necks and one of them, a big Dalmatian, had a bow of pink ribbon tied to its tail.

If the beggars represented want, the Saturday markets held in the boulevard des Lices represented plenty. The stalls lined both sides of the boulevard and they stretched from beyond the Post Office all the way downhill. They were always crowded and their variety was astonishing. The fish-stalls displayed huge cuts of filleted and unfilleted monsters and smaller varieties – many like the Saint-Pierre unknown outside the Mediterranean area. There were eels and glutinous, flabby squid; beady-eyed lobsters; spider-crabs; tunny; fat glossy mackerel; rose-red *rougets*; and sardines and other tiny fish in rainbow colours. They were spread out on white trays packed with broken ice; or in plastic tubs; or layered in soggy cardboard boxes. The wafting smells of fish mingled with the sharp tang of cheeses, the soft-sweet smell of fruit, the hard perfume of flowers and the warm feathery smell of ducks and poultry. Vegetables of every imaginable variety and colour were piled on coverlets of dyed-green hessian. I feasted my eyes on the wonders of a bread-stall – the fancy plaited loaves, the immense rounds of black-crusted bread dusted with flour, squares and oblongs and various sizes of *baton* and *baguette* – all warm to the touch and golden-brown, smelling as bread ought to smell; totally different from the plastic-wrapped supermarket productions at home which tasted, as Compton Mackenzie put it, 'like powdered tomb-stones'.

Qumquats from Morocco; sparkling heaps of Spanish oranges; huge red-and-yellow Starking apples such as I used to buy in the Camargue; ripe bananas and large, pale, luminous grapes, their bloom catching the sunlight, the sunlight in every mouthful. A voice in my ear cried: '*C'est pas cher, mais c'est pas un cadeau!*' – and another voice broke into a torrent of complaint, as I turned to see the stall-holder and an old crone in black tugging fiercely at the ends of an enormous, purple Arlésien sausage. I tried the green and black olives, picking them from their big terracotta bowls one by one until I had eaten my fill and then salved my conscience, quite needlessly, by buying a litre of olive-oil, a first-pressing from Salon. It cost 40 francs, about £4 and the quality was superb.

Among the stalls of the poultry-sellers I discovered that a duck sold for 70 francs; hens for 35 francs apiece; while cockerels went for 15 francs a kilo. All the birds were sold live from cages stacked along the pavement, where they squatted blinking in the full glare of the sun. The birds appeared to be clean and healthy, even the guinea-fowl I saw tightly-packed in boxes not much bigger than a milk-crate.

In a booth near the poultry there were paintings on display – gaudy-coloured, sugary landscapes some of which depicted famous buildings and monuments at Arles and Nîmes. The artist introduced herself as Madame MacKillop and told me that she was the wife of a computer-programmer from, of all places, Dumbarton, on the River Clyde. The MacKillops had come back to Arles, her home town, after living in California and Madame MacKillop somehow managed to find time for art lessons and painting between looking after the house and three small children. Some of her pictures were quite pleasing, especially when she had 'done her own thing' instead of attempting to reproduce the style of other artists – the most popular models being Van Gogh and Cézanne. She admitted with touching frankness: 'I'm always a little unsure of myself. Maybe that is why I try different approaches. I like to paint what is there in front of me and make it look real. I'm really useless at perspective. Look at this picture of the Pont du Gard, for

example. The colours are nice but the drawing is *exécrable*! That's why I've priced it at only 150 francs. I doubt that anyone will pay more than that.'

I asked Madame MacKillop whether she painted from life. She replied, no – not always. The Pont du Gard had been copied from a postcard like some of the others. I felt that here was part of her problem. She would have benefitted by taking more time to master the basics of her technique – instead, she had been too impatient, too eager to begin selling her work. She painted only what she thought the tourists might buy. When I moved on, I saw disappointment reflected in Madame MacKillop's jade-green eyes. She called after me: 'I enjoyed our talk, *monsieur*, but I'm sorry nothing took your fancy!'

Glimpses of Arles street-life recur as snapshots. An advertisement in a menswear shop-window epitomized the Gallic sense of priorities: 'Why drive a comfortable car if your trousers aren't a comfortable fit?' A few streets away, LE SWEATERIE is a woman's outfitter specializing in imported designer-woollens. Book-matches I picked up at a *bar-tabac* were labelled '*L'Instant Passion*' – the smoker's aphrodisiac. A red van dashing past in a narrow alley, so fast that some terror-stricken pensioners flattened themselves against a wall, had its sides lettered-in block-capitals: SECOURS URGENT DES ASPHYXIES ET DES BLESSES ('URGENT RESCUE SERVICE FOR THE ASPHYXIATED AND THE WOUNDED'). Near the river, a tiny restaurant, closed for the winter, was called Le Poisson Banane: *Quel mélange!* Was its speciality really fish and bananas, or could it be a banana-shaped fish? I am left wondering. . . . A great flock of sparrows made a terrific volume of chirping noise, but the birds were totally invisible among the ivy shrouding a derelict house. Nearby some women were giving a tourist directions for the Alyscamps. I noted the bell-like chimes of their voices. For 'Alyscamps' they would say: '*Alice-cong*'. Someone says: '*Demeng meaten va bieng*' ('Tomorrow morning is all right'). I love this sound.

I was accosted by the spokesman of a bus-party, a tall,

bronzed fifty-year-old with curly grey hair, an open-fronted
Technicolor weather-proof jerkin and a bunch of keys jangling
at his belt. Keeping his options open, the man addressed me first
in French, then in English. I recalled a remark made by an elderly
Glaswegian when I was eighteen: 'The English chew their
words. The Italians sing them. The Germans vomit!' The grey-
haired man was a vomiter. *'Je viens d'Autriche! Autriche – vous
savez?* Ach so! You're English, ja? That's good. Just now I tell
you that I am an Ostrich!' Having failed to bridge the linguistic
gap, the humour of it escaped him – but then he came from a
country where a joke is no laughing matter.

More Snapshots: posters advertising a spiritualist meeting.
Here in the Rhôneland the paranormal seems to have a peculiar
fascination. Such meetings are usually well attended. The chief
participants are Dr C. Chris and Monsieur Gadmer. Gadmer is
bald and wears rimless spectacles; his dreamy gaze suggests that
he is not of this world. Dr Chris bears an uncanny resemblance
to the former SDP leader David Owen. There is a floating figure
of a woman in the background. She has a beaded Turkish
head-dress and the tormented eyes of a 1920s silent-film actress.
The posters are printed in appropriately spiritual colours – ·
purple, black and silver – a mixture also favoured by undertakers
and certain branches of European royalty.

At the Actes-Sud complex in the rue Dr Fanton, I found an
exhibition of photographs which I thought might shed some
light on the history of Arlésien costume and other dress-styles of
the region. However, an English-speaking assistant with an
American accent in the Actes-Sud bookshop, informed me that
the exhibition, entitled 'La Passion des Étoffes' (The Passion for
Drapery), was 'seriously WEIRD!'

The sepia photographs, I soon discovered, were all of women
in Arab dress. They had been taken in Morocco, in villages of
Fez Province whose romantic names – Fas Bali, Fas Djedid and
Azemmour – conjured up images of palm-fringed oases. The
photographer, a neuro-psychiatrist, Dr Gaëton Gatian de
Clérambault, had been from 1905 the assistant medical officer at

a Paris asylum, the Infirmerie Spéciale des Aliénés, attached to
the Préfecture de Police. Born at Bourges in 1872, Clérambault
was related through his mother's family to Alfred de Vigny
(1797–1863), the lyric poet, dramatist and leader of the early
Romantic movement. Clérambault studied painting in Paris at
the Ecole des Beaux-Arts, before turning to medicine. Having
been awarded the Croix-de-Guerre, he spent part of the 1914–18
War in Morocco, recovering from a bullet-wound. There he
indulged in 'the pleasures and seductions of Moorish life'. By
then Clérambault had developed a revolutionary theory linking
styles of folded drapery with racial groups and tribes. In Fez
Province, he photographed hundreds of Bedouin women,
thus obtaining a unique collection which eventually numbered
more than 40,000 plates.

The exhibition at the Actes-Sud gallery was accompanied by
flute-music and the nasal wails of a female Arab singer. I noted at
the time: 'It creates a sense of being drawn against one's will into
a strangely disturbing, sinister and yet somehow beautiful
private world. A dream-world which offers temptation without
tangible satisfaction. Wraithlike figures in white robes appear to
hover in a twilight zone between Life and Death. Exaggerated
poses against shadowy backgrounds – elaborately-carved door-
ways, ornate grilles, floor-tiles laid in severe geometrical
patterns. The women's shrouds give almost no hint of their
form – only the eyes, hands and feet are exposed. The enigmatic
images remind me of Resnais' film, *L'Année Dernière à
Marienbad*. They create a feeling of impenetrable mystery,
perhaps even of mystification for mystification's sake. I find
myself repelled, yet at the same time fascinated by these ghostly
forms which are like the nightmare visions of an embalmer.'

As a police-psychiatrist, Clérambault had specialized in the
interrogation and treatment of women whose bizarre sexual
attraction for fabrics such as silk, taffeta and velour drove them
to become uncontrollable kleptomaniacs. A dress-maker's sister
convicted of theft admitted: 'Stealing silk is delicious; buying it
never gave me the same thrill.' Clerambault recorded many of
their case-histories in a thesis, *Le Passion érotique des étoffes chez la*

femme, published in 1908. The mere mention of silk, in certain patients provoked reactions which escalated from a prickling sensation in the finger- and toe-nails to violent orgasms. Some of the married women who confessed that they preferred masturbation to normal sex, told Clérambault how they had achieved a climax by caressing themselves with items of silk *lingerie*. The texture and the rustling of silk excited the most extreme fetishists to the point of hysteria.

It appears that Clérambault himself became obsessed by their weird passion. He lived alone with an elderly housekeeper in a quiet Paris suburb, surrounded by eyeless, chiffon dolls and full-size wax female dummies which he spent hours meticulously dressing in rich Eastern fabrics. Haunted by money-worries, dreading permanent blindness following a cataract operation, in December 1934, at the age of sixty-two, Clérambault committed suicide in front of a mirror, shooting himself through the mouth with a service-revolver.

A few days later I attended a debate at Méjan when some visiting psychologists and an ethnophotography expert dealt at considerable length with Dr Clérambault's art and assessed his medical career. The language of the debate was uncompromisingly technical and, I regret to say, for the most part left me none the wiser. A speaker invited to explain the role of the 'Psychic Envelope' gave as examples nuts and sea-shells, a baby's experience of the womb and the newborn infant's response to its own skin. A gremlin in the slide-carrousel caused a carefully arranged selection of negatives to appear back to front, upside-down, out of sequence or totally blank, which provoked laughter among the audience and left the young projectionist protesting her innocence, almost in tears. During a discussion of tactile fetishes, a Persian cat which had wandered in off the street added an unexpected dimension of Virtual Reality by parading between the rows of chairs and rubbing itself against the audience's legs – bringing uncomfortably alive the images of Clérambault's excited unhealthy probing among silks, taffetas, cotton, velour and lace!

The Arlésien dress in its present form dates from the reign of

Louis XV (1710–74). By the time Lelée arrived at Arles in 1902, the eighteenth-century model had changed, influenced by changing fashions outside Provence itself. The hair-ribbon, or *ruban* had been shortened to its current length and the puffed-sleeve (*manche bouffante*) had been replaced by the pagoda style (*manche pagode*).

The Arlésien dress of Mistral's day is still worn by the Queen of Arles and her Maid of Honour, by the Queen of the Félibrige – whose predecessors naturally included Madame Mistral – and at Les Saintes-Maries' pilgrimages and other festivals by the wives and daughters of the Nacioun Gardiano. The evolution of the costume is exhaustively illustrated at the Museon Arlaten, where a room has been furnished with many actual examples as well as drawings and paintings by Lelée and other artists including Théophile-Henri Mayon, Jules-Armand Ronin, André-Spitz and Father Hérain. Léopold Lelée's prolific sketches in watercolour and gouache in many cases showed the method of dressing from various angles – the costume details being carefully emphasized in contrast to Lelée's figures sketched in his Provençal Art-Deco style, often with blank features.

Anxious that the Arlésien dress should be preserved as a living tradition, Mistral awarded diplomas, which Lelée designed, to its wearers at the Festo Vierginenço and decreed that the dress-style should remain as it was in 1904 – the year of his Nobel Prize award, when the seventy-four-year-old poet saw his Provençal crusade carried by Folco de Baroncelli-Javon to the Camargue and there established by the founding of the Nacioun Gardiano.

I spent an interesting evening with members of the Reneissenço association which met every Thursday in a rather drab, dimly-lit school hall in the rue de la Paix. The ladies of the Reneissenço and their instructors, Madame Castanet, Madame Marchard and Madame Niel, were amused and intrigued by my desire to learn about the Arlésien costume. There were about sixteen women in the hall and each of them was eager to have her say. I found myself deluged with information. It was impossible to make notes, since all the women talked at once; but their enthusiasm was both touching and impressive. Madame Niel showed me a copy of her privately printed book on Arlésien costume and hairstyles, *L'Art du costume d'Arles*, which she had illustrated with her own excellent pen-and-ink drawings. Madame Castanet gave me copies of an article which, among other things, revealed that a *ruban* dating from Charles X or Louis Philippe (1773–1850) nowadays fetches between 2,000 and 3,500 francs, or even more. Many of these original garments and accessories, handed down through several generations, are still worn today and I had already seen some wonderfully preserved examples at Les Saintes-Maries and Arles. If nothing else, the high values showed the importance placed upon them, not only by collectors but also by their owners who preferred to wear these beautiful clothes rather than part with them – an attitude of which Mistral, I am certain, would have strongly approved.

A teenage girl in a black jersey and black pantaloons, with the pale, drawn features of a habitual insomniac, crept up and whispered that she had spent 'a whole year' in England. She said: 'I was all the time in Surreyshire, learning the dialect of Farnborough.'

She went on: '*Monsieur*, I have for you one question, please. For a long time I have desired to know – are your Scottish *châteaux* still very much troubled by the phantoms?'

With my faculties strained to the limit and all my efforts concentrated on making sense of the complex Arlésien costume, the sudden change of theme caught me unawares. I replied rather lamely: 'It all depends whether or not you believe in such things. Are you particularly interested in ghosts?'

The girl shook her head very emphatically: '*Mais* NON, *monsieur*! You see, I wondered. . . .' And with that her voice trailed off in a tiny outburst of shy laughter. It transpired that she had been merely looking for an excuse to practise her newly-acquired Farnborough dialect. She had heard that I came from Scotland and the subject of haunted castles had seemed as good an ice-breaker as any other.

I first saw the Arlésien costume worn by the daughters of

Henri and Riquette Aubanel, as recently as 1984 when we drove to a lunch given by the Nacioun Gardiano. Despite its quaint, old-fashioned style, it has never struck me as out of keeping with the modern Rhôneland. The Arles dress almost invariably enhances the wearer. I have heard younger women complain that the bodice, the shawls and the fullness of skirt makes them appear squat and dumpy. Others say that the dress ages the wearer – an eighteen-year-old girl might pass for a woman of thirty. This may be true in certain cases. But generally speaking the effect is elegant, graceful and, of course, it is perfectly feminine. At the same time, I realize that, in some quarters, this must be unpopular. I have a strong suspicion that Arlésien costume and Women's Lib, for example, would be totally incompatible. Few of the Rhôneland women I met had much time for Women's Lib or its protagonists. The women of the Camargue sometimes worked as hard as the men. They dressed in jeans or a divided skirt and rode out after the bulls. Yet these same women wore the Arlésien costume with pride, without any feeling of being compromised or being relegated to an inferior role in a man's world. Their feelings were summed up by a *manadier*'s wife who told me: 'We wear our costumes because they're part of our traditional life. *C'est normal, monsieur.* I don't understand these Liberationists. *What is it* that they're trying to escape from, may I ask? If they don't want to marry or have children, that's their own affair. No-one is forcing them to do so! The business of wearing clothes of one sort or another is simply an excuse. What a woman *feels* she is, *knows* she is, is what really matters. Character is not like clothes which you put on or take off as the occasion demands.'

I asked: 'Don't you ever resent the fact that your dress-style was actually decreed by a man? The fact that Mistral gave out diplomas to encourage the girls to go on dressing themselves like their grandmothers?'

'Not at all, *monsieur*! On the contrary, it is largely thanks to Mistral our ceremonies have been preserved. The poetry, the songs, the dances are our heritage. The Arles dress likewise. Can you picture the *farandole* being danced by girls wearing tee-shirts and denims? The music, the dance and the costumes all go together. Take one away and the result is spoiled – the whole meaning is lost. After all, we still read Mistral's poetry in the language it was written. *Mireille* was published nearly 150 years ago. What about your English Shakespeare who wrote centuries before that? Surely you're not suggesting that Mistral and Shakespeare should be translated into modern language? That would be *absurd*!

'The Arles costume is the same. *C'est une realité, monsieur* – just as you're a man and I'm a woman – and that's all there is to it.'

I often arrived at the Museon Arlaten in the morning to find the Arlésien guides, wrapped in their long black *manteaux*, waiting for the doors to be opened. Madame Mineff was tall; Madame Palazon and Madame Dibon were average height; Madame Boullin was very *petite*. Standing in a group by the great doors of the Museon, with youngsters flashing past on skateboards, the last of the tourists in denims, Bermuda shorts and coloured weatherproofs and the townspeople of Arles, *chic* and up-to-date, going about their daily affairs, the Arlésiennes nevertheless managed to blend with their surroundings.

Their elegant costume, like Arles' beautiful old buildings and monuments, was merely another facet of the town's varied street-life. Once inside the Museon Arlaten, it seemed to me, odd as it may appear, the guides did not merge so effectively. Here in the shadowy stillness they seemed unexpectedly obtrusive, living models of a bygone age – like Mistral's tableaux brought to life – as they dealt with visitors's queries or sat knitting or sewing like the old nurse who watches over a young mother in the *Visite à la couchée* display.

Nothing was too much trouble for the Museon's guides. They loved their work and they entered into the spirit of it to the full. In their various fields I found them to be very knowledge-able: Madame Dibon who looked after the Félibrige room and other exhibits on the first floor; Madame Boullin who needed to stand on tip-toe on a chair to read the inscriptions of drawings hung in the corridors; Madame Mineff who tutored me with such patience on the intricacies of Rhôneland costume.

'I know my good fortune,' said Madame Mineff, 'for indeed I am very lucky to pass my days among such beautiful things. Yes, I can't complain' – she crossed her hands in her lap and smiled with placid satisfaction – 'I can tell you honestly that here I have found what so many of us seek, that is my true *métier*. After all, who could possibly wish for more interesting work than this?'

14

The Painter of the Arlésiennes

An 'ambassador of charm', is how Lelée has been described by his biographer, Michel Gay; and in many respects Gay's description is a very apt one. Léopold Lelée is best known for his drawings and paintings of women in Arlésien costume. Many of his paintings have been used to illustrate books about the Rhôneland and other parts of France including the Auvergne, and they are famous for their delicacy and scrupulously accurate detail.

Lelée was born at Chemazé, in Mayenne, on 13 December 1872. In March 1902, aged twenty-nine, Lelée came to live at Arles and there he married Rosa Tourrel. The couple had two daughters, Mireille and Yvonne.

I had the good fortune to meet Yvonne Lelée (now Madame Jules Moulard) through her son-in-law, Julian Panichi. Madame Moulard's flat was on the second floor of a modern block built close to the railway line. I found her waiting for me on the landing: very *petite*, stoutish and welcoming, with short-cropped white hair and tinted glasses, dressed in a black skirt and a black ribbed-wool jersey. Her only jewellery, apart from her wedding ring, was a pair of gold ear-rings and a tiny pendant suspended on a fine gold chain.

Madame Moulard's husband was still convalescing after an

operation and spent most of the day in bed. This explained why in the flat the central heating had been turned on full blast, even though out of doors it was warm and sunny. Madame Moulard apologized: 'You will probably find the sitting-room very hot and stuffy,' she said, 'but I daren't open the windows. The trains make so much racket that we shan't be able to hear ourselves speaking.' She sighed: 'How I miss my little courtyard with its tree and its flower-beds! *Ah, monsieur . . . ma cour me manque!*' I noticed she pronounced the word *'manque'* as mank, in the Arlésien fashion. She was now seventy-nine years of age and her husband was eighty. They had given up their house in Saint Martin-de-Crau a few years before and moved to Arles to be nearer to their daughter, Nelly, and son-in-law.

Yvonne Moulard told me that she and her sister had had a happy childhood at Fontvieille. She said: 'Mireille was eight years older than me. She died a long time ago, alas! Father didn't earn a great deal from painting, but we were never short of food or clothing. Father was gentle and kind, but he could be severe if we didn't attend to our schoolwork or misbehaved. Of the two, Mother was perhaps the stricter; but our life at Fontvieille was as happy as any I could have imagined.'

All his life Lelée had worked tremendously hard, producing hundreds of drawings, besides often quite large paintings in gouache and watercolours. His early works tended to reflect the classic, representational style – what in France could be termed the Beaux-Arts tradition – popular at the turn of the century. As so frequently happens, in later life Lelée's technique broadened; his compositions and his use of carefully juxtaposed and balanced flat colour-washes gave his paintings a deceptively simplified poster effect; his interest in form and space, to some extent at least, replaced his youthful preoccupation with detail. Gay observes that Lelée invented a style which might be described as Provençal Art-Deco. This technique was also perhaps influenced by Lelée's need, rather than his *penchant*, for mass-production. His subjects gradually became less and less individualized, their features and expressions merely being suggested by a few deft brush-stokes, or lines of graphite or crayon. His Arlésiennes, especially the larger groups, were latterly the equivalent of a highly sophisticated cartoon, stylized shapes whose main emphasis lay on the clothes and hair; their limbs gracefully arranged and entwined to show the Arlésien costume to best advantage, describing the movements of a traditional dance such as the *farandole*.

In these later paintings, even the clothes themselves were reduced to their basic elements: the waisted dress with its full, flowing skirt; the bodice, *fichu* and *dentelles* with their decorative old lace; and the long black shawl, or the hooded cloak worn out of doors. The distinctive tulip-shaped Arlésien hairstyle with its velvet *ruban* also lent itself very readily to the artist's ingenious and instantly recognizable shorthand.

Madame Moulard fetched a glass water-jug and a bottle of sweet cordial, the taste and colour of which reminded me of lichees. She invited me to smoke if I wanted to: 'Father always smoked while he was working,' she said. 'Never less than two packets of Gauloises *sans filtre* every day! He drank a little wine with his meals, or he might have taken an occasional glass with a friend at the café. . . . Nothing excessive. . . . He was a serious artist – but also a man who cared for his wife and family.'

With considerable pride, Madame Moulard showed me a photograph of her mother standing arm in arm with Mistral. Mistral had been an enthusiastic admirer of Lelée. Mistral's poetry and his ardent encouragement of Provençal traditions and ceremonies influenced Lelée, inevitably – not least the Festo Vierginenço, when Mistral presented a diploma designed by Lelée to the women and girls who attended wearing Arlésien dress. It might be said that, in his own way, Lelée created images which were a pictorial equivalent of Mistral's poems – by which I mean their descriptive passages. The *capoulié*, or head, of the Félibrige, Marius Jouveau, called him a true 'son of Provence'; but it was Mistral himself who described Lelée as the 'Painter of the Arlésiennes'.

Michel Gay's remarks about the 'charm' of Lelée's paintings are in no sense meant to be derogatory. They point instead to the lyrical appeal of Lelée's art. This comes across very clearly in Michel Gay's excellent study, *Léo Lelée: un angevin chez les félibres* (1989), of which Madame Moulard assured me she heartily approved. The book has been criticized by scholars of the Provençal renaissance for being too *uncritical* of Lelée; and for providing a text which offers a commentary upon rather than a critical discussion of Lelée's work. In the absence of a translation which English readers could judge for themselves (and since the book is only available in a limited edition in Provence – at least for the time being) I will simply add that, while Gay has written no mere eulogy of Lelée, such criticisms have some merit. What is equally important – indeed I would venture to suggest far more important in this instance – the author's informed selection and arrangement of the illustrations provides us for the first time with clear pictorial evidence of the development of Lelée's unique lyrical style – including what Michel Gay calls his Provençal 'Art-Deco' period.

Yvonne Moulard showed me a beautiful gouache landscape of *gardians* and bulls in the Camargue – the horsemen with their tridents, the grazing herd and a *cabane* (the *gardian*'s hut) in the middle-distance, and a sunlit blue panorama of *sansouires* with the blue water of an *étang* and a cloudless sky of delicate *eau-de-nil* merging at the horizon. The picture was of a size and format popular with Lelée in the 1930s and 1940s, about 480 cm long by 1130 cm wide. The shape of the painting, Madame Moulard explained, had been dictated by the paper her father used for this and other similar works. It was a plain brown wrapping-paper which Yvonne's mother brought back from the butcher's shop: Yvonne, then in her late teens, was given the job of dabbing off the worst of the blood-stains, trimming the edges where the dripping meat had stained the paper beyond repair and, finally, ironing out the wrinkles! Lelée's extensive use of gouache made it possible to work on such comparatively crude material, which would have responded less satisfactorily to the lighter, transparent watercolours used for smaller works – for example studies of gipsy women, and the mills of Fontvieille.

As far as I can gather, Lelée painted on butcher's paper only because it cost nothing and was in plentiful supply. Between 1901–1903, another great Rhôneland artist Auguste Chabaud, worked at Graveson drawing on butcher's paper – or paper from the village fishmonger's – with blue and red carpenter's chalk. Unlike Lelée, Chabaud chose his material primarily for aesthetic reasons. A recent work by Hervé Solignac has suggested that the thick wrapping-paper with its coarse-grained surface used by Chabaud 'corresponded to the temperament of the artist'. According to Yvonne Moulard, Lelée made no such self-conscious decision; instead he merely took what was readily available, the only drawback being that, unless the artist took care to avoid using fugitive colours and applied the paint with some forethought, the pictures were liable to fade and discolour more rapidly than others painted on purpose-made watercolour papers.

If Madame Moulard had inherited much of her father's character and temperament, then Lelée must have been an utterly charming, delightful person! He was introduced to the Rhôneland by a friend he had met at the Beaux-Arts in Paris, Visconte Gaston de Luppé, a wealthy, talented sculptor and painter who lived and worked in a large seventeenth-century house in Arles, facing the arena, which he bought and restored in 1905. Both the Visconte de Luppé and Lelée were married and had children; and, although both were committed artists, they lived – each according to his circumstances – conventional family lives, the only real difference being that, while Gaston de

Luppé had a considerable fortune which he had inherited as a young man, Lelée had to work hard to make ends meet, despite his popularity and success as an artist and an illustrator.

Madame Moulard offered little information about her father's friendship with Gaston de Luppé; and of course she had been too young to remember Mistral, who died when she was little more than an infant. 'Father made some wonderful illustrations for Joseph D'Arbaud's Christmas story, the *Nouvè Gardien* – you know, *monsieur*, the one set in the Camargue. D'Arbaud often came to our house – a very elegant man, always carrying a cane.' This certainly sounded like D'Arbaud – one side of his character at any rate – and there is a story told how, when he was desperately short of money, he had unexpectedly come by 1,000 francs (this was before the First World War I may add) and blew the lot on a fine new pair of riding-breeches!

The old lady spoke with deep affection of the poet, Charloun Rieu, a member of the Félibrige, whose great kindness – '*Quelle bonté monsieur!*' – had made an indelible impression on her. Charloun Rieu himself had had a hard life – years of unrewarded literary toil, which in the end Mistral persuaded the French Government to recognize. Charloun Rieu was awarded a pension of 300 gold francs a year. According to Aldington, it is also possible that in 1904 he received a small share of Mistral's money from the Nobel Prize (or to be more exact, half-prize), a sum which had been reserved by Mistral not for the Museon Arlaten but for 'a poor *félibre* for whom Mistral had a great respect'. I was much interested by Aldington's shrew observation that 'the range, subtlety and power of Mistral's art could never command the instant response of the poor in spirit as did the naïvely touching poems of Charloun, who humbly solicited approbation by composing his poems to the tunes of popular songs of the day'.

Among Lelée's other friends were the Marquis Folco de Baroncelli-Javon and Folco's biographer, Jean des Vallières. A fine watercolour by Lelée of a *gardian* on horseback, which he presented to Folco de Broncelli , was afterwards given by Folco to Jeanne de Flandreysy and bears the Marquis's inscription and signature. Despite the fact that he was courted by aristocrats – the Visconte de Luppé, the Marquis of Javon – and had won the admiration, friendship and patronage of the great Mistral himself, none of this went to Lelée's head. He remained as he had always been – plain, unassuming, a tireless worker, a dedicated artist and a responsible, devoted husband and father. In Michel Gay's *Fontvieille* (1990) there is a photograph of Lelée painting in his studio and another which shows him drawing at a small wooden table. The studio was quite spartan: apart from the table, there were a few rush-matted kitchen chairs, some bookshelves and a hard-backed settee. Compared to the large sculptor's studio in Arles where his friend, Gaston de Luppé, drew and modelled superbly-detailed figure-studies and animals, Lelée's work-room at 31 cours Hyacinthe Bellon in Fontvieille had been modest.

A few weeks later, Madame Moulard invited me to dinner. Her husband joined us for the meal, but he had still not fully recovered from his operation and retired to bed immediately afterwards. Jules Moulard did not talk a great deal. He was also slightly hard of hearing. I should have liked to hear his views on the *corrida* and the Course Camarguaise – for according to Julian Panichi, Monsieur Moulard was an *aficionado* of tauromachy and very knowledgeable, Unfortunately, however, his false teeth irritated his gums and he had removed them. He chuckled and his cheeks compressed like a punctured bladder. 'What muth you think of me, *mithew* – I've jumped out of bed and come thraight to the table in my drething-gown and carpet-slipperth. No teeth and – look here! – no troutherth either!' The absence of trousers mattered less than Monsieur Moulard's missing dentures which, combined with his strong country dialect and deafness, made any conversation with him somewhat difficult. He was a very likeable man, the son of a shepherd, and spoke of Lelée with genuine admiration.

Dinner was excellent. Madame Moulard had shopped and prepared the meal entirely by herself. For an *apéritif*, we had a glass of fresh orange juice. The *hors d'oeuvre* was a cheese soufflé, timed to perfection; the main course, roast lamb, was served with potatoes fried in bread crumbs, which looked like large orange-coloured marbles and required some determination to spear with a fork. A green salad, which Madame Moulard had mixed to go with the cheese course, to her distress had to be thrown away. A flick of the wooden spoon revealed an enormous beetle sprawled among the lettuce-leaves. Madame Moulard wailed and clucked her tongue: '*Sale bête!*' she cried. 'The central heating was so warm that I left the kitchen window open, trains or no trains, to get a breath of air. This dirty creature must have flown in!' The beetle was plucked from among the salad and carefully inspected. It was quite dead, as far as I could tell, and had either drowned or had been asphyxiated by the potent salad-dressing.

The *gardian* cheese, made of ewe's milk, had an exceptionally tart, metallic after-taste. Eaten with a piece of fresh bread, it tasted delicious. After a fruit salad followed by coffee, Madame Moulard cleared the table, refusing politely but firmly any offer of help; and then she showed me her collection of books, including several illustrated by Lelée. The finest of them was a specially bound copy of D'Arbaud's *Nouvè Gardien*, which contained several of Lelée's original drawings.

Madame Moulard also produced folders containing some rough sketches on brown paper which Lelée had made during the 1914–18 War. These portraits of his companions in the trenches were economical, powerful and demonstrated Lelée's mastery of expressive line as well as his ability to capture mood and atmosphere spontaneously, with absolute precision. Some of the books she bought in the early 1970s had cost between 2,000–3,000 francs each. She agreed: it was a *lot* of money. But, she said: 'I think it's only right. . . .' – meaning that it was right that she should take an interest in her father's work and help to keep his name alive.

I found it hard to decide which among the framed pictures in the sitting-room most appealed to me: was it the blue Camargue landscape on butcher's paper? Or a splendid oil-on-canvas portrait of Yvonne's mother, Rosa, and her grandmother,

Marie Tourrel? Or, perhaps, a watercolour of a gipsy girl made with a 'full' brush (that is, Lelée let the brush soak up plenty of colour instead of working with it half-dry), the tangled curls of blue-black hair suggested by a few rapid squiggles. I noticed how Lelée took pains to get the drawing right; how he used the watercolour washes mainly as 'infill'. Some studies of Arlésiennes made in pencil using a light, sandy paper had been strengthened with gouache – or else white had been used to create an illusion of depth, for example, the hightlights on a nose and cheek-bones which brought them closer than the other features. In the end, I felt I liked the Camargue landscape best, with the gipsy girl coming a close second.

When Léopold Lelée died on 26 June 1947, eight years after his friend and exact contemporary, Gaston de Luppé, he was given a lavish public funeral at Arles. The Arlésiennes turned out in their hundreds – like one of Lelée's great crowd-scenes come to life – led by their Queen, Gabrielle Boissy and many local dignitaries. The hearse, covered with a black cloth canopy, was pulled by a team of black horses. 'It was a wonderful tribute!' said Madame Moulard. 'So many people! It seemed as if the whole of Arles crowded into the cemetery to pay my father their last respects.'

15

Shadows of Van Gogh

'And presumably you are going to write something about Van Gogh?'

This remark had been dropped into the conversation by someone I'd met quite by chance shortly before I left London. He was merely an acquaintance: agreeable enough in his own way, but not someone with whom I was on close terms. His remark was the throw-away sort people use when their store of polite, neutral questions is exhausted. Without really thinking, I replied: 'I expect so. But Van Gogh's two years at Arles have been explored fairly thoroughly already. I honestly doubt that there is anything left to be discovered.'

Many of the places associated with Van Gogh's stay were badly damaged or totally destroyed by the Allied bombardment of Arles in June 1944. These included the modest *pension*, the Carrel, at 30 rue Amédée-Pichot, close to the place Lamartine, where Van Gogh ate and slept for several weeks after his arrival on 22 February 1888, and the famous Yellow House in the place Lamartine itself, where he installed himself in May that year. This was where Gauguin eventually joined him for a few tempestuous months during which they painted together, had violent arguments and lived on a meagre diet, spending what remained of Van Gogh's allowance from his brother on tobacco, absinthe and occasional visits to the brothel. It was here, after an explosive quarrel with Gauguin, that Van Gogh mutilated himself by slicing off part of his ear with a razor. The Yellow House was completely destroyed by bombing on 25 June 1944 which also damaged the nearby porte de la Cavelerie.

Not very far from the place de la République, the 'Espace Van-Gogh' was inaugurated on 17 February 1989 as a cultural centre, consisting of a médiathèque (which includes the municipal library, an extensive video library with viewing accommodation and a host of other facilities), a university-centre and a college of translators. The complex was formerly a hospital, the Hôtel-Dieu du Saint-Esprit founded in 1573, and here Van Gogh recuperated and painted during 1889.

Arles is proud of its associations with Van Gogh, although at the time the painter lived there many of the Arlésiens were cruel to him, mocked his red hair and blistered, sunburned face and laughed openly at what they considered to be his eccentric behaviour. '*Fou-rou*' they called him: the mad, red creature. Even Madame Calment, the oldest woman in France, who remembers Van Gogh buying bread in her mother's shop, had few kind or flattering words to say of him. To be fair, Van Gogh in some ways had been his own worst enemy. He suffered from hereditary epilepsy and nervous depressions which were exaggerated by heavy drinking, too much smoking and too little food. His manner was often abrupt to the point of rudeness. His excitable, drunken moods and unsociable temper alienated the townspeople who, perhaps understandably, since they did not realize that Van Gogh was also shy, vulnerable and in poor health, thought him quite deranged. This, however, does not excuse his treatment by the Arlésiens, many of whom (including the proprietor of the *pension* Carrel) over-charged and cheated him. Few people in Arles, except for the postman Roulin and his family, showed Van Gogh any kindness or sympathy.

Thanks to Alain Marion, the Deputy-Director of Tourism at Arles, I was able to meet Madame Jeanne Calment and question her in private about her recollections of Van Gogh. Madame Calment has become something of a celebrity. She was born on

162 *Wild Thyme and Saladelle*

21 February 1875; thus Van Gogh arrived in Arles the day after Madame Calment's thirteenth birthday. Since the age of 110, she has lived at the Maison du Lac, an old people's home which stands in beautifully landscaped grounds near the hospital.

It was a fine, bright sunny afternoon with a stiff breeze when I set off to walk from the centre of Arles, through the Fourchon – the recently developed business-quarter on the town's south side – to the Maison du Lac, a distance of no more than three kilometres.

I crossed over the boulevard des Lices and then turned down into the boulevard Emile Zola with its walled gardens, where a party of schoolchildren marching along in Indian file, to their teacher's embarrassment, greeted me with Nazi-style salutes and mystifying shouts of '*Eclair!*' Just below the level-crossing, by the canal, I stopped to admire a beautiful old house with a wide verandah covered with ivy, standing in a wild, untended garden in the shade of some large chestnut-trees, their branches tossed by the wind. The brown chestnuts lay on the gravel-drive and the lawns in their hundreds. The house was in bad repair and the garden a tangled wilderness; but they had a romantic, forgotten charm which made them an attractive subject for a sketch. While I was busy sketching, the owner came out to check the mail-box. He was very tall and thin with a mop of long black hair blowing every which way in the wind. A pharmacist, he and his family had lived there for eight years. He insisted on showing me round, inside as well as out. The rooms had a comfortable, lived-in atmosphere. It was a quiet, inward-looking sort of house such as a writer or a musician might choose. And yet the wild garden which presented a different aspect from every window, seemed to be a part of the interior and to flow through it.

The pharmacist asked if I liked jazz music and my tour of the house was accompanied by a wonderful recording of a local pianist whose name sounded like 'Pariancciani'. He played like Dave Brubeck, cascades of intersecting complex melody, a sparkling abstract of sound in a style which was, nevertheless, entirely his own. Pariancciani's playing, which was technically brillant, seemed to breathe from the depths of his spirit and his soul. The pharmacist said: 'You'd never think so to hear him play, but Pariancciani has been deformed since his birth. To do no more than sit at a piano and move his fingers over the keyboard, causes him difficulty. The piano is Pariancciani's life, his love, his whole expression. When he plays jazz, his whole being becomes at one with the instrument, at one with the music.' I thought: how like Van Gogh! For the painter, too, had suffered a kind of deformity; a deformity not of body but of mind, a mixture of nervous illness and paranoia which warped his spirit and bred distrust and bitter resentment. Yet when Van Gogh began to paint, like Pariancciani at his piano, he was transformed. Like the crystal cadences of the jazz that followed us from room to room, Van Gogh's canvasses mirrored the depths of his inimitable genius.

The wind blew from the northwest along the disused railway tracks. The willows by the canal reflected in the soupy-green water which the wind ruffled, catching the sunlight's glitter. Beyond the motorway bridge the countryside appeared very much as Van Gogh must have seen it a hundred years before: the fields of shining stubble divided by thin, ragged hedges; the mistral gusting through the trees and bushes, brushing the pile of their dark-green leaves almost pure-white in the sun. I tried to picture Van Gogh, alone there in the open fields, his face reddened by sunburn until it resembled a lump of raw meat, muttering and gesticulating like a man possessed as he struggled to paint at his wind-whipped canvas. For months he had worked like a painting-machine, totally oblivious of the need for food or rest. Mentally as well as physically the effects of this on Van Gogh had been catastrophic. I had often read about this period of tortured ecstasy when he produced many of his finest works, but somehow I never fully grasped the reality of it until I came here and saw for myself these brilliantly lit, restless landscapes which had caused Van Gogh such an effort of suffering to portray.

Near the gate of the hospital, a lane wound uphill through some woodland between rounded, undulating meadows where the grass was sprinkled with flowers the colour of bluebells.

A small crowd of local journalists and television crews from the French national network, TF-1, and Télévision-Monte Carlo, had gathered outside the Maison du Lac to report the unveiling of a sculpture by the main entrance. The unveiling was to be performed by the Queen of the Arlésiennes, Carole Bressy, and Madame Calment. From the journalists' point of view, Madame Calment was the main attraction.

Before the unveiling ceremony there was a tea-party. About a dozen of the Maison du Lac's elderly residents, some of them in wheelchairs, appeared with their nurses and sat in rows in a big, airy room furnished with pink and white chairs and formica-topped tables and enormous tubs containing rubber-plants, vines, ferns and clumps of variegated foliage. Madame Calment, in a chromium-plated wheelchair, sat apart from the others in royal isolation. Most of the old people were in their late nineties. One old lady was 103. Madame Calment, then 116 and eight months, easily outstripped the rest; not only was she much older, but she had the looks and vitality of a healthy woman of little more than eighty.

There was something wonderful, yet at the same time awful, about the scene. It was the opposite extreme of a children's tea-party, and yet this was what it most resembled. Instead of mothers and nannies, the old people's nurses fed them with cakes, biscuits and lemonade, wiped their faces clean after they had finished eating and shepherded them discreetly away when they demanded to go to the lavatory. A few who were incontinent perched on comodes, blissfully unaware of their gurgling bowel-movements which now and then interrupted the speeches by the hospital's Director and representatives of the town council. Many of the elderly seemed very frail; some were quite deranged; others disabled in some way. An old Spanish woman of eighty-five, with yellow broken teeth, hobbled up and sang to me in a cracked, high-pitched voice, then invited me to join her dancing a *jota*. An old man in a brightly-coloured jersey struggled to his feet, trembling all over and gasping; then, as if propelled by an electric motor, he shuffled away, his carpet-slippers making little sharp squeaks on the polished linoleum. In a way they were like children: trusting, dependent and vulnerable – but their courage and cheerful spirits were also very moving. A pretty nurse told me: 'This is my calling, *monsieur*. It's what I like to do best. And, after all, they are only what we ourselves will become, one of these days.'

The statue, unveiled by Carole Bressy and Madame Calment, looked like a piece of freshly-chewed-and-spat-out toffee, many times magnified, mounted on a plain stone pillar. The sculptor, in a black leather jerkin, had a large, flashy diamond stud in his left ear. He posed obligingly beside his creation for the TV cameras, but the sculpture itself was as incomprehensible to me as the reasons for Madame Calment's extraordinary longevity.

After the ceremony, when the journalists had gone, Carole Bressy introduced me to Madame Calment and translated my questions. Madame Calment's fine head of white hair had been permed for the occasion. She wore a smart dress of navy-blue-and-white cotton and a navy-blue cardigan and matching navy-blue sandals. Her skin, I noticed, was very white and filmy, her bare legs were lightly veined and patched with red and blue markings, her face and hands were speckled with dark blotches. Her eyes looked red and sore. The left eye appeared little more than an empty socket. Both were a watery-blue colour and filmed by cataract. Her mind and body still functioned quite normally. She wore a hearing-aid in each ear but could barely understand my Anglified French pronunciation, which did not altogether surprise me. Carole Bressy and her nurses she could make out without any difficulty.

When I asked her how she felt in herself, Madame Calment replied: '*Je me défends!*' This put it in a nutshell, for she had become like a defence-system, fending off age, decay and death minute by minute, hour by hour, day by day. Her nurse explained: 'With such great age, it seems as though the life-cycle enters a new phase. It's a kind of "re-start", if you like. The machinery slips into another gear. The body free-wheels like a car running downhill in neutral. Or else, you might compare the process to a swimmer being carried along by the tide.'

Jeanne Calment had no theories, and made it perfectly clear

that as far as she was concerned there was no 'secret', about the reason for her unique health: as a matter of fact, she had seldom given it much thought, she said. Her life had been fairly humdrum, but carefree. She had smoked a few cigarettes and she enjoyed a glass of wine. Perhaps an unusually strong constitution was the answer; or it might have been something she'd inherited. Or maybe it was just good luck.

The nurse told me with a grin that Madame Calment thoroughly enjoyed her new-found fame which is due to two things: her age and the fact that she had met Van Gogh. She has been interviewed so frequently that – as one might expect – her replies to questions about the painter have become rather stereotyped. On the other hand, when Madame Calment gives a slightly different version, journalists have been apt to sigh and remark that her memory is failing at last.

The fact is that Jeanne Calment's memories of Van Gogh are a child's memories of more than a century ago! She probably did not speak to Van Gogh herself, except to wish him *bonjour* now and then, or bid him *au revoir*. She does, however, remember her mother's brief conversations with him.

Once Van Gogh came into their bread-shop complaining of terrible sun-burn, with his head and face aflame and his eyes wild and staring 'like a mad-man'. And there had been another occasion, she said, when 'I remember him telling my mother what trouble he'd had with a painting of a star-lit night.' (This was the painting of an Arles street-scene with the stars, like Catherine-wheels, madly whirling in an ultramarine sky.) 'My mother felt that he would paint better if only he didn't drink so much.' (I cannot be sure, but I have a suspicion that Jeanne's mother told Van Gogh as much, without mincing her words.) It seems that her mother disapproved of Van Gogh, although this might be explained by his habit of staggering into the little *boulangerie* in the early morning to buy his few sous'-worth of bread, still half-drunk and incoherent after a night-long binge at the Yellow House, or in one of the cafés. 'He had a frightening appearance sometimes,' said Madame Calment. 'His cheeks were all caved-in and he looked like skin and bone.' I sat quietly beside Madame Calment as she dredged her memory for other anecdotes, prompted occasionally by Carole Bressy who knelt by the wheelchair and gently stroked the old lady's hand as she spoke. However, it seemed the well had run dry – for today at any rate. As we were leaving, Madame Calment gave a hoarse little cry: 'His voice!' she exclaimed, 'I forgot about his voice! It was so harsh! So rough! But then what can you expect from a drunken Dutchman?'

One day I happened to be strolling beside the canal in the Fourchon quarter when I noticed a track leading to some tumble-down buildings which gave every impression of having been long since abandoned. It seemed that visitors were unwelcome, however, since the track which led down to a derelict farmyard overshadowed by some trees, had been roughly barricaded off by a telegraph-pole balanced on two rusty oil-drums. An open gateway in the farmyard wall gave a glimpse of a house which had a garage and another shed of some sort built on to it in rough blockwork; and opposite the house there was a large open-sided shed littered with farm implements and ancient machinery including the chassis of a pre-war tractor. The farmstead occupied an island site in the middle of the Fourchon and seemed entirely out of place among the chalet-style modern hotels, supermarket warehouses and car-manufacturers' spare-parts depots which surrounded it on the east and south sides. Between the farm buildings and a row of apartment blocks marking the limits of Arles' southeast suburbs, lay the canal and the railway line. On the far side, and less than 100 metres from the courtyard, clearly audible and within sight of the house, a stream of cars and lorries sped back and forth along the motorway linking Nîmes and Marseille.

I had been wrong in imagining the farm was abandoned. There were some hens and ducks scratching and waddling about in the yard; and then a moment later the owner came striding across from the tractor-shed and asked me quite bluntly, none too politely, what I was doing there apparently loitering at his gate.

'You must forgive me, *monsieur*,' I said, 'but I was rather surprised to find your farm so close to Arles and among all these new buildings. No-one has ever mentioned it to me before, but now that I'm here, with your permission, I should very much like to make a sketch or two. That is, of course, if you don't object.'

The farmer looked very suspicious at first. He was a stout, powerfully built man of about fifty, in an old pullover and tattered trousers; as he lowered his head, like an inquisitive bullock, to peer at me his thick horn-rimmed glasses slid forward, and almost fell off the end of his nose. 'Don't you know where you are?' he enquired. 'And if you don't, why do you want to draw my farm?'

When I explained that I had come to the Rhôneland to draw and paint and gather material for a book about the writers and artists and the daily life of the Camargue, the farmer relaxed somewhat. Gradually he opened up and I even detected the merest flicker of a smile, as he began to tell me the story of the farm and his ancestors in a slow drawling voice which struck me as at the same time both eager and hesitant; the voice of a middle-aged, shy bachelor, who had been accustomed to observing rather than talking. He lived alone with his dogs and cats; he was the self-reliant sort who neither needs nor actively seeks company. 'You say that you're an artist, *monsieur*, so what I'm about to tell you will mean more to you than it would to most people round here. This old *mas* was built somewhere about 1860. My great-grandfather was the first of our family who lived here. After him, there was my grandfather; then my father. None of them lived to a great age. Now there's just me. It was over there that Van Gogh made his famous painting of the bridge over the canal. The German troops blew it up when they were retreating, in 1944. You can still see the old foundations beside that monstrosity of a road-bridge they've built alongside it. What a horrible-looking thing it is – and all these new buildings cluttering up the place! All this used to be open countryside in my grandfather's day. People were allowed to live in peace in those days. Just look at the place now! Hotels, roundabouts – that blasted motorway behind us with drivers rushing back and forth like maniacs! If this is what you call progress, as far as I'm concerned you can keep it!'

The farmer shoved his loose-fitting spectacles further up his sharply curving nose and cleared his throat. 'Anyhow, I'm losing the thread of my story . . . where was I? Ah, yes – Van Gogh and the old bridge. Well, as I was saying, Van Gogh came and painted here, soon after he arrived in Arles. If I remember correctly that was between February and May, 1888. He painted the bridge, standing with his back to the house, so of course you don't see it in the picture. But afterwards he made some sketches right here in the farmyard, including the house and the trees – yes, these trees are the very ones – but of course they've altered a bit since then.

'My great-grandfather used to chat to Van Gogh and Van Gogh sometimes left his paints and his easel in that little shed by the front door. Pity he never gave my great-grandfather one of his drawings! I don't suppose my great-grandfather ever thought of asking for one, either. Isn't it perfectly damnable?

Even a scribble on the back of an envelope by Van Gogh would be worth thousands of francs nowadays!'

Asking me to excuse him for a few moments, the farmer went indoors and reappeared with a book which contained a coloured photograph of Van Gogh's painting of the canal bridge. The page had been marked by a white envelope, from which he took some cheap postcard reproductions of Van Gogh's Arles landscapes including a view of Arles painted while he had been working close to the farm.

The farmer chuckled ruefully: 'That's my Van Gogh collection, such as it is! Just one more thing: please don't mention any of this to anyone in Arles. Especially the Tourist Office! I don't want crowds of visitors snooping about here, or knocking at the door and pestering me with silly questions. I value my privacy, *monsieur*' – with this the man turned and shook his fist at the motorway traffic roaring by – 'at least, what's left of it!'

I readily understood the farmer's outraged feelings, having seen our village on the River Clyde in Scotland wrecked by over-development – a factory erected within a few hundred metres of the lovely old Parish church, where my parents were married and I was christened, and a motorway driven through the fields near our cottage. To my delight, he suggested that I should come again in a day or two and, if I felt like it, draw or paint in the farmyard – provided of course that the weather stayed fine.

The following Monday I paid another visit to the farm. It was a beautiful, windless morning. The farmer gave me a white plastic garden-chair and filled my water-jar from a tap in the garage. When he felt quite certain that I had everything I needed, but not until then, he went off to attend to some chores behind the tractor-shed, leaving me to my own devices. Despite the dull roar of the motorway traffic in the background, which after a while I hardly noticed, it was very peaceful sitting there in the yard in the warm sunshine, with the hens pecking about at my feet, or from time to time being chased away in a flurry of feathery cackles by the cockerel. (The farmer, incidentally, had been overjoyed when I told him that very morning I'd heard a cock crowing from my room at the Campanile. This was the selfsame bird and the farmer gleefully interpreted its cries as a rude gesture aimed at the Campanile, and the Fourchon's other hotels which he so openly detested.)

I worked rapidly and when the farmer appeared again after about half-an-hour, a sketch of the house, washed in lightly with watercolours, was almost complete. He stood by quietly, watching while I gave the sketch a few finishing touches and, when it was done, he nodded approvingly: 'You artists don't waste much time!' he said, with a grin. 'That's taken only a few minutes. *Mon Dieu*! No time at all! I suppose it was the same when Van Gogh painted here a hundred years ago. They say he, too, was a fast worker!'

Hastily disclaiming any comparison between my efforts and those of Van Gogh, I offered him the sketch as a present. The farmer accepted it without a moment's hesitation. He was a pleasant fellow but also very shrewd in his way; I had the distinct impression that he considered even a rough drawing by an unknown artist well worth having. After all, he observed, Van Gogh had never sold a single picture in his entire lifetime! His great-grandfather had let one artist slip through his fingers and the farmer was not about to make the same mistake. His frankness amused me at the time. But I was pleased that he liked my little sketch, which he promised to have framed.

I remember his earnest expression as he begged me to be sure and write my name and the date on the sketch before I left. 'For *monsieur*,' said the farmer, 'what is the value in years to come of a picture without a signature? Damn it all, a thing like that might have been painted by anybody!'

I crossed Van Gogh's path once more at Arles when I paid a visit to the Galerie la Rose des Vents owned by Madame Maité Dubosquet. Madame Dubosquet has studied the life and work of Van Gogh and Ganguin very extensively – she is an acknowledged expert on both of them, although being a modest woman she would disclaim that. Small-boned, dark-haired, with large brown eyes and an infectious smile, always busy and full of laughter, Madame Dubosquet's life has been actively involved with the poetry, art and traditions of the Rhôneland. Throughout the region, including the Camargue, her work is valued and highly repected. As her friend, Madame Barnicaud, observed: 'Maité is unique – *une femme incomparable!*'

She had invited me to her gallery in the rue Diderot on this occasion for a very special reason. When I arrived punctually at eleven, she led me upstairs to the *salon*. 'Wait here, Alexander,' she said, 'I have something interesting to show you.' In a moment she reappeared with a package wrapped in brown paper, from which she produced a large square of black cloth. She shook out the cloth, which I saw had been divided into two pieces of equal size, and held them up for my inspection. 'This is the shawl – *the very shawl* – you have seen in Van Gogh's portrait of the *Arlésienne!* It belonged to Madame Domergue whose great-aunt sat for Van Gogh's picture. She was Madame Domergue's great-aunt Ginoux, formerly Mlle Marie Julien. The shawl was left to Madame Domergue and her sister which is why the old lady cut it in half – a pity, but there it is.'

When Madame Domergue gave the famous shawl to Madame Dubosquet, she also gave her a letter of provenance, dated 26 October 1980, a copy of which I have in my possession. The shawl was beautifully woven and had a textured pattern which was revealed when Madame Dubosquet switched on the light, like a message written in invisible ink.

16

Out of the Crucible

While there is no real connection between them, when I come within sight of Les Baux, by the winding road through the valley below, I am reminded of Stephen Graham's descriptions of the 'wind-carved pyramidal mountains' he found, riding through New Mexico in the winter of 1922. Or else, I think of wild corners in the Pyrenees, such as Héas, where the magnificent landscapes of jagged rock and tumbling streams are known as a 'Chaos'. It is said that the Val D'Enfer near Les Baux inspired Dante's *Inferno*. Here, Queen Joanna, whose pavilion Mistral copied for this tomb, held her famous Court of Love in a walled garden with shrubbery-enclosed paths and arbours hung with sweetly-scented flowers. The echoes of these harsh, romantic times lives on at Les Baux. Its dizzy heights and windswept crags are as much the home of troubadour legends as Aigues-Mortes' ramparts evoke the Crusader past and deeds of chivalry. Les Baux was the troubadour's ultimate refuge and 'the very rocks pulsate in sunlight, quiver in moonlight, to the rhythm of his song'.

In *Calendal*, Mistral compared the princes of Les Baux to eagles, which brushed this 'crest of all the heights' with their soaring, outspread wings. Even the gentle-hearted Mireille, Mistral's heroine, confessed that, should her wish be granted, she would make Les Baux her 'capital'.

I made several journeys to Les Baux where one of the greatest Provençal artists of recent years had lived, at the nearby Mas de Méjeanes: Yves Brayer, who died in May 1990, whom alas I was never able to meet. When I came in November, a year after Brayer's death, I found many of his paintings and some of the artist's memorabilia displayed in the newly-refurbished Hôtel des Porcelets, the Porcelets' ancient family home which before the Second World War had been the village schoolhouse. The dignified little building stands beside the church of Saint-Vincent, but, as one traveller has observed, 'Less dignified is the origin of the name. . . .' The story goes that 'A legendary ancestress – an advocate of birth control it seems – reproved a begging woman for the undue number of her progeny. The beggar, being a fairy, and therefore in league with children, condemned the unwilling lady to bear as many babies as there were to be piglets in the litter of a nearby sow. Nine there were, and the nine sons and daughters to which the dame gave birth were dubbed, according to the tale, *les porcelets.*'

The first of Yves Brayer's drawings I ever saw hung in the drawing-room of Le Simbèu, the Aubanel family's house near Les Saintes-Maries. This was a simple sketch of the Camargue, showing a *gardian* on horseback, a subject which Brayer returned to again and again in the late 1940s and indeed all through his later career. In Armand Lanoux's monograph, published in 1976, Brayer testified to his deep feelings for the Camargue, writing: '*C'est une terre pour les poètes, que savent que la nature est plus riche que la civilisation*' ('It is a country for poets, who know that nature is richer than civilization').

Wherever Brayer travelled, he painted and drew from life, translating the realities he saw into a more powerful, hard-edged – if you like, a more savage – form of Lelée's Art-Deco where details of faces or musculature were sacrificed in his pursuit of form, the subtle balances of colour and strongly constructed composition. *Le Bonheur en Camargue* is a good example, showing the *gardians* and their wives in simplified, yet instantly-recognizable Arlésien costume, in a late-summer landscape with a sunlit *mas* and a wind-bent tamarisk, also

catching the sun, against a sombre violet-coloured sky. The same broad treatment of horses and the marsh landscapes can be seen in Brayer's studies of *Chevaux aux Saintes-Maries-de-la-Mer* and another in which a rough track, *La Route en Camargue*, leads us towards the church of Les Saintes-Maries, sunlit at the horizon.

Brayer's pictures glowed with 'a brilliancy of colouring such as it is not easy either to imagine or describe'. This was Basil Collier's impression of the Provençal coast where he found the blue sea 'bluer than any one has ever painted it, a colour entirely fantastic and incredible'. Brayer's coloured landscapes, just as 'fantastic and incredible', evoked the same surprise when compared to the more muted autumnal shades I had seen round Les Baux. Even at the height of summer, these Rhôneland landscapes often appeared more in keeping with Gertrude Bone's impressions of Spain, 'a country of light so intense that colours are subdued and simplified. A splendid and sombre glowing'. But the colours of Spain are harsher than those of Provence and here, like Brayer, I had seen wonderful sunlit days when the sky, the pine-clad hills and the soil radiated shades of blue, green and tawny-red as powerful and as pure as the colours of a stained-glass window.

I have seen many photographs of Yves Brayer at work, sketching horses at a *mas*, duffle-coated against the winter cold; or drawing from his seat in a rowing-boat, his thinning hair capped by a chequered-tweed deerstalker; or painting on the beach, with his long legs in narrow-cut *gardian* moleskins, stretched out in front.

Again and again, Brayer reiterated his ingrained philosophy: '*J'ai besoin du contact avec la nature.*' ('I need to have contact with nature') and the shrewd reminder to his critics and others that '*On ne peut bien connaître un artiste en voyant ses œuvres isolément,*' which might be translated as 'You cannot really know an artist by studying his works in isolation.' When he began to draw, Brayer wrote 'my ideas take flight' – like his friend, Jean Giono, he believed that drawing represented the crucible in which thoughts bubbled, white-hot like liquid metal. '*Rien n'est plus intelligent qu'un dessin.*'

At the Hôtel des Porcelets, I spent a long time looking at Brayer's large, bright watercolours and rich gouaches, many of them painted on thin semi-transparent papers, which he used to make the first strike of the outline in pencil, then overlaid with another sheet which he used for the finished painting, tracing the other in bold, free brush-strokes and washes of colour without too much weight of detail. Brayer's watercolour brushes, a 3 and a 10 made of pure sable and a box containing an astonishing twenty-two half-pans showed signs of heavy wear. (I say 'astonishing' for I was always taught to work with as few made-up colours as possible, just the basic primaries and a few others such as Lamp Black and Chinese White. This apparently was the direct opposite of Yves Brayer's method.) Brayer had been Provençal, as it were by adoption, like Ivan Pranishnikoff before him. He was born near Versailles in November 1907 and he worked and travelled extensively in Europe, including the Mediterranean islands, until the age of seventy-seven, when an illness in 1984 left him paralyzed on his left side.

The paintings Brayer made in his last years, a period when he was honoured and became the Director of the Musée Marmottan in Paris, suggest that his work ceased to develop and it was almost as if he had been content to paint in the distinctive shorthand of line and colour-washes that rendered his pictures immediately recognizable. Even so, I flinched when I heard a gallery-owner remark, 'Nothing would induce me to show Brayer's paintings, for they are tainted with the *vert-de-gris* of hard cash.' The man's criticism may have had a grain of truth in it, but, to me, it seemed unjustifiably harsh.

Even more than the Brayer collections at the Hôtel des Porcelets, I was fascinated by the workrooms of Les Baux's master-printer, the artist and typographer, Louis Jou. The artist's *atelier* is almost unknown to the summer tourists and the few who visit it rarely see its most intimate hidden treasures. Michel Gay introduced me to the President of the Fondation Louis Jou, Andéri Macchia. We met him one evening at his house off a small courtyard in Les Baux's cobbled rue Frédéric Mistral, when the village lay wrapped in medieval gloom after a stormy, wet afternoon and the pungent-smelling smoke of wood-fires suffused the damp air. The wind had dropped and Les Baux was still, except for the doves which fluttered about Monsieur Macchia's blue and white tiled *pigeonnier*. Monsieur Macchia led us out into the street, and then through a heavy door which opened onto a room lined with glass cabinets where Louis Jou's sumptuously bound books and delicate wood-cuts were displayed. The books included Jou's magnificent reproduction of a Gutenburg Bible, *Don Quixote* and Montaigne's *Essays*, besides other more modern works by Wilde, Gide, Suares and Marie Mauron, who wrote the classic accounts of the Camargue bulls and the old shepherd life of La Crau, *Le Taureau* and *La Transhumance*, which should be read by everyone interested in the region. The quality of Jou's wood-cut illustrations for these and a Life of Joan of Arc were astounding for their beauty and the craftsmanship which the fine shading of hair's-breadth knife-cuts revealed. But it was more than sheer skill, incomparable technique and mastery of his materials that showed through. These were the productions of a great artistic talent and they rivalled, indeed surpassed much of what I had seen before in the Rhôneland – or for that matter, anywhere else. Louis Jou had been born in Spain, on the outskirts of Barcelona, in 1882 and died at Les Baux in 1968. His champion, Andéri Macchia, was slightly built, bald, bespectacled, grave and professorial. Jou himself, in complete contrast, judging from a mounted photograph we saw, had looked like a Martigues fisherman: heavy-bodied, heavily jowled with square peasant features and glinting heavy-lidded eyes. His big grinning features seemed better suited to a man whose life had been spent among nets and fishing-boats or working on a farm and his coarse fingers holding a fat white cigarette appeared incapable of performing the delicate, surgically precise tasks of the master wood-engraver. 'Louis Jou's emblem was the bull,' said Monsieur Macchia. And it struck me that this choice had been remarkably appropriate. Andéri Macchia seemed to read my thoughts, for he added: 'It is true, the artist's appearance and his fine workmanship appear to clash. Look carefully, however, and you will see what an emotional power, what depths of sensitivity lie behind his gaze. His physical strength, far from being a hindrance, assisted his work and it gave him the stamina and control he needed to carve these larger, finely detailed illustrations.' To a degree, such physical strength was important. The Camargue artist, Hermann-Paul, had had to abandon wood-engraving after a car-crash which damaged his shoulder; while at Cagnes, near Antibes, in frail old age Renoir painted 'with the brush strapped to his wrist'. Indicating a plate from Joan of Arc, a close-up of footsoldiers in helmets and chain-mail, Macchia said: 'Imagine the hours of hard labour that were needed to project such a wealth of detail, the tiny links of mesh, each perfectly placed, each formed with the patience and precision of the finest needle-work. How many expert seam-stresses do you imagine could not only create these intricate patterns with thread but also draw them afterwards? I would venture to suggest very few! See the lines he has cut to make the "roundness" of the soldiers' helmets and the fine wood-grain along the haft of a lance? These lines never interrupt the general scheme. They sink back into the composition for they are nearly invisible to the naked eye; but take a magnifying glass and you will see that they exist all the same. Each of these unobtrusive, delicate lines has its own small part to play, like a semi-quaver or a crotchet in an orchestral score. Take even one away and you still have a fine picture; but it is no longer the work of Louis Jou.'

When Jou designed a page of lettering, a page of Montaigne for example, in order to justify both sides so that the print was set out in perfectly parallel columns, he sometimes used cunning little tricks such as including two or three ampersands ('&') of slightly varying shape and size which allowed him to spread or tighten the spacing of lines much as one would stretch or compress the bellows of a concertina.

The 'intimate hidden treasures' I mentioned earlier were Jou's beautiful wood-cutting tools and the original wood-cuts them-selves which were kept locked away in a big Provençal cabinet in the print-shop opposite the building in which the books and prints were housed. The tools, oiled and shining, their blades sharp and unmarked, and the wood-cut blocks spoke volumes for the artist's care. Here, too, stood the great printing-press Jou had used, still in immaculate working-order. And there were the priceless *incunabula*, the early editions of Petrarch, Dante and the Holy Scriptures from which Jou's sometimes even more splendid copies had been made. The glittering array of carver's chisels and knives made the tools of Brayer's, even Cézanne's trade seem almost crude and amateurish!

The Fondation Louis Jou was certainly a discovery. Until our visit to Andéri Macchia at Les Baux, I am somewhat ashamed to admit that I had never heard of Jou, let alone seen examples of his work; and later on, when I made further enquiries in London, I was surprised to find that even among the most prestigious antiquarian booksellers and specialist galleries, he was virtually unknown.

There was an element of mystery, too, surrounding the country *atelier*, near Graveson, a few kilometres from Les Baux, of another great Rhôneland artist – among the greatest of modern times, a contemporary of Louis Jou – Auguste Chabaud (1882–1955). Having seen several fine Chabauds at the Galerie Saint-Michel, including a superb still life of earthenware vases against a landscape, I had felt deeply moved by their melancholy beauty. It was this same melancholy that I found in the depths of the Camargue marshes – the strangely unforgettable yearnings evoked by space and sombre colours and the evanescent shadows cast by lovely transient things to which we attach, perhaps from necessity, a sense of permanence.

Chabaud's still life left me spellbound, puzzled, delighted; an effect like first love which, they say, never can be quite repeated and which leaves its matchless imprint for ever on our hearts and minds.

Auguste Chabaud was born in 1882 at Nîmes and studied painting under an influential master, Pierre Grivolas, at the Beaux-Arts in Avignon, and afterwards in Paris. He served for three years in the army in Tunisia between 1903–1906, where he painted military scenes and studies of Tunisian architecture – the

familiar domed houses with roofs like white, upturned breasts, set against strongly contrasting skies of dark Prussian Blue. Like Mistral in his landscape poetry, Chabaud never sought to describe merely for description's sake. Here in North Africa he learned to observe and remember, registering, dissecting and preserving the essence of fundamental detail which characterized his later work. Returning to Graveson in 1906, he began his career as an artist. Still an *exposant*, Chabaud at first exhibited his paintings and sculpture, but eventually worked apart from the mainstream of contemporary art and seldom showed his paintings, even going so far as to buy back some of the earlier works which had been sold.

Much of Chabaud's active life was spent at the Mas de Martin, a family property where he built a house for himself and his family in 1921. That year he had married Valentine Suzini, with whom he had eight children, four girls and four boys. Here at the Mas de Martin, two of his sons, Jean and Pierre still lived and worked; Pierre as an artist, a picture-restorer and a frame-maker.

Michal Gay and I arrived one overcast windy morning and were received by Jean Chabaud's charming wife, Marie-Paule, who led us to her father-in-law's immense studio, a stone-walled *bergerie*, across the courtyard from the main house. Sheep had wintered in the *bergerie* before Chabaud converted it and here we found dozens of Chabaud's powerful, instantly arresting canvasses. Besides the North African paintings, there were Provençal landscapes with figures, which expressed the artist's incessant pursuit of religious truths. Although a Protestant, Chabaud frequently discussed religion with the Catholic priests at Graveson. Other figures with diabolical, leering, mask-like features emerged from a nightmare world inhabited by Chabaud's fears and doubts. *L'Ecurie*, an oil-painting of a stable interior was dominated by a horse's head in profile, with the manger suggested by a few lines and the atmosphere built from simple tones of light and shadow. There was a beach-landscape with hills – the curve of sand and the sea again reduced to a minimum showing little more than the dramatic interface of land and water. Some sketches had been drawn on butcher's paper and were gentle, almost ethereal; a rainbow above a *cabane*, *L'Arc en ciel*, *Deux Jeunes Filles*, and *La Famille au soleil*, dappled by sunlit patterns chalked in white with a carpenter's pencil. Many of Chabaud's paintings hung on the rough-hewn walls of the *bergerie* and seemed part of them; as elemental and tactile as the small Cubist sculptures which Marie-Paule Chabaud encouraged me to pick up and handle, as sculpture should be handled, she said, 'as if you were shaking hands with Chabaud himself'. The *bergerie* had safeguarded sheep and paintings alike, with a sort of benevolent indifference to the simplicity or greatness of its charges. Its destiny and purpose had been as eloquently defined in slate and stone as the statue of the Virgin I had seen in Graveson, near the famous *roubine*, whose inscription read: 'You have put me here to take care of you.'

Such was the impact of Chabaud's work on my imagination that, for a considerable time after leaving Graveson, I saw its images and colours everywhere – in the bleached white sky, the jagged ridges of La Montagnette and the twisted, gnarled shapes of the trees.

17

In Cézanne's Footsteps

Although Aix lay beyond the boundaries of the Rhôneland, I went there merely for the pleasure of visiting this beautiful old town with its fine seventeenth- and eighteenth-century buildings, its tree-lined boulevards and its fountains. Aix has been called the Athens of Provence, the City of Fountains. The largest of them, La Rotande, in the place du General de Gaulle, is the first you see when entering Aix by road coming from Arles. There are many more besides: in the cours Mirabeau, the Fontaine du Roi René showing the monarch holding a branch of the muscatel grapes which it is said he introduced into Provence; another in the place d'Albertas which commemorates Cézanne; and at the junction of the rue du 4 Septembre and the rue Cardinale, the famous Fontaine des Quatre Dauphins, an obelisk with four dolphins spouting water at its base. It is only a slight exaggeration when you are told that in Aix the sound of falling water is everywhere.

One evening, standing near the great fountain, La Rotande – built in 1860, two centuries after the cours Mirabeau was opened – I experienced a curious optical illusion. It was already getting dark. The rush-hour traffic was nearing its peak. I noticed that when the cars circling the fountain slowed down as the lights changed, the rush of water from the fountain appeared to falter; as the cars picked up apeed, the jets flowed faster. Once when a police car came hurtling round and twice circled the fountain, its headlights flashing, its klaxon blaring, the water fairly spurted, or so it seemed.

Not everyone I met at Arles had a good word for Aix. Some complained: 'It has too many students roaming the streets. There's too much traffic and hurly-burly for our taste.' Others dismissed Aix as 'a *bourgeois* town with a stand-offish atmosphere'. And an acquaintance had sniffed and said: 'Aix suits the northerners used to Paris and the TGV life. I dare say after London you'll find it a provincial backwater. Compared to Marseille, I should certainly find Aix tolerable, but I would never choose to live there.'

With a population of more than 150,000, Aix-en-Provence is about the size of Nîmes, twice the size of Avignon and about three times as big as Arles. But Aix has a southern atmosphere and a character quite its own. Such comparisons are really pointless and these criticisms I felt were largely unjustified and unfair.

When I arrived there on Armistice Day, the sun was shining, the air was crisp and clear and plane trees along the cours Mirabeau seemed ablaze with light which filtered through their branches, dappling the pavements. Almost at once I was stopped by a pretty teenage girl, a student from the University, who begged me for directions. I couldn't be of much help, but a dark-skinned Yugoslavian woman came to the rescue and then said she would accompany me up the cours Mirabeau where she wanted to buy a telephone-card at one of the many *bars-tabacs*.

We chatted as we walked along. She told me that her husband was a local man, a schoolmaster, and they had a friend from England staying with them. Admittedly she was a foreigner, but she was anything but stand-offish. She laughed: 'Our guest is a Geography *professeur*. He is really my husband's friend. He's nice enough, but he has an eye for the girls! He divorced his wife after nearly thirty years and now he has turned up with a new one, half his age. She'll probably kill him. I said so to his face. Maybe I talk too much. My husband tells me I'm indiscreet. Do you think so?' And before I could reply, she continued: 'But of course you do! Men are all the same. Think what you like, do what you like – but keep it quiet! That's men for you. Ask any woman. She'll tell you I'm right.'

We parted company opposite Aix's famous literary haunt, Les Deux Garçons, the café frequented by Cézanne, Zola and many other writers and artists, where I sat at a table among the barrels of evergreen shrubs and watched the morning shoppers laden with fruit and vegetables and the crowds of students loitering, smoking, eating ice creams or racing about on motor-scooters taking it in turns to ride pillion in and out among the rows of parked cars and delivery vans.

Les Deux Garçons was close to the site of Veuve Renaudet, the long-since vanished printers where Mistral's *Trésor du Félibrige* was first published. Inside, the café's original decorations gave some reminder of those bygone days – the huge mirrors, the carved panelling painted in gilt and *eau-de-nil*, the gilt lamps with their etched-glass globes, the cool, shady rooms with their high ceilings. The stone façade had been 'refreshed' in a rather-too-violent shade of yellow-ochre, a hot colour like the fumes of hot cooking-oil wafting from the kitchen, as the waiters in smart white monkey-jackets, black bow-ties and black trousers served coffee and cold drinks, sliding easily between the little round tables where pigeons strutted at the customers' feet. I sipped my black coffee from a green and gold cup and scribbled snapshot notes on the passing scene: The filtered sunlight's 'pointilliste' effect among the leaves. Associations I am unable to explain: the streets of Barcelona, illustrations from a pre-war novel belonging to my mother, *The Wraith of Raeburn*. Pale classical façades above the shopfronts. Grey-painted shutters, grey doors, the grey and yellow trees. The dull rumble of traffic coming in waves. Light-bulbs strung at intervals among the branches. Cooking smells, the odour of burning wood, a sudden draught tainted by cigarette smoke. Washing hanging from balconies in a side-street. Solitary people gazing at the street, their gaze ignored by passers-by. A waiter emptying ash-trays pockets someone's tip with a shrug and mutters something I cannot quite hear.

On the cours Mirabeau, further down I saw a young woman in a black velvet *gardian*-style jacket selling glossy coloured cards on which were printed poems titled 'The Smile' and 'My Brother'. She told me that she had composed the poems herself and that she worked with a group of 'independent poets', all of whom hawked their verses as she did, selling them at 50 francs the half-dozen. The asking-price struck me as rather steep, for her poems were not much better than greeting-card doggerel, or at best like the sentimental rhymes Patience Strong used to write for *Woman's Own*. I was just about to hand them back, when a voice boomed nearby: 'Watch carefully! Don't be tempted to try any of this!' The warning had been so perfectly timed that even the poet herself managed a wry snigger.

The speaker turned out to be a down-at-heel gipsy in a torn cardigan and crumpled trousers, a street entertainer round whom a little crowd had gathered. The man looked desperately thin and undernourished, his gaunt cheeks hazed by several days' growth of stubble. His limited repertoire certainly held the crowd's attention for it consisted of him swallowing double-edged razor-blades and lighted cigarettes which he produced singly or in batches stuck to the tip of his tongue before they disappeared – as we were led to believe – down his scrawny throat. Each swallow produced a ripple of OOOHHHS! and AAAHHS! from the onlookers. The performance no doubt would be repeated until a policeman appeared and moved him along, but meanwhile these dangerous tricks earned the gipsy a precarious living while the seller of poems went unrewarded.

At Aix, again and again my thoughts turned to Cézanne. This was inevitable – and there were obvious reminders of the great painter wherever one looked. Some were admittedly less flattering than others. The cinema Le Cézanne in the rue Goyrand was showing *Terminator 2*, starring Arnold Schwarzenegger, which had been playing to packed houses all week. Le Cézanne was a modern multi-screen cinema and also showing were *Croc-Blanc*, a dubbed version of Jack London's story, *White Fang*, and a film about Van Gogh. Several of Aix's restaurants had picked up the Cézanne theme, of which Chez Paul in the cours Mirabeau was a typical example.

A trail of bronze plates let into the pavement provides visitors to Aix with a clearly-marked itinerary which corresponds to the main episodes in Cézanne's life in and around the town. The plates are captioned with the letter 'C' and beside it 'Cézanne' set out vertically, so that merely by checking that these are the right way up you are always sure of walking in the right direction. The little plates are only about 125 mm square; thus they remain quite unobtrusive, but are much easier to follow than signs fixed to the wall. You are led to the Collège Royal Bourbon where Cézanne took his *baccalauréat* in 1858 and met Emile Zola. In the place St Jean de Malte, there is the Musée Granet which houses examples of Cézanne's work and was the academy where he studied drawing. From the rue Pavillon, you come to No 28 rue de l'Opéra, where Cézanne was born on 19 January 1839 and so on until you reach the house in the rue Boulegon, No 23, where he died, aged sixty-seven, on 23 October 1906.

It interested me that Cézanne, like Mistral, studied law at Aix; and that afterwards he became Provence's greatest artist, while Mistral became the region's greatest poet. As far as I know, Cézanne and Mistral never met, nor did their paths cross in any other way. It seems strange, especially as they had friends in common, including the writer Joseph D'Arbaud who sometimes dined with Cézanne and Edmund Jaloux at Aix. In his book, *Cézanne: A Memoir with Conversations*, Joachim Gasquet quoted Jaloux's description of Cézanne's curious manner of speech, 'nasal, slow, meticulous, with something thoughtful and caressing', and how Cézanne used to characterize his painting, saying: 'An artist has to make his work, as an almond makes its flowers, as a snail makes its slime.'

These allusions to humble, country things would have touched Mistral's heart, I feel certain. But whereas Mistral was genial and accessible, even in old age when he won international acclaim (an exception being Augustus John who, for some reason or other, Mistral refused to see when he turned up at

Maillane), Cézanne became increasingly reclusive and un-
approachable and was taunted, even had stones thrown at him
by local villagers. In 1937, the travel-writer and gourmet Basil
Collier, munching his way through Provence, was given a
modest lunch of wine and custard made with goat's cream at
Tholonet by an old farmer and his wife who remembered
Cézanne in the days when he painted at the Bibemus quarry.

Cézanne used to leave his painting materials at their farm.
They told Collier: 'He was a very pleasant gentleman . . . but
not what you would call friendly; and in the village, near which
he sometimes stayed, he had a reputation of walking about the
roads at night.'

I found the cemetery of Saint-Pierre where Cézanne was
buried, opposite some tennis-courts just off the Tholonet road.
Apart from a few people carrying wreaths and bunches of cut
flowers for the soldiers' graves, the cemetery was deserted,
silent except for the birds and the occasional scrunching of
footsteps along its gravel paths. The tombs stood on the yellow,
sandy soil among umbrella-pines and olives, lining the
cemetery's twenty-one *allées* planted with lavender and red
roses. Near the entrance, an immense stone commemorating the
French ex-patriots in Algeria and Madagascar bore an inscription which read: 'The real tomb of the dead is the heart of the
living.' Everywhere I looked there were flowers in abundance:
roses of all varieties and colours, yellow chrysanthemums,
dahlias, marguerites in sprays and vases lined with ferns. There
were mausoleums of stone which had tiny windows of royal-
blue and amber glass; statues of winged angels and infantrymen
with rifles; metal crosses in delicate filigree, painted gold and
silver; black-marble graves of modern design, lettered with
gaudy gilt, some of which were inset with coloured cameos of
the dead.

In the sunshine, sheltered from the wind, the stillness was
almost as tangible as the grave-stones themselves. A little
rounded hill, thickly covered with trees, marked the Tholonet
road in the distance.

Somewhere among the clouds, an aeroplane droned like a

wasp trapped against a window-pane. I heard the faint whunk of tennis-balls from the courts and the hollow dribbling of water as a woman filled her plastic bucket from a stand-pipe beside one of the graves.

When she had finished re-arranging the flowers on the grave, the woman with the bucket came over to the bench where I was sitting and passed the time of day. She was in her sixties and I learned that her in-laws had been monumental sculptors at Aix since the nineteenth century. Her father-in-law, Louis Barnier, had studied at the Beaux-Arts in Aix and had designed, built and restored many of the cemetery's tombs. The Barniers' workshop was somewhere nearby and after Louis died in 1947, aged eighty-nine, his son, Marcel – Madame Barnier's husband, carried on the business until his death in 1984.

'And now it is the turn of my son, Maurice,' said Madame Barnier with evident pride. 'Poor Maurice, sadly for him the "art" has gone out of his profession. His grandfather designed the War Memorial down there in *allée* No 3 (she knew the layout of the cemetery backwards and was very precise when describing its features) and many of these fine family tombs you see all around. All that had changed by the time my husband died and nowadays nobody will pay for elaborate workmanship.' She indicated a black slab near my bench. 'This material is quite popular – granite imported from Labrador. It's a simple affair, but even so it costs a great deal – 20 or 30 thousand francs, perhaps more. May I enquire why you have come, *monsieur*? Is it possible that you have a relative buried here?'

'No,' I replied, 'I am searching for Cézanne's grave and the grave of Zola.'

'Ah, you mean Zola's father, François. That's easy. Just go to the top of *allée* No 11, walk towards the wall and you will find Zola *père* on your right. Now, Cézanne . . . let me think . . . of course, he is buried in *allée* No 6 only a few steps from where we are now! So many famous people are buried here at Saint-Pierre. . . . Death comes to us all. People will tell you that Death is the great leveller' – Madame Barnier used a different expression which I have forgotten for the moment, but the meaning was identical – 'however, I don't see it like that. Everyone who lies here did something different with their life. The tombs are not all quite the same either – and of course, being a mason's wife, it is only natural that I should pay heed to such matters.'

I recalled a remark made by Michel Gay's friend, the writer Yvan Audouard, who said: 'The best compliment I ever had was someone saying that I gave the words on the page their voice. The printed word is silent. It is the writer's job to make it speak.' I told Madame Barnier this and she smiled gently: 'That's true,' she said. 'And you know, the same might be said of these grave-stones. They too have a tale to tell, and I'd like to think that my father-in-law and my husband helped in some way. . . . I know they'd have liked the idea.'

Cézanne's tomb lay within earshot of a little trickling fountain, in a quiet corner flanked by pines where the air smelled of box-leaves and lavender. Compared to Mistral's pavilion at Maillane or the imposing monument erected for Ivan and Joséphine Pranishnikoff at Les Saintes-Maries, for example, the Cézanne's family memorial seemed a remarkably modest affair. The smooth unpolished granite slab, fronted by a simple plaque, had the painter's dates and the legend in incised capital letters: 'ICI REPOSE PAUL CÉZANNE.'

Someone had left a little spray of white marguerites and there were some rust-red and yellow pansies scattered beside a violet-coloured plastic container made to resemble a wicker basket, filled with pale-pink and white imitation roses. A terracotta pot held a single white pansy in which a tiny brown spider had made its home. Unlike the other tombs, no one had bothered to clear away the flowers left by the summer visitors weeks or months before – withered sheaves of chrysanthemums and the remains of some purple dahlias which were already 'going over'.

18

Village of the Lagoons

Aix-en-Provence is the City of Fountains, but Aigues-Mortes, in the Camargue's far west, is almost entirely *surrounded* by water. The marsh lagoons, the Canal Maritime and, above all, its proximity to the Mediterranean, produces wonderful, lustrous effects of the kind we associate with Pacific islands where the colours of the spectrum fill the sky at dawn and sunset. The local author, Maurice Barrès wrote: 'The sunsets are prodigious at Aigues-Mortes,' while Amy Oakley pictured the village floating 'ethereal as will o' the wisp or glamorous mirage', as though 'wrapped in the center of a fantastic iridescent bubble of sky and shimmering wet sand . . . bathed in ghostly light'.

At Aigues-Mortes, Basil Collier found 'a sort of Carcassonne, shorn of some of its most romantic features and set on level ground instead of on a hill'. Henry James, who seems to have been among the less robust of the late nineteenth-century travellers, recommended observing Carcassonne's battlements from a diligence, complained that Arles' rough cobble-stones bruised his feet and, exercising typical restraint, merely remarked that Aigues-Mortes, 'a very small sister of Carcassonne' was nevertheless 'extraordinarily pictorial'.

Aigues-Mortes, when approached either by land or water, even to this day, evokes the romance of the Middle Ages with its high ramparts and the iron-shod spire of the Tour de Constance – its impregnable prison-tower – projecting 40 metres above them at its northeast corner. Coming from the east by Vauvert, on a road which skirts the marshes and the lonely Tour Carbonnière 3 kilometres from the village, you find yourself entering a Crusader world, magical and unreal – and for a moment the bland modern surroundings of Nîmes you have left behind you are forgotten. It is as though you have slipped backward through time and are confronting the landscapes of a bygone age.

This is not quite as fey as perhaps it sounds. I am thinking of a November day when I travelled to Aigues-Mortes by the local bus, driving through the sprawling suburbs of Nîmes in pouring rain. The sky was blanketed by unbroken grey clouds. The wet grey road led through a forest of advertising signs and gigantic motorway hoardings, through a wasteland of suburban supermarkets, hypermarkets, DIY warehouses, car-showrooms and petrol-stations, beyond which lay a plain segmented by vineyards and fields of cereals – colourless, desolate and even more depressing than the kilometres of characterless commercial clutter that lined the road out of Nîmes for more than half-an-hour. In Nîmes itself, among the grey classical façades of the town-centre, dominated by the arena, I had felt less oppressed by the noise and bustle – the tense, heavy undertone of the city traffic, which brought to mind the opening bars of Delius' nocturne, *Paris*. Gazing from the window of the bus at the rushing road and the slick, smooth lines of the cut-price stores, I felt almost mesmerized by them – and the glittering filaments of rain slanting past; and for a moment it seemed as though I were being sucked away into a depth of infinite space.

On the outskirts of Nîmes we passed a burnt-out office building and the charred remains of a signboard above the door which read: 'Specialists in Fire Insurance'. Further along the road, a tiny *mas* on an island site between the tarmac forecourts of two vast garages cowered sheltering behind a thicket of dark-green trees. Swamped by the tide of commercial development, the Fire-Insurance building and the *mas* seemed hopelessly adrift and out-of-place among their faceless neighbours. It was as if the Fire-Insurers had taken courage and committed a desperate *auto-da-fé*; while the *mas* simply hid away in horror, for not so much as a window but only its roof and a chimney were visible among the dense foliage. These images lingered in my mind as we neared Aigues-Mortes, which may explain – at least to an extent – why I found my impression of the village so startlingly and refreshingly different.

After Aimargues and Vauvert, the weather began to clear. The first glimpse of weak sun shed a pale ghostly light, something like Amy Oakley's description, which added a hint of romance. In a way, coming upon Aigues-Mortes was like finding Avila's incredible towers after the long drive north from Plasencia. Here, like Avila, many of the permanent residents lived outside the walls; but compared to Avila with its broad windy squares and great churches, Aigues-Mortes had been conceived on a much smaller scale, like a medieval crossword, and it was possible – if you felt so inclined – to walk the length and breadth of the old village in a few minutes.

Today it is Aigues-Mortes' antique appearance and its intimate size, combined with a striking position on the coastal plain, which makes the greatest appeal to visitors. In 1936 Mrs Oakley could still write: 'The rhythm of life at Aigues-Mortes is set to the leisurely measure of barges gliding past its walls.' To a lesser degree the same might be said of the present. But then as now, as Mrs Oakley pointed out, it had been the approach to the village of the 'Dead Waters' which thrills the eye – unfortunately, 'Upon entering, the spell of the past dissolves.'

Aigues-Mortes has always appeared to me like a beautiful anachronism. In contrast to Arles and Avignon, like Les Baux, Aigues-Mortes is almost wholly sustained by tourism. Being small and isolated, it is Aigues-Mortes *itself* which draws visitors. At Arles and Avignon, visitors flock to the remains of the old town contained within the modern sprawl and ignore the rest.

Of Aigues-Mortes' founder, King Louis IX, Saint-Louis whose black-painted statue commands the square, Sir Theodore

Cook wrote in 1905 in *Old Provence*: 'With him, died the kingly chivalry of the Middle Ages.' In a sense, this was probably true. It is interesting, however, that only a year earlier in 1904, Mistral's Félibrige society had celebrated its fiftieth anniversary – a society among other things dedicated to reviving time-honoured traditions, and the old language of Provençal chivalry in which the Troubadours had immortalized knightly deeds of bravery and unrequited love. And the Nacioun Gardiano, then recently founded by Baroncelli-Javon, Pranishnikoff and other *aficionados* of the Camargue life, had at its core something very like the ancient code of chivalry – the noble ethics of the *chevalier* which became the *gardian*'s model.

At Aigues-Mortes, strolling round the ramparts, I could easily imagine the scene as the great army of 30,000 soldiers led by King Louis embarked with their horses and waggon-loads of provisions in the fleet of thirty-eight ships which carried them away to the Holy Land in July 1248 for the Seventh Crusade. Apart from the army encampment which must have been an immense affair, Aigues-Mortes had a much larger population than it has nowadays. The army's embarkation made an unforgettable spectacle that lasted six weeks. But Louis on his return 'put aside wordly vanities' and afterwards was seen no more resplendent in 'gold . . . silk . . . [or] costly furs; nothing brighter than small gray or vair'. He then set about constructing the village's defences, assisted by the military architect, Eude de Montreuil, who designed the thick crenellated walls with their long arrow-slots which enabled archers to shoot great distances. This layout and system of construction was later repeated throughout the Middle East, in Syria and Palestine, wherever the advancing army erected its outposts. Louis IX did not live to see his work at Aigues-Mortes completed, for he died of typhus in August 1270, at the gates of Tunis, near the beginning of the Eighth Crusade. The ramparts remain the village's outstanding feature and their perimeter measurements, including ten gate-ways and fifteen towers, extends to more than 1,600 metres.

When I arrived at Aigues-Mortes in early November, the streets off the place Saint-Louis were still thronged by tourists in search of the village's many souvenir-shops, postcard-stalls, fast-food bars, restaurants and places of interest, such as the Early Gothic church of Notre-Dame-des-Sablons, the Capucines' Cloister and the seventeenth-century Chapels of the Grey and the White Penitents.

The tentacles of the tourist trade have engulfed this gem of a medieval village like the rash of ivy covering the walls of a country mansion. It is this parasitic growth that you notice first; and now – even in the '*morte saison*' – the tourists were almost as numerous as the ivy's leaves. It was virtually impossible to escape the babbling voices, or the hissing walkmans they carried dangling at their necks with the earphones unplugged and fully functioning to the beat of Heavy Metal and Punk Rock.

At a newsagent's I commiserated with an elderly arthritic shopkeeper, who told me that he was always relieved when the tourist season was finally over. His family still lived in the village, in a terrace-house facing onto the ramparts. He had an odd habit of pursing his lips and blowing a loud raspberry when, as frequently happened, he was either stuck for words, or – being also rather puritanical and prudish – he meant to say something rude without actually resorting to expletives.

'I've had my fill of these BRRRRZZZZPPPP foreigners asking their BRRRRZZZZPPPP stupid questions about BRRRRZZZZPPPP nothing at all,' he complained, rubbing his nose until it, too, glowed bright raspberry-red. 'In the days when I was a – a BRRRRZZZZPPPP – a youngster in my teens, the village was worth living in. Now it's all gone to BRRRRZZZZPPPP!' Overcome with emotion, he thumped his fist on the counter, upsetting a tray of enamel brooches which crashed to the floor, scattering in all directions.

'There now – BRRRZZZPPP! Look what I've gone and done! You only have to mention these BRRRZZZPPP people and something like this happens!' He bent down to pick up the trinkets, but jammed like the hands of a grandfather clock at half-past-three, massaging his ribs and grumbling. Independent, as we would say in Scotland *downright carnapshus*, he refused my offer of help with a gruff *merci*. 'Hell's teeth, I'm getting too old for this,' he muttered and gave a little groan. 'Time I chucked this BRRRRZZZZPPPP life and retired like any sensible man of my age. I'll be eighty-five next year, God willing. Not much longer to – to – BRRRRZZZZPPPP – to go! Maybe I'll give it just one more summer and then BRRRRZZZZPPPP-off out of it!'

I have said that it was almost impossible to escape the hordes of tourists, but this is not quite correct. They poured through the streets all morning and congregated at shop-windows, church-doorways and at noon they disappeared into the village's excellent restaurants all of which appeared to do a roaring trade. From the most expensive, such as Les Arcades, Les Capucins and La Camargue, which offered well-cooked specialities of the region, to snack-bars with diverse names like Manhattan, Glacier and Le Constance which sold beef-burgers and Coco-Cola, from midday until mid-afternoon they were packed wall-to-wall with footsore, hungry diners who devoted themselves to eating and drinking with an almost religious fervour. The preoccupation with food and wine always left me feeling like a heretic and an outsider, since I seldom eat a cooked lunch –as my friends at Arles and Les Saintes-Maries observed with much amusement, poor qualifications for someone who had come here intending to write a book about Provence.

Instead, I ate my tramp's lunch consisting of bread and cheese and an apple on a bench facing Saint-Louis' statue and pondered the extraordinary appetites of travelling gourmets such as Basil Collier, who wrote passionately about Provençal cooking, describing dozens of meals from the sublime to the indifferent; gargantuan feasts and – to him at any rate – meagre snacks, in his entertaining account of a journey, made 55 years ago, from Cerbère to the Riviera, *To Meet the Spring*. Mr Collier's descriptions of Provençal menus were undoubtedly the fruits of personal experience and they were written with gusto, straight from the heart. I could never compete with him as a trencher-man, but I enjoyed reading about food, and would sometimes pore over a menu with the same pleasure as I derived from a bookseller's catalogue.

In common with other Provençal villages and towns, Aigues-Mortes' restaurants specialized in *bouillabaisse*, the fish-stew which was once the homely fare of country-folk and the *gardian*'s staple diet. *Bouillabaisse* nowadays, as everyone knows, is regarded as a delicacy and it is apt to be overpriced by restaurants in consequence. Its quality, as might be expected, varies greatly. The dish includes at least four of the following varieties of fish: conger-eel, rock-fish, monk-fish, weevil, scorpion-fish, rascasse and white rascasse; and it is garnished either with *aiöli* – known locally as 'the Devil's mustard' – a mayonnaise made from crushed garlic and olive-oil, or more commonly with *rouille*, which is *aiöli* mixed with red pepper to make it hot. Garlic is an essential ingredient of much traditional Provençal cuisine. It was banned from the court of Alphonse de Castille in 1378, but a valuable garlic-tithe was paid to the meridional bishops. In Provence, it was believed garlic cleansed the bloodstream, eased colic and corns, cured the plague, purified polluted water and fortified manual labourers. Croutons are sometimes served with *bouillabaisse*, but usually it is flavoured with saffron and eaten with fresh bread. As far as I know, there is no hard and fast rule about the wine that should be drunk with *bouillabaisse*, though in his book, *La Camargue*, Michel-Droit suggested that a sweet *rosé* is appropriate.

Roy Campbell wrote: 'No decent fisherman will eat *bouillabaisse* without *rouille* (the "rust"), which is the spur and rowel both of one's thirst and one's appetite. . . . East of Marseilles you seldom see the *rouille* which requires the stomachs of jousters, tamers of horses, and punchers of cattle.' According to Campbell, the rascasse, or scarlet sea-scorpion is '*the* prime necessity for a *bouillabaisse*'. The rascasse is a fearsome creature. Perhaps it is just as well that innocents dining on typical fare at Aigues-Mortes and Les Saintes-Maries don't know much about it. For those of a less nervous disposition, 'the rascasse has to be trimmed of the sixteen or seventeen venomous fangs which, with poison glands at their bases, protrude from its diabolic scarlet bulldog countenance, prickly fins and spiky back. A single sting from a rascasse will make you sick for a week, like the bite of an English adder: but his venom, like that of even a mamba or a cobra, is edible, provided you have no cuts in your mouth, and, like snake poison, it is completely neutralised by boiling.'

'The *bouillabaisse*,' Campbell wrote, 'is always celebrated *au cabanon*; that is in the little country cabin that every Provençal family possesses in the pines: or, if it is fine weather, as it usually is, you cook it outside in the woods, or on an open fire.'

The dish was apparently one of Basil Collier's notable failures: though I suggest that an edge of real hunger, rather than a palate blunted by over-indulgence, might have altered his opinion of it. He dismissed it somewhat dispeptically and wrote: 'Eating *bouillabaisse* is like walking through a half-familiar landscape on a foggy day.' This was at Aix-en-Provence. How he fared at Aigues-Mortes, he doesn't tell us.

L'Aïöli was the title given by Mistral to a journal which he founded in January 1891 with money from the Prix Jean-Reynaud, awarded for the *Trésor du Félibrige*. Like the garnish, Mistral's *L'Aïöli* involved a 'stirring up' of Provençal affairs by contributions written in the region's own language. *L'Aïöli* was one of Mistral's rare flights of self-indulgence, edited and produced by Folco de Baroncelli-Javon at the Palais du Roure, where the original printing press can still be seen. Published three times a month on the 7th, 17th and 27th – dates which reflected the poet's obsession with sevens – in contrast to the *Armana Prouvençau*, *L'Aïöli* never caught on and it was discontinued in December 1899.

It was hardly surprising to find at Aigues-Mortes many shops and small businesses which supplied mainly the holidaymakers and souvenir-hunters. These included a sports-shop selling fishing-tackle, shotguns, air-rifles, sheath-knives and knuckle-dusters, besides a wide selection of vicious-looking stilettos – the 'switch-blades' beloved by gipsies and American students – the sale of which I was positively assured did not result in any noticeable increase in violent crimes. This shop and the church next-door to it seemed equally popular with Aigues-Mortes' visitors, who drifted from one to another casually oblivious to the jarring contrast of deadly weaponry and stained-glass images of the Apostles. But, perhaps after all, this was merely a throwback to the village's Crusader heritage, the reflection of an age when knights had knelt to pray before a crucifix made of the same two-handed broadsword they had used to slay Saracens in battle.

There was a boutique further along, run by a family of Hungarian soap-makers, where the owner and her nephew mashed brightly dyed pellets of soap in tin baths on the pavement, then fed the strong-scented greasy paste through a mincing-machine before it was finally moulded into a variety of shapes and subjects. The saddler's shop nearby was run by an American from Arizona and his wife, a local girl, whose stained roughened hands would have provided the Hungarians with a worthy challenge. They turned out everything imaginable from handbags, hats, waistcoats and pistol-holsters to Camargue-style saddles – for which the girl admitted there wasn't much demand – at prices which undercut the competition at Tarascon and Nîmes by as much as 50 per cent. These saddles, fashioned according to the thirteenth-century Crusader pattern, took 100 hours to complete and they sometimes cost the *gardians* a whole year's salary. The Aigues-Mortes' saddler reckoned he could supply one for 5,000, maybe 6,000 francs; but elsewhere the price had been fixed between 8,000 and 9,000 francs, and this was regarded as fair and reasonable.

Least frequented by the *morte saison*'s tourists was an exhibition of paintings by two local artists, which had been set up near the Mairie in a Tourist Office annexe off the place Saint-Louis.

Most of the paintings were typical Camargue scenes, with bulls and horses dotted about the *sansouires* in dramatic lights ranging from piercing-blue winter skies to blood-red summer sunsets mirrored in the lagoons. Whatever the artists may have lacked in draughtsman's skills they more than made up for by lively brush-work and the lavishly uninhibited use of colours. Like the aging concert-pianist, of whom it was said that he still played all the right notes though not always in the right order, passion rather than precision was the hallmark of the artists' work.

Both men were in their late fifties and had other jobs besides painting, which to them was really more of a hobby. They had each dressed for the occasion in painterly costume – one in a loud green-and-white-check country suit, the other in a bulky black-leather bomber-jacket with numerous (mostly redundant) zip-fasteners and bits of chromium-plate rivetted to the chest and sleeves.

Making a little bow, the bomber-jacketted one said: 'Be so kind if you will as to sign our *Livre d'Or*, and then we shall know how to greet you properly when you next return.'

'From the artist's point of view Aigues-Mortes has no equal in the Languedoc.' Such was Amy Oakley's opinion, and who was I to disagree? A panoramic view by Edouard Doigneau which I had seen at the Palais du Roure, *Gardians et taureaux de Camargue sous les remparts d'Aigues-Mortes*, painted about the turn of the century, is a fine example of a much-repeated theme. Naturally Aigues-Mortes is a venue much favoured by the Nacioun Gardiano and a perfect setting for their bull-drives, the *abrivado* and the *bandido*. Throughout the summer months, the Course Camarguaise is held there and, as an added attraction reminiscent of roman antiquity when the Nîmes arena was flooded and sea-battles were staged for the jaded spectators bored by lions disembowelling Christian martyrs, the 'Toro-Piscene', bull-fights held in a swimming-pool. 'Or maybe it should be called the "Toro-Obscene"!' I heard a lady remark who had been dragged round the Rhôneland arenas for a fortnight and by then had had her fill of tauromachy.

It is strange to think what memories one carried away from places like Aigues-Mortes. Such memories seldom had anything to do with the tourist literature's recommendations, or regional spectacles like the Course (except for special occasions), or the noble architecture, or even the delights of Provençal *cuisine*. For my part, I remembered the view of the western ramparts from the edge of the lagoon – the Tour de Constance fired by the weak November sun against a background of heavy clouds and the

odour of salt sea coming with the breeze. Better even was the village at dusk, while I waited for the evening bus by the Boulodrome, listening to the click of the *boules*, watching the lights of the marina, the orange floodlights against the porte de la Gardette and the flicker of car headlights among the trees.

Just across from the bus-stop I saw a young family – a husband and wife and two car-weary children, tumbling out of a Renault-5 by an unpretentious little shoebox house, unloading the week's groceries and hurrying indoors. The couple were laughing, kissing, teasing the children and evidently glad to get home, probably after a day's shopping at Nîmes. Here at Aigues-Mortes, this brief glimpse of everyday ordinary family life seemed exaggeratedly real and unexpectedly moving in the village's theatrically unreal setting.

With nightfall, the breeze strengthened and a heavy shower broke just as the Nîmes' bus drew up at the modern glass shelter in the boulevard Diderot. As the bus swung away from Aigues-Mortes, past the ramparts' orange flush silhouetted against the blackness of sky, I heard the patter of rain on the roof and at the same instant, so perfectly synchronized with the sound that I laughed out loud, the voice of Gene Kelly and 'Singin' in the Rain' on the driver's radio.

19

Saints and Saladelle

'*Nul ne nait ni ne meurt en Camargue.*'

The Camargue is a flat terrain without obvious features such as hills, and this some people eventually find boring. As a friend of Yvan Audouard observed cynically: '*tu montes sur une chaise, et tu as tout vu!*' ('you climb on a chair and you've seen the lot!').

The little blue and white Cartreize bus for Les Saintes-Maries sped away from Arles, through the leafy suburbs of Trinquetaille, out into a bleak marshy terrain here and there divided by rice-fields. To the west, beyond the Mas de Pioch, lay vines and rough pastures where the strong sunlight reflected on patches of still water the size of an English pond. To the east, the marshes bordered some larger salt-water lakes – the famous *étangs* of the Camargue delta. Wherever I looked the entire countryside appeared to be in a state of perpetual motion: it was a combined effect of light and wind – the quivering grasses, the heaving brown tussocks of marsh-samphire, the shivering gnarled tamarisks and clumps of tall, feathered rushes whipped and bowed by the mistral's raging blasts.

The restless windswept plain, weathered pale by months of spring and summer sun, was exactly as Daudet had described it in *Lettres de mon moulin*: the light 'lashed by powerful blasts . . .

dispersed and scattered, only to be flickeringly united again.'
Directly in front of me, to the south, the hard blue sky shone
like tempered steel, its colour bleached by the explosion of
brilliant rays thrown back from the sea. I saw the pale-red roof-
tops of Les Saintes-Maries-de-la-Mer at the horizon with the
church-tower sunlit, hovering above them like a plume of
yellow flame.

The village has been called 'the spiritual capital' of the
Camargue. A century ago, it was still one of the remotest
corners in Europe at a period when the Camargue was
effectively a *terra incognita*, very wild, desolate and sparsely
inhabited.

In those days Les Saintes-Maries consisted of little more than a
handful of white-washed, thatched cottages and an inn or two,
clustered round the twelfth-century fortified church; and the
villagers made a hard, at times precarious living as fishermen,
shepherds, wildfowlers and herdsmen, or *gardians*, employed by
a few scattered *manades* which bred the black Camargue bulls.
For the most part, the people were uneducated: a deeply-rooted

attachment to superstition counterbalanced their religious faith and their belief in the miraculous powers of the saints to whom the village church was dedicated.

There were a great many versions of the village's name – more even than versions of the legend of the Holy Marys on which its early history and much of its reputation had been founded. It was called Villa-de-la-Mar; Sancta Maria de Mari, or Sancta Maria de Râtis; Nostra-Dona-de-la-Mar; Notre-Dame-de-la-Mar; Notre-Dame du Radeau; or Notre-Dame de la Barque. In popular usage also were Nos Dames de la Mer; Les Deux Maries de la Mer; Les Maries; Les Trois Maries; or simply Trois Mères. The modern name, Les Saintes-Maries-de-la-Mer is something like a compromise between them all and was adopted after 1838. Today, among the 'Saintins' themselves, the village is usually referred to as Les Saintes-Maries, Les Saintes, or merely as Saintes.

It occupies the site of a sixth-century BC encampment which the Greeks later knew as Oppidum Râ and was thus established long before the Roman conquest of Gaul. According to the legend, it was at this point on the Camargue shore that the Holy Marys landed, having fled from Palestine soon after the Crucifixion of Christ. A simple cross of weathered wood at the beach-head marks the saints' landfall, after their stormy voyage across the Mediterranean in an open boat (the outcast's *barque* of antiquity) which had neither sails nor a rudder. There was Mary, the mother of Christ; Mary-Jacobé and Mary-Salomé, the wives of Cleophas and Zebedee; the risen Lazarus and his family; Martha; Mary Magdalene, whom the novelist Blaise Cendrars called 'the lover of Jesus Christ, the only woman who made Our Saviour weep'; and several of the Apostles. The number of the boat's occupants varied according to the different accounts. Of course, this story has been written off as a mere fable and the miraculous arrival in the Camargue of the storm-tossed boat-load of biblical characters has given disbelievers and cynics a field day. However, if we accept as a matter of faith other New Testament miracles, there may be less reason to dismiss the so-called legend of the Holy Marys out of hand. But as the stuff of heroic poetry, like the creation of the world told in the Book of Genesis, the saints' story is none the less moving or inspiring for all that.

There has been much speculation, too, about the origin of the Marys' servant or handmaiden, Sara-le-Kâli – 'Black Sara' as she is sometimes known – whose painted effigy stands in a corner of the ancient crypt below the altar. One version of the legend states that Sara had no direct connection whatsoever with the Marys, but instead she was the chieftain of a tribe living in the marshes, who rescued the saints and gave them food and shelter. Despite the fact that Sara has been so far unrecognized by the Catholic hierarchy, her claim to sainthood is stoutly upheld by the gipsies who flock in their thousands to Les Saintes-Maries every year for the pilgrimage rites of 24 and 25 May.

The May pilgrimage is the feast of Saint Mary-Jacobé. Later in the year, on or as near as possible to 22 October, follows the Feast of Saint Mary-Salomé which does not involve 'Black Sara' or the gipsies. In May, during the procession when the boat containing the robed statues of Mary-Jacobé and Mary-Salomé is carried shoulder-high down to the shore, the gipsies accompany them with Sara's effigy, crying *'Vive sainte Sara!'* in response to the shouts of *'Vivent les saintes Maries!'* Before the procession, the gipsies, or *gitans*, hold a night-long vigil in the crypt by candle-light. This is an intensely private ceremony to which only the gipsies themselves are admitted. Their role in these pilgrimages received the Church's approval only as recently as 1935, thanks to Folco de Baroncelli-Javon who interceded with the ecclesiastical authorities on the gipsies' behalf. The pilgrimages were founded in 1449; but during the French Revolution and from about 1793–1797, when the saints'relics were hidden, the pilgrimages were temporarily discontinued.

There may be some connection between 'Black Sara' of the *gitans* and the Black Virgin of Guadaloupe in Spain. Likewise, the ritual of the saints being carried to the sea finds echoes elsewhere – at Saint Tropez and Algeçiras, for instance, and as far afield as Bali.

Whatever the facts may or not be behind the saints' legend, the site of their landfall is even more debatable. It has been suggested that the Quatre-Maries farther to the west beyond the point where the Petit Rhône flows into the sea at the Grau d'Orgon, is the true location. But an even stronger case has been made for a site close to Les Baux, since the Camargue's shoreline of today lies many kilometres south of its position 2,000 years ago, when the Mediterranean penetrated inland as far as Arles.

The character of Les Saintes-Maries has altered drastically since the Second World War. The tiny hamlet of fishermen's cottages and herdsmen's *cabanes*, which Folco de Baroncelli-Javon first saw as a boy of six in 1875, has expanded as a major tourist attraction and a much-frequented seaside resort with many souvenir-shops, boutiques specializing in *gardian* clothes, hotels, restaurants, trekking centres and, since 1984, a modern harbour. It is far from exaggerating when I say that the village has changed beyond recognition; though I wouldn't go so far as to admit that it has been hopelessly ruined, as some critics claim. The spirit of Les Saintes-Maries and the Saintins is much too durable for that.

As the bus drew closer to the village, we passed converted *mas* buildings with the same message repeated again and again on their painted signboards: 'Rooms to let'; 'Hotel service with meals'; 'Heated swimming-pool for the use of residents'; and 'Horse-trekking over the marshes' – the ubiquitous *promenades à cheval* – which in the words of Michel-Droit (a member of the Académie-Française and an *aficionado* of the Camargue) encourages tourists to hire 'reasonably docile horses in order to venture into that Camargue which is so exciting in their imagination'. Lines of dejected-looking white or brown ponies stood side by side in open sheds in the hope of attracting the dregs of end-of-season visitors. The horses may have had a few drops of the wild Camargue blood in their veins; though to judge by their appearance, not much. Their harness was of a kind you find almost anywhere. None had the traditional high-backed *gardian's* saddle with its medieval 'chair'; nor the elongated basket-stirrups evolved from a type favoured by the sixteenth-century knights.

This was only to be expected in these commercial establishments concerned with the tourist trade; but even at the working *manades*, which organized trekking as a lucrative sideline, the best Camargue horses were kept, almost invariably, for the *manadier* and his *gardians'* exclusive use and, of course, the same applied to the harness and other equipment.

Approaching Les Saintes-Maries from the north across the sunlit windswept marshes, despite these changes, I still found much that remained beautiful and appealing. There was the limitless vault of blue autumn sky and the streaming wind-torn clouds which projected their vast irregular patterns on the dry tawny earth and the shimmering surface of the lagoons. I saw flamingoes flying in a thin, rose-pink line above the Etang de Gines; and a small herd of bulls, several of them with white cattle-egrets perched on their backs, grazing a few hundred metres from the roadside.

The flamingoes, like the hardy black bulls with their distinctive lyre-shaped horns, are permanent symbols of the wild Camargue. Baroncelli-Javon wrote of the flamingo, the *flamant rose*, as 'a flower that flies / Over Malagroy and Gines. . . .'; and the bull, which reigns 'Over the Mediterranean peoples / In joy, in art and in blood'.

Horses, bulls, egrets and flamingoes; I half-expected to hear the few tourists among my fellow-passengers complain, as visitors do sometimes – those who keep strictly to the main roads through the Camargue – of the disappointing scarcity of animals and wild birds. It is as if they felt cheated by an absence of wild creatures systematically arranged and neatly tabulated like the inmates of a zoo.

Those who know the Camargue better, however, also realize that a little effort is required; that given, the dividends are enormous – and there are few sights in nature to compare with a dawn-pink cloud of flamingoes at a nesting-site, or an evening flight of duck raining down on a lagoon in hundreds, a mere fraction of the 100,000 that winter here in the marshes every year. There are mallard, teal, widgeon, coot; sandpipers, avocets, egrets and purple herons; the rare glossy ibis and bittern booming in the reeds; moorhens and many species of gulls. The marshes are home to wild boar (*sanglier*) and beavers – *lou vibre* in Provençal, after which Baroncelli-Javon named one of his favourite horses.

Besides the rich abundance of wildlife there was a great diversity of plants, flowers and trees in these 'grey wastes of dread' which confronted the casual observer with an illusion of emptiness. Most obvious was the marsh-samphire, or *engano*, whose spring-green, summer-grey colours had by now turned reddish-brown, like Highland heather, patching the dry alluvial soil. There were the tall, plumed sea-rushes fringing the irrigation-canals between the rice-fields or growing in wind-lashed clumps by the *étangs*; reeds of many kinds, wild iris, sea-purslane and water-mint. Among the Camargue's trees the silver bursts of tamarisk and, far from the road, in the Bois-des-Rièges, thickets of *mourven*, the Phoenician juniper which, together with the pine-woods of Clamador and Brasinvert, are all that remain of the delta's vast forests of antiquity.

Deceptively fragile, quivering in the *mistral*'s bitter gusts, I pictured the violet-blue flowers of sea-lavender, the *saladelle* which is the Nacioun Gardiano's emblem, whose unpretentious beauty is rivalled only by the sky-blue *pervenche* of the Félibrige.

I felt excitement, and a thrill of anticipation now that I was returning to these wild landscapes of mirages and lagoons; and I remembered the beautiful words of Baroncelli-Javon's prayer: '*Mon Dieu, abreuve-moi les graces du Désert/ – de silence, de paix, d'eau limpide et d'espoir!*' ('O God, let me drink of the wilderness' blessings – silence, peace, clear water and hope!') Despite the changes I had seen, I had faith in the Camargue's ability to absorb them, to turn some to its advantage, to overcome the disadvantages caused by others. It had been Baroncelli-Javon's imperishable belief in the Camargue which inspired Mistral to write: '*Ton trident, ô Folco, avec ses pointes fières, tel que la lune nouvelle, va se lever au ciel ardent, pour notre gloire de félibres: les ailes de ta foi planent sur la terre salée, plus haute que celles des goëlands.*' ('Your trident, Folco, with its trusty points like the new moon, will be raised to the burning sky for our brotherhood's glory: the wings of your faith glide higher above the salt-marshes than those of the gulls.')

I found Les Saintes-Maries swept clean by the gale, its low white buildings and dusty streets steeped in brilliant sunshine, the narrow lanes and alleyways a patchwork of sunlight and shadows. From the bus-stop in the rue des Razeteurs, I made my way down to the esplanade, skirting the place Mireille with Antonin Mercié's romantic bronze statue of Mistral's heroine, across the draughty stone-paved place de l'Eglise and along the rue Sadi Carnot to the Hôtel-Restaurant L'Abrivado, which overlooked the arena and the white masts and rippling blue water of the Port Gardian.

When I arrived, the Abrivado was in a state of homely chaos. The owners' small grandson squatted defiantly under the table in the reception-area, nursing a cut finger and sobbing. A raven-haired girl barely out of her teens, whom I took to be his mother, knelt at his side doing her best to console him. The owner's wife, pale and exhausted, her hair dishevelled and straggling, was bent over an ironing-board in the breakfast-room. Through the open door I saw her surrounded by huge heaps of crumpled bed-linen like a miniature Alpine diorama, sheets and pillow-cases draped over the chairs and tables and piled high on the shining linoleum-tiles – a prospect as daunting in its way as the Alps' glaciers and ice-mountains might have been to a weary climber. She bade me '*bonjour*' and laid aside her iron with the dazed, defeated grin of a long-serving captive.

'Every year, *monsieur*, I ask myself the same question: why do I go on with all this? Hotel-work is a real killer! From morning till night I'm on my feet, cooking meals, shopping, ironing and making beds for the guests. . . . I tell you, *monsieur*, it's hard graft. My dear husband says: don't lose heart, soon we shall retire. We'll go off and live in the mountains. Put our feet up. Go on holiday if we feel like it and have others to wait on us for a change. . . . Dear man! He's such a dreamer and so kind-hearted!' She sighed and flicked away a strand of hair from her brow. 'Meanwhile, we have to struggle and save every *sou*. Who knows? If God wills and we manage to survive, we might get to the mountains one day. . . .'

The summer tourists had long since gone, but the hotel was still fairly busy – which explained the quantities of laundry – mostly short-stay visitors from Germany, Switzerland and America, besides a trickle of French families, she added somewhat disparagingly, 'from north of the Loire'.

She led me upstairs to a comfortable room – not as I'd hoped a room facing the sea, but one with a small window screened by fine wire-mesh against insects, which looked onto the cinema and a lurid poster, streaked with gulls' droppings, advertising *Les Plaisirs du Paradis*. The good lady evidently registered my disappointment, for I had hardly begun to unpack when she reappeared, insisting that I should move instead to another larger bedroom from which, by negotiating an enormous padded writing-desk in the corner and craning my neck it was just possible to glimpse a postage-stamp-size view of the harbour. It seemed hardly worth the effort, but she was adamant and touchingly eager to please. Besides, I had discovered that my budget did not stretch to a room with a terrace overlooking the esplanade.

Afterwards she introduced me to her husband, a cheerful, easy-going man with thick horn-rimmed glasses and a two-tone tweed cap, which throughout my entire stay I never once saw him remove, who instantly reminded me of a famous actor, the late Sir Bernard Miles. The couple's name was Bedot, which I misheard and, as a result, for some days rendered as Bidet until in exasperation Madame Bedot painstakingly, but very firmly corrected me. Monsieur Bedot immediately launched into a long animated conversation on his favourite topics which were the Course Camarguaise, the life of the Camargue *manades* and, above all, *boules* of which he had been for some years a local champion at Aigues-Mortes as well as Les Saintes-Maries. He became very excited when I mentioned that I knew several of the *manadiers* round the village; but his enthusiasm knew no bounds when I begged to be initiated into the mysteries of *boules* which, until then, I had found as confusing as the rules of cricket.

This must have struck a chord, for when I returned to the Abrivado that evening after dinner, I discovered that my bedroom had been changed for a third time and my things were carefully laid out in one of the sea-facing terrace rooms, for which Monsieur and Madame Bedot positively assured me there would be no extra charge.

In the afternoon I tramped along the nearly deserted shore in the sun and wind towards the Mas Le Simbèu, where in the past I had spent many memorable days listening to stories of the old Camargue told by my friends, Henri and Riquette Aubanel. Henri Aubanel was one of the region's most famous *manadiers*. Until very recently the Captain of the Nacioun Gardiano, a poet and an orator, he had also written two highly-acclaimed prose-works, *Je suis manadier*, published in 1957, and a collection of exquisitely-wrought tales, *Camarguaises: un gardian en hiver*, which in 1983 was awarded the Prix Broquette-Gonin of the Académie-Française. Although born in Paris, Aubanel's life had been spent almost entirely in the Camargue. A descendant of Théodore Aubanel who, with Mistral and Roumanille, had founded the Félibrige, Henri had worked as a *gardian* at L'Amarée for Folco de Baroncelli-Javon. In 1933, he married the youngest of the Marquis' three daughters, Marie-Sarah-Caroline-Joséphine-Françoise-Frédérique – known to her family and friends simply as Riquette – who had been a god-daughter of the great Frédéric Mistral himself.

Riquette Aubanel truly was one of the Camargue's great women. Another was Riquette's elder sister, Nerte, whose horsemanship, bravery and enthusiasm for the bulls won the admiration of even the most reactionary and *macho* of the *gardians*. Yet another Camargue heroine, the *manadière*, Fanfonne Guillierme, whose hawkish features and eyes with their drooping lids gave her expression a kind of menacing stillness, had been among the first women to wear the *culottes* or flared, divided riding-skirt like the gaucho's loose *bombachas*. In doing so, from about 1935 Madame Guillierme set a fashionable, practical trend which some Camarguaises still adhere to – my friends, Madame Bellon and Madame Nou, for example, whom I saw dressed in nearly-ankle-length *culottes* at the Course in Les Saintes-Maries. Many Camargue women were striking in appearance, fresh-faced and healthy-looking if not actually pretty.

I met Riquette Aubanel for the last time in September 1988 when one blazing-hot day my wife and I drove to Les Saintes-Maries from Arles. For several hours we sat and talked in the cool, dark shade of the *mas'* dining-room where, in spite of the afternoon heat, a fire of tamarisk logs and driftwood burned in the great, smoke-blackened hearth. With her jet-black hair and Roman profile, Madame Aubanel bore more than a passing resemblance to her father, the Marquis, of whom she spoke always with the deepest affection in a voice that trembled with nostalgia and passion.

And now, as I walked by the tumbling waves, in sight of Le Simbèu's white roofs and thatched *cabanes*, the memory of those conversations came flooding back – and the old couple side by side at the beautiful old table, talking in turns, exchanging glances as every so often Henri Aubanel paused and gently patted his wife's hand.

I remembered the fine, blustery spring morning when I walked to Le Simbèu and found its low buildings clustered beside a muddy pool a hundred metres from the breakwater. That was almost ten years ago, but the excitement of the moment thrills me still whenever I think of it, or read the brief description I scribbled in my diary. I wrote: 'Here at the Camargue's edge, "poised between sky and water", I find myself at the frontier of two worlds. Behind me, to the southwest, glittering ocean rollers heave and crash incessantly against the bleached sea-wall. To the north, as far as the eye can see, the grey-brown marsh landscape stretches beyond a shadowy green lagoon. Above the dull thunder of waves and the roar of white surf, the gulls' melancholy crying echoes down a sapphire sky. An ancient ruined *cabane* stands on the shore near La Simbèu. A flourish of wind-whisked tamarisk casts its trembling shadow on the wall. Half the roof has gone and, through the open doorway, I see some of its rotted timbers partly buried by drifting sand. The owner is long since dead and now the only occupants are sparrows which flutter about in the remains of the thatch and the tamarisk's branches.'

The little hut may have existed when Alphonse Daudet visited the Camargue with a shooting-party one bright, wild December day when a shrieking *mistral* scoured the marshes where Daudet found every scrap of vegetation 'bowed and twisted, leaning southwards as if in an attitude of perpetual flight'. The *cabane* where they rested was made entirely of reeds and consisted of 'a single vast windowless room' with a glazed door which after dark was covered by heavy shutters. The *cabane*'s walls were rough-cast and daubed with a coating of white-wash. Daudet's *cabane*, like this ruin on the shore, looked like an upturned boat. Its north-facing wall was curved, offering a minimum of resistance to the *mistral*; and at one end of the roof there was a sloping white cross like a flying gull. The blasts of fierce winter wind, Daudet wrote in 1866, battered his *cabane* door like the horns of an angry bull.

Just off the route d'Aigues-Mortes, on the landward side of Le Simbèu, lies the tomb of Folco de Baroncelli-Javon. The stone sarcophagus bearing his arms is raised on a stepped foundation forming three concentric circles. Since 1951, when Folco's remains were brought here from Avignon and reburied, the tomb has been the focus of a memorial service held every year on 26 May, the Jour Baroncellien, which follows the pilgrimage of Saint Mary-Jacobé. There used to be a plaque by the tomb with the inscription: '*A LA MEMOIRE*/ *du MARQUIS de BARONCELLI*/ *Qui fut L'Ami de Gitans*'; but now it had been replaced by a white stone with the words, '*A notre pélote –regretté*' ('To our late proprietor') lettered in gold. My rendering is inadequate; but in the Camargue the term *pélote* means the owner of a *manade*, the master of its bulls and horses.

Folco's funeral cortège had been escorted to Le Simbèu by a procession of gipsies and horsemen of the Nacioun Gardiano. In 1960, the Marquis' former *baïle-gardian*, René Barbut, recalled: 'the bulls understood what was happening. On each side of the embankment they accompanied our procession, and many of them bellowed as though it were Ramadan.'

Baroncelli-Javon built the Mas Le Simbèu in 1931 as an almost exact replica of L'Amarée, his first *manade* near Les Saintes-Maries. The name means 'the symbol' and it usually refers to the *dompteur* bull, or herd-leader. When Amy Oakley met Folco four years after he moved there, he explained: 'I vowed . . . if ever I built a *mas*, it, too, should be named Lou Simbèu . . . you find me in it.'

The original farmhouse was destroyed by German troops in 1944, a year after the Marquis' death. The present cottage which Henri Aubanel built on the site was a more modest affair, with five rooms and a *cabane* by the entrance where a *gardian* or an overnight guest sometimes slept. Here Henri and Riquette Aubanel had lived with their three daughters and their son, Pierre. But Pierre had long since removed to Saint-Gilles where he had a *manade* of his own; and, to my sorrow, I learned that Riquette had died in 1990, leaving Henri, Marie-Caroline, Jacqueline and Nerte.

When I arrived at Le Simbèu, Monsieur Aubanel, now aged eighty, was resting, while Marie-Caroline and her sisters had business to attend to at Aimargues. Marie-Caroline herself had been confined to a wheelchair for the past seven years, after a bull charged her horse at an *abrivado* and she fell heavily onto a cobbled road breaking her back and severing one of her vocal cords. Despite her terrible injuries, and a long, frustrating convalescence, Marie-Caroline's spirit was quite remarkable. I found her courage and her cheerful determination very moving as she told me: 'I must be strong! Strong for myself, for my brother and sisters, for Papa and for the sake of Mama's memory!'

Although I knew the family well, in the circumstances I thought it better to keep my visit fairly brief. Having arranged to visit the Aubanels on a more convenient day, I walked back along the shore to the village and afterwards took a sketchbook and watercolours and made some drawings of the coastguard's house and the fishermen mending their nets at the harbour.

The wind in the vessels' rigging made a tinkling sound like a carillon of tiny bells; but I found the heavy gusts and the showers of flying sand and grit a maddening distraction. Yves Brayer had worked out of doors at Les Saintes-Maries for many years and made his large watercolour paintings on flimsy paper which must have been very difficult to control in these conditions. By contrast I used small sheets of 135 gsm attached to a ring-binder, but even with the addition of a strong clip the paper shifted constantly, while a layer of fine sand gradually silted up the watercolour box and textured the damp washes with a 'five o'clock shadow'.

As I sat with my back to a rock, engaged in this losing battle with the wind and sand, I was joined by three Pakistanis in long mackintoshes who came and squatted beside me. They were day-trippers from Avignon, a very youthful looking father and his teenage sons. The boys' father spoke haltingly in English: 'We wish only to observe, sir. You must understand immediately, please, that we are not wishing to buy a picture! We shall remain for five minutes only, provided we are not being troublesome to you.'

I replied that they were quite welcome to stay as long as they liked. In any case, I assured him, my sketches were not for sale and I was painting entirely for my own pleasure. It appeared that the man didn't quite believe that – why, I cannot say. The three sat perfectly still, their arms resting on their knees, their thin brown fingers limply dangling. The man paid little heed to my drawing, but from the corner of my eye I could see him watching me as though he were trying to fathom what drew a foreigner to this deserted beach in autumn and what possible pleasure there could be working in a cold wind for no reason. When he judged the five minutes were up, the boys' father glanced at his wrist-watch, nodded and said that they must be on their way. He added with a perplexed frown: 'Dear me, 'South of France is a jolly place, you know. But everywhere we are spending too much money. To enjoy life here, truly one would require the silk purse without bottom. When we return next week to Karachi, people will be amazed by the stories I have to tell them. But I tell my sons: to know life you must also see how others live. I pray that they will learn from these experiences and find contentment.'

★

How very different Les Saintes-Maries was when Van Gogh came here to paint in June 1888. Delighted by the sight of the gaily painted fishing-boats drawn up along the beach, he wrote how the 'greens, reds, blues, such pretty shapes and colours . . . made one think of flowers'. The blinding glare of the reflected sunlight and its subtle effect on the sea's colours stunned Van Gogh as he wandered up and down the shore in a frenzy of excited bewilderment: 'The Mediterranean has the colours of mackerel,' he exclaimed, 'changeable I mean. You don't always know if it's green or violet, you can't even say it's blue, because the next moment the changing light has taken on a tinge of pink or gray.'

The fishermen I met by the harbour seemed preoccupied and taciturn. Even among themselves, it seemed they spoke very little as they threaded the veils of nylon-mesh with metal leaders, making quick stabbing thrusts with their rough weathered fingers which I could never follow in time to record. In their own way, they too appreciated the lovely colour changes of the sea and the windy lagoons from which they gathered their living. Fishing offshore in spring and summer, they caught mackerel and sardines – the large blue Mediterranean variety; and in winter the catch from the *étangs* and the *roubines* consisted mainly of eels, crabs, prawns and mullet. A kind of local shellfish, known as *tellines*, included in almost every restaurant menu at Les Saintes-Maries, were dredged from the sand at low tide.

That evening, at the Esperado restaurant, I shared a table with a Swiss couple – an enormously fat man who seemed to consist entirely of stomach, and his blonde wife. Never in my life have I watched anyone eat with such undisguised relish as the fat Swiss, or in such unbelievable quantities! They drank glasses of *pastis* while the food was being prepared and, to fend off starvation, my gigantic neighbour devoured the contents of their large bread-basket and then mine, without so much as a by-your-leave. This performance drove his wife hysterical with laughter. Two vast oval-shaped platters heaped with *tellines* arrived, one for each of them; and as soon as his plate had been cleared, the man set about his wife's portion, which she had hardly begun, and gobbled that up, too. The *tellines* were accompanied by a bottle of dark-red wine, an excellent local vintage, which the Swiss poured down his throat like beer and soon emptied while his wife sipped her thimbleful, laughing uncontrollably. Between mouthfuls of *tellines* and gulps of wine, the man somehow managed to order another bottle and more bread. And then he attacked an immense plate of mutton, fried potatoes and fried mushrooms and after that comman-deered his wife's equally generous main course of shell-pasta which he devoured ravenously, grunting like a hungry lion as it rips apart its kill.

The cheese course which followed was dispatched in seconds; and then several large helpings of sickly-sweet chocolate mousse. Having cleared this mountain of fairly rich food, the Swiss colossus glared about in desperation, his gargantuan appetite seemingly unsatisfied. His eyes fell on a paperback of Daudet's *Lettres de mon moulin* which I had been reading during the meal and I nodded to it, unable to resist the opportunity, and said: '*Peut-être vous voulez manger aussi ce petit morceau?*' at which the Swiss and his wife laughed uproariously. The man confessed that he felt perpetually hungry, even now after a heavy dinner, and blamed this on the fact that he had recently given up smoking sixty cigarettes a day. It was probably my imagination, but throughout the meal it seemed that his already vast body swelled to even vaster proportions as though it were being inflated. The more wine he consumed the redder, fatter and shinier his face grew, until his beady black eyes almost vanished altogether in the folds of taut, beetroot-coloured flesh where his cheeks and eyebrows met.

The Esperado was popular with the locals which I took to be a recommendation. The taped background muzak was discreet – 'Volare' and 'Blue Moon', besides many variations of Spanish flamenco. Through the glazed doors I could see the restaurant's lights reflected on a blue Renault van parked in the pitch-dark street, and I heard the awnings snapping and fluttering in the cold night wind and the glassy jingling made by the strings of fairy-lights. Some *gardians* came in for a drink at the Esperado's tiny bar which was not much bigger than a telephone-kiosk. The proprietor, in a black silk suit, with a dapper Ronald Coleman moustache and a long cigarillo between his teeth, drank with them, while a waitress in blue denims and huge brass gipsy ear-rings joined the group from time to time, or else loitered seductively by the serving hatch, winking at the customers and gossiping with the chef who worked and chain-smoked in the cadaverous submarine gloom.

Some of the *gardians* were fine-looking fellows. A very tall man with long black hair curling up at his shirt-collar was dressed in royal-blue jeans and had a cheap, flashy gold watch with a gold bracelet and big gold rings on both hands. He was very swarthy, deeply-tanned and had a carefully managed growth of 'designer-stubble' which the waitress admired. Another younger man was square-jawed, fair and classically Teutonic in manner. Yet another, in white *gardian* moleskins, stood with his arms akimbo showing off his fringed suede cowboy-jacket, his thumbs stuck into a leather belt which had a big Mexican silver buckle, while a fourth man, older than the rest, had his thinning long brown hair greased and slicked back like Elvis Presley's and grizzled 'mutton-chop' side-boards.

By 10 pm the wind had dropped and, before I turned in, I went and sat on the terrace in the starlight and listened to the sea. The rushing of waves and the faint buzz of a motor-scooter somewhere in the village were the only sounds I heard. As the waves crashed they left intervals of silence in their wake, like the hush that follows the crowd-roar when a bull dashes in from the *toril*, or brakes sharply, pawing the dust, glowering at his tormentors. Tonight the sea was in a bullish mood; poised for the attack; the fragments of stillness tensed and full of menace; the waves' ebbing sighs like those of a hard-breathing animal gathering strength and about to attack again.

The fortified church at Les Saintes-Maries stands at the site of a sixth-century chapel, Sancta Maria de Râtis – or Saint Mary of the Island – which between the eleventh and seventeenth centuries was owned by the monks of Montmajour Abbey, near Les Baux.

In the twelfth century, a larger building was erected, enclosing the chapel, with a square bell-tower on its north side. The church, and the tiny hamlet which surrounded it, remained vulnerable and were attacked frequently from the sea until, in the fourteenth century, the church was fortified with battlements and the hamlet encircled by massive ramparts. The ramparts survived until the Revolution, when they were demolished, but until the late eighteenth century they appeared on maps of the Camargue and showed an arrangement of gates and crenellated walls very similar to those found at Aigues-Mortes.

The church, which Alain Albaric's delightful guide to Les Saintes-Maries describes as the 'last fortress of the lagoons' owes much of its fame to Good King René, the last Count of Provence, who, in December 1448, obtained Papal consent to excavate the sixth-century chapel. Shards of pottery with Christian symbols and part of an ancient sarcophagus were unearthed; and buried close by the diggers uncovered two skeletons, one of them with its arms folded on its breast, which the Bishop of Marseille, Nicolas de Brancas accepted without question as the remains of Saint Mary-Jacobé and Saint Mary-Salomé. At the time, there was no means of proving or disproving their identity. The skeletons might have been buried long before the saints' alleged arrival in the Camargue in 43 AD, or else King René's workmen perhaps had uncovered an obscure medieval grave. But quite simply because the King and the church authorities wanted to believe that they had discovered the saints' remains – thereby giving substance to what, until then, had been mere hearsay – the somewhat fortuitous evidence was deemed sufficient.

King René's wholesale excavations wrecked the original chapel. But, on his orders, the crypt was dug out and cleared, the nave extended by two further spans and, above the altar, a high chapel was constructed to house the holy relics. The church was altered in minor ways during the centuries that followed, including a comparatively recent extension to the campanile which artists such as Bonaventure Laurens and Ivan Pranishnikoff sketched in 1852 and again in the 1880s, showing only two of its present four supporting arches.

The fortifications which give the church its distinctive character have been described by many travellers and students of military architecture. They were carefully examined by T. E. Lawrence (whose important thesis, *Crusader Castles*, was published in 1936) when he visited Les Saintes-Maries with Augustus John. Lawrence demonstrated to Augustus John how the church's walls had been designed to repel invaders at a period when the building and its surroundings were inundated by the sea. Heavy stones which were dropped from the battlements rebounded horizontally from the splayed footing and wrought havoc on enemy vessels. This simple device produced similar results, and was every bit as effective as the medieval war-engines – great catapults like the scorpion and the ballista which were the forerunners of modern field-guns and rocket-launchers.

Another of Augustus John's friends, Roy Campbell, took a delight in pointing out the associations between the church's Christian foundations and the site of an earlier Mithraic temple which had not been exposed when King René excavated the crypt. Campbell himself saw the temple uncovered and he believed that the crypt-site might have been older than those of Saint Peter and Saint Clement in Rome. There was no doubt that it had been the site of a pagan altar. Campbell found no reason to discredit the church's links with Cybèle, the Anatolian mother-goddess worshipped by the Greeks, or Diana the Huntress, goddess of the moon. Nor indeed with Mithras, the Persian sun-god, whose connection with bull-worship in the Camargue had a particular significance – especially for Folco de Baroncelli-Javon who tried but failed to stage a Mithraic ceremony at the church over a bull's carcass. Campbell neither sought to discredit the many 'beautiful legends which have since been woven round the doings of the saints of the Rhône', the Holy Marys. After all, he wrote somewhat ingenuously: 'I have also seen the Holy Shroud at Turin.'

In the nave of the church, votive tablets and thanks-offerings attribute innumerable miraculous cures to the Marys, and describe many catastrophes averted by their intercession. Some of these miracles I found again, illustrated by a nineteenth-century coloured lithograph in the Baroncelli Museum nearby. On the feast day of Saint Mary-Salomé, in October 1591, a child fell from a height of almost 14 metres and was miraculously saved; in 1596, an outburst of rioting at Arles was suppressed thanks to the saints' intervention; while on 25 May 1871, the feast of Saint Mary-Jacobé, a crippled woman from Mezé, near Montpellier, recovered the use of her wasted limbs. According to the lithograph, the very existence of Les Saintes-Maries was due to the saints who caused a spring of clear fresh water to appear at the site where the village now stands.

The building-up of Les Saintes-Maries since the last war has left the church rather hemmed in; even so, it is possible to get a fairly complete view of it from the forecourt, where girls and young men in Provençal costumes dance a *farandole* after the spring and autumn pilgrimages. The tower dominates the village's skyline and it can be seen on a clear day from as far away as 10 kilometres.

The church has been painted and photographed countless times over by visiting artists and tourists and, over the years, I suppose several million postcards featuring the church have been sold to the holidaymakers, 200,000 of whom, I am told, pass through Les Saintes-Maries every season between April and September. The artists who have worked here over the past 150 years, have left their mark – Bonaventure Laurens, Pranishnikoff, Hermann-Paul, Lelée and Brayer among them. One I met recently, Nicolas Barrera, a Russian emigré, has come to paint at Les Saintes-Maries for six months every year since the early 1960s. He never seems to tire of painting the village and its church from his *cabane* which faces east across the Etang des Launes; and he has faithfully represented this scene in all kinds of weather, at every season of the year.

At the suggestion of Madame Barrera, to whom I had been

introduced some time before by Michel Gay, I called on her husband one morning on the way to Le Simbèu. I found the artist working outside their *cabane* which stood at the water's edge, at the end of a muddy track by the village monument – the famous emblem made of crossed tridents, a heart and an anchor which symbolize Faith, Love and Hope. Two elderly *gardians* were mending a wooden fence by the gate and there were some horses grazing by a little pond, fringed with pale yellow reeds.

I waited for a few moments until Barrera got up from his chair and stood back to inspect the picture. He greeted me and waved me over. Of middle height, stocky, sunburned with a lined face and piercing blue eyes, Barrera was perhaps seventy years of age, dressed in olive corduroys, a short white smock like the kind worn by dentists and a purple woollen bonnet like a Cossack's hat. He asked me to wait while he added a few strokes of paint to the oil-sketch he was making of the lagoon and then we went into the *cabane* where there were dozens of canvasses stacked round the walls and others he had recently completed hanging up to dry. I saw many views of Les Saintes-Maries and the church – some painted in bright sunlight, others which showed the church-tower sunlit against a stormy sky of dark-blue. Again and again he had painted the lagoon with egrets and the white Camargue horses in the foreground and he appeared very drawn by the effect of the white birds and horses, brightly-lit, dramatized and contrasting with the shadowy water of the Launes and the landscapes of dark marsh-samphire.

Michel Gay had told me: 'Monsieur Barrera is a romantic, a painter of the old Leningrad School.' Romantic he was certainly, and, like Ivan Pranishnikoff, he had brought the Russian spirit to these atmospheric portrayals of Camargue scenes which he painted rapidly and vigorously in a mood of intense excitement which his canvasses reflected. He didn't smoke, but offered me a glass of whisky instead which, I suspect to his disappointment, I refused.

Monsieur Barrera talked as energetically as he painted, his blue eyes glinting and lively, in a husky voice which matched his powerful build and Cossack character. 'You say that you're interested in the Camargue's artists,' he said. 'Well, why shouldn't you be? *Pourquoi pas?* Quite good, some of them, I dare say. It all depends what you like. I can't tell you much about Pranishnikoff or Yves Brayer. The details of their lives you can get from books – if you think such things matter, that is – but, of course, you need to look at their paintings. Reading is all very well, but the pictures tell the real story. The same goes for musicians. Painting and writing are entirely different, of course.'

He made a dismissive gesture, as though waving someone goodbye, and went on: 'There's really a tremendous lot of rubbish talked about art these days. The loudest talkers are usually people who have never laid hands on a paintbrush or a pencil in their lives. I've no patience with that sort! To be more exact, I hardly give them a second's thought! If you were to ask me which of the great masters I admire most, I'd say straight away Turner and Velasquez – no question about that. And I also admire Constable and Goya.'

I interjected: 'What about the French artists?'

Barrera sucked his teeth and pondered: 'Off the cuff, d'you know, I can't think of any. . . . None I revere as I revere Velasquez. . . . One or two Impressionists, perhaps? That's possible, eh? . . . The modern crowd are a different story. What do you think of Dyf, for instance?' (Marcel Dyf 1899–1985, a Parisian artist, was best known for his landscapes of Brittany and Provence. His sun-filled canvasses were, to my mind, *recherché* though easy on the eye. I could never warm to Dyf's chocolate-box portraits of his model, Claudine, a girl with enormous eyes and an elongated neck like a gazelle. Michel Gay, who knew Claudine, told me that these features had not been exaggerated.)

Barrera continued: 'Personally I can't see why people make such a fuss over Dyf.' He crooked a finger and thumb, imitating a duck's bill: 'To me, Dyf is like that – a very minor artist. Actually, none of this interests me in the slightest. I paint in my own way, just as it suits me. I don't give a damn what anybody says about my work.'

In this mood, Monsieur Barrera reminded me of the painter, Jean Hugo, who I met shortly before his death in 1984. A grandson of Victor Hugo, he had known many of the Surrealists including Dali and as a young man he had worked closely with Jean Cocteau. His autobiography, *Avant d'oublier*, had been praised by the critics but, I was told, obliged everyone to consult a dictionary! We met at the artist's house in Lunel, northwest of Les Saintes-Maries, one dark stormy night and I remember the wind and rain lashing the trees round the *mas* and the firelight's wild reflection in the painter's eyes. For some reason, I asked Hugo what he thought of Gauguin, to which he replied vaguely, 'Oh indeed, a fine painter. But I can't say he interests me a lot.'

And so it was with Nicolai Barrera.

'A word of encouragement is agreeable now and then,' said Barrera, 'but as for the critics – as far as I'm concerned they can rant and rave to their heart's content. Look outside: what tranquillity! What beauty!'

He shrugged: 'As for making money – as long as we get by, who cares? My wife's an artist, too. She feels the same as I do. My son lives in Paris and he's in the computer business. He's probably worth 6 million francs by now. Well, I say good luck to him: that's fine by me. But I'm happy to go on painting. All the wealth I could desire, I have here. Every day the weather is different; the light is different; and the view of the village and the church. Every day brings something new. And that keeps me on my toes.'

20

Gipsies and Pilgrims

It is almost always the May pilgrimage at Les Saintes-Maries which writers choose to describe. This is mainly because of the colourful atmosphere lent by the thousands of gipsies, the hordes of visitors and the fact that spring is in the air. Amy Oakley portrayed this scene in 1936: 'Roguish young Romanies, in gay fringed shawls and scarlet dresses . . . buxom mothers, babes at ample breasts, scraggy grandmas eager to tell fortunes. Caravans were drawn up between the inn and the Mediterranean shore. Tawny, lustrous-eyed men tossed hay to horses or fed the cocks which were to wake us before the dawn. . . . The wind was blowing from the sea. . . . Crowds were everywhere – on the beach, jamming the narrow cobbled streets. Humanity choked the portals of the church; ant-like forms moved upon its parapetted roof. The statue of Mireille . . . was in the midst of a mundane hurly-burly of swinging boats and carrousels.'

By 1961, when Michel-Droit wrote *La Camargue*, the gipsies' horse-drawn *roulottes* had been largely replaced by motorized caravans and trailers pulled by battered, gaudily-painted sedans which, together with their carts and waggons usurped every scrap of space in the village squares, even the narrowest side-streets. At night, for a week or more, the air of

Les Saintes-Maries was filled with the strong spiced odours of the nomads' cooking and the plangent melodies on a score of gipsy guitars.

For centuries the arrival of the gipsies in the Rhôneland was dreaded by the inhabitants of Arles who locked their wives and daughters indoors and barricaded their houses. Nowadays, while the people's reaction is less extreme, the gipsies are at best tolerated and viewed with suspicion. At Les Saintes-Maries, the gipsy women and girls are apt to make themselves a nuisance, foisting their trinkets and charms on passers-by and pestering them for money in exchange for tiny metal badges of Saint Sara. Their movements are graceful and rapid; their darting black eyes miss nothing.

Once, years ago, I remember being accosted by a haggard Romany woman and her daughters in the place Mireille. Rigged in fluttering shawls and multi-coloured flowing cotton skirts, their approach was less aggressive than usual and for a while we talked without any mention of money, or haggling over their wares. I asked the older woman where they lived – actually meaning, where had they made camp? For I knew that there was a big encampment of gipsies near the cemetery on the Arles' road. The woman thrust aside a lock of raven hair: 'We have no home, *monsieur*. We are travellers – sons of the wind.' Her gaze seemed to be filled with inexpressible pathos. Meanwhile her daughters fidgetted, scrutinizing every item of my clothing. At last the woman's mendicant nature could be restrained no more. She begged outright for some money. I handed her a few francs. She glanced at the coins with a muttered, '*Zut!*' and immediately pressed me for more: '*quinze . . . vingt . . . trente!*' She clutched my arm: 'Understand, *monsieur*, the money isn't for us, it is for Saint Sara!' But when I tugged my coat away and replied, 'Take this for yourselves and, if you wish, save a few *centimes* for a candle,' she accepted the offering with an air of weary resignation. At that moment two *gendarmes* appeared in the square and the gipsies melted away.

Another encounter I once had with two drunken Romany youths near the cemetery gates, threatened to turn violent. I was

alone on the deserted road and had stopped to take a photograph, when the gipsies came roaring up in a rusty pink saloon
and braked hard, leaving long skid-marks on the gravel
forecourt. The driver yelled at me through the open window:
'Hand over ten francs! That's our land you're photographing!'
But again, the situation was saved: this time by a farm-truck
which I saw approaching from the distance. I pointed to the
truck and said: 'Let's stop these people and ask them who owns
the land?' At which the gipsy driver crashed his old car into gear,
drove it round in a circle showering me with gravel and,
mouthing some quite unprintable obscenities, sped away
towards Les Saintes-Maries.

Later the same day, I heard that the same youths had started a
fight in one of the village bars and, when the police arrested
them, they were found to be carrying flick-knives. This sort of
behaviour did the gipsies no good; but, I believe, on the whole it
was exceptional.

The Romanies are one of three distinct gipsy types who make
the annual pilgrimage to Les Saintes-Maries; the other two being
the Gitans and the Manouches. The dress of the Romany
women is easily recognized. The married women wear a silk
scarf tied round their head; and the better-off have necklaces
made of gold coins. Many Romany women are fortune-tellers,
while the men sometimes work as boiler-makers or gilders,
living on the industrialized outskirts of Lyon, Lille and Paris.
The Romany language, which George Borrow described in
Romano Lavo-Lil, derives from Sanskrit; and the Romanies
guard their language, legends and traditions with what one
might call a 'Mistralian' fervour.

The Manouches, like their cousins the Sinti, sport distinctive
black moustaches and goatee beards, but are usually harder to
identify than the others. The Manouches live in caravans and
make a living as packmen, scrap-metal dealers and, in some
instances like Mireille's lover, Vincent, as basket-weavers. The
Manouches and the Sinti love music and many have formed
tzigane orchestras or like the Manouche guitarist, Django
Rheinhardt, won fame as solo-instrumentalists or singers.

The flamenco guitarist, Manitas de Plata, is of Gitan origin; for this group has spread widely throughout Spain, from Catalonia to Andalusia, as well as the Midi in France. The Gitans are swarthy and speak a dialect, *le kalo*, which tragically seems fated to vanish. These gipsies are most closely identified with 'Black Sara' whose image they worship in secret at the church of Les Saintes-Maries. And there would seem to be an obvious connection between the Gitan tongue, *le kalo*, and the suffix, *le kâli* which is frequently attached to Sara's name. Of all the gipsy groups, the Gitans are by far the most numerous. At the May pilgrimage they appear in their thousands and, for this reason, all the gipsies seen by tourists between Arles and the Camargue tend to be carelessly labelled 'Gitans', which of course is incorrect.

In 1910 Baroncelli published *Les Bohémiens*, a sympathetic portrait of Les Saintes-Maries' gipsies, in a limited edition of 300 copies printed on *chinois* and *vélin*. He took up the travellers' cause, fought the government to preserve their traditional camping grounds and immersed himself in their history. The gipsies, he discovered, hailed from all corners of the globe: from the Hungarian steppes, Spain and the Basque country; from Yugoslavia, Greece and Turkey. Baroncelli-Javon believed that the gipsies shared a common ancestry with North American Indians and the Incas of Peru. His 'Bohemian genealogy' linked groups found in the Western Pyrenees, Egypt and India. The nomadic, tawny-featured race, like the Sioux warriors of North and South Dakota, were horsemen and, as such, 'the first occupants' of the Earth. The Marquis carried his theories still further and identified the gipsies with the ancient Mithraic cult which also embraced his beloved Ligurian black bulls. This eccentric, though sincere philosophy formed the basis of another shorter work, *L'Ame rouge*, or 'The Red Soul'.

Nobody reads *L'Ame rouge* today. And I should imagine the young Gitans who haunt Les Saintes-Maries' streets today are as familiar with the writings of Folco de Baroncelli-Javon as the Tziganes of Spain might be with George Borrow.

Baroncelli-Javon had wondered whether, like the American Indians and the Basques with their unique language, some Gitans outlived the cataclysm in which Atlantis perished. Writing in July 1922, the *gardian* André Viallés again posed this vexing question and noted how Baroncelli had been surprised by customs which Gitans and Red Indians shared, 'such as the simple action of inspecting the teeth of a horse'. Viallés continued: '[Baroncelli] noticed curious answers to the question, "Whence did your people come?" "From where the sun rises," says the Indian. "From the sunset land," say the Gitanos. These speculations are strengthened by sayings of Gitanos who take part in the pilgrimage to "Li Santo". A snowy-bearded patriarch said: "We are to the human race what the Camargue horse is to his – the sole survivors of a vanished world." '

The October pilgrimage is followed by another ceremony, the Feast of Revelation held on 2 December, which marks the discovery of the saints' relics by King René's excavating party in 1448.

On a previous visit to Les Saintes-Maries that autumn, I attended the Feast of Saint Mary-Salomé, a much quieter affair than the May pilgrimage, which is celebrated mainly by the Saintins themselves and members of the Nacioun Gardiano.

Again, I arrived at the village on a bright, dry day with the *mistral* blowing hard across the *sansouires*, the sea-air cold and luminous. At the side door of the church, a small crowd gathered – filtering inside in ones and twos, mingling rather uncomfortably with the congregation which by 10 am had packed the nave to overflowing. I joined the queue, which thrust its way forward, threading like a wavy current of water among the worshippers who stood shoulder to shoulder in the aisles and the open area behind the pews. The people seemed cheerfully indifferent to the mêlée as ribs and elbows collided, shins were barked and toes trampled in the good-humoured confusion of rustling arms and legs. Whispered greetings and excuses, laughter and pained exclamations, counterpointed the priests' gutteral sing-song relayed over the crackling loudspeakers. All round me, the people shivered in a cold draught from the side door which a steady stream of latecomers and others who chose not to stay the course opened and closed continually throughout the service.

The electric lights mounted high up on the walls of the nave bathed the church's interior in a soft amber glow. The altar candles shone like points of starlight in the sea-green gloom shed by the apse's stained-glass windows; while at the back of the nave, a score of camera-flashlights burst from the shadows at intervals, like sheets of wildfire.

I felt deeply moved by the mass which the priests delivered in French and Latin, and by the harsh, belling intonation of the hymns. Most of all, I was impressed by the words of a pilgrim chant which rose and fell on a rich, sonorous tide of organ-music: '*Salut, salut, O Saintes Maries, Salut, salut, O Saintes Maries.*'

From time to time, a muffled rhythm of echoes rippled through the church in a long drawn out sequence, as the seated congregation nearest the altar rose to their feet, knelt to pray and afterwards resumed their places, in not quite perfect unison.

Behind the altar, in a semi-circle, the *gardians* and *manadiers* sat with their wives and daughters: the men in their black velvet jackets, white or dark-blue trousers piped with black and black

cravats and string-ties; the women and girls resplendent in their Arlésien finery with coloured ribbons in their hair.

The morning mass, which was dedicated to Saint Mary-Salomé, included eight hymns – each with a good many verses – and several lengthy invocations. At last the order was given for the church doors to be opened and the saints' effigies in their little boat, placed on a litter draped with blue cloth to represent the sea, were carried in slow procession out into the bitterly cold, sunlit forecourt where they were immediately surrounded by cheering onlookers and the congregation following hard on the heels of the white-robed priests, *gardians* and Arlésiennes.

The procession made its way from the church in a great clockwise arc, through the windswept dusty streets towards the shore. The saints' litter was escorted by four *gardians*, mounted on white Camargue horses, each man shouldering a long trident. One of the *gardians* smiled down at me and remarked that the gusts of wind were apt to make the horses nervous. '*Faites attention, monsieur!*' he warned, as someone jostled his pony's flanks. '*Faites attention, il vous lancera une ruade!*' ('Watch out! Or he'll kick you.')

Away from the protection of the houses, on the exposed beach, the *mistral* blew with terrific force, billowing the saints' little white gowns and streaming the black hooded-cloaks of the Arlésiennes, who appeared like a coven of beautiful witches flying low across the sand. The bishop and the priests stood in a blue-painted rowing-boat drawn up just above the tide-mark, where the saints' carrying-party, tousle-haired villagers in rough fisherman's jerseys, assembled; while the *gardians*, led by their captain, André Dupuis, holding aloft the Nacioun Gardiano's gold and crimson banner, urged their horses out, knee-deep, into the surf. The horsemen turned to face the shore, forming a wide crescent: the white horses, with their long white manes and tails roughened by the wind, the white-capped breakers splashing their legs and the glaring white burnished sky and the glittering sea, surrounding the riders in an aura of dazzling, blinding light. From the boat, over a portable microphone, the bishop blessed the sea, the land and the pilgrims – his words almost completely drowned by the wind and the waves crashing at the sea-wall in explosions of ragged foam.

Many of the crowd, myself included, had the waves lapping round our ankles and later I saw numbers of Arlésiennes whose long skirts had been spattered with wet sand and hung, bedraggled, stained and muddy well above the hem. Apart from the visitors with video-cameras and SLRs, in their bright wind-proof jackets, caps and head-scarves, the scene was as dramatic and colourful as Léopold Lelée's fine watercolour of a May pilgrimage, painted about seventy-five years ago, which I had seen at the Palais du Roure. As usual, Lelée used the opportunity to portray Arlésiennes of all ages, in varying dress-styles of the period. The result was a charming set-piece, lit by a bright southern sun, with the tiny figures of the saints looming unnaturally large at its centre. But in every other respect Lelée's picture was so vivid and so real, that, looking at it, you could almost hear the blurred rush of the wind, the plashing waves and the gulls' plaintive crying.

21

Kingdom of the Bull

Madame Bedot rightly prided herself in the *petit déjeuner* she served at 8 o'clock sharp every morning in the Abrivado's cheerful breakfast-room. She made excellent coffee; and the rolls and *croissants* were produced from the oven, piping hot, moist and delicious with plenty of fresh butter and jam.

Monsieur Bedot always ate his breakfast with the guests, sitting a little apart at a table in the corner, his tweed cap pulled down so that it almost rested on his thick spectacles, engrossed in the morning paper. It wasn't only Bedot's weatherbeaten features or his infectious, crooked grin which made his resemblance to Bernard Miles so extraordinary. The pitch of his voice – even his mannerisms – made the likeness uncannily perfect. It occurred to me that Monsieur Bedot might have done for the *croissant* what Bernard Miles did for Mackeson's stout. When he wished me *bon appétit* from across the room, touching his cap and jerking a finger at the steaming contents of my bread-basket, I half-expected him to shake his head in an expression of gnarled country wisdom and mutter: 'They looks good! They tastes good! And, by golly, they does you good!'

Sometimes Monsieur Bedot would read to me aloud a few paragraphs from the newspaper – a report of the Course Camarguaise held in a nearby village, perhaps, or the results of a local *boules* tournament. One morning, when we had the breakfast-room to ourselves, Monsieur Bedot volunteered to teach me the principles of *boules*.

He tossed aside his paper and came and stood by my table.

'Boules,' said Monsieur Bedot, 'is played in two different styles which are called *pétanques* and *longuistes*. The *pétanque* style consists of standing still and throwing your *boule* at the mark, the *bouchon*, from a distance of 6 to 9 metres. For *longuistes*, you take a run at it, three long strides, and you throw the *boule* between 15 and 21 metres. Anything less than 15 metres, we count a bad throw, but a little over 21 metres is still all right. You throw the *boule* palm-downwards. That's not for back-spin. It's just a good aiming technique. If your *boule* hits the marker and comes to a rest touching it, this is the best possible result. If your opponent's *boule* lands further away from the marker than yours, obviously you win the round. We play the best of thirteen rounds. Two players use three *boules* each. When there are four or six players, each man uses two *boules*. It's just a case of keeping the number of *boules* on the ground to a sensible figure, otherwise we'd lose count.'

The solid metal *boule* is surprisingly heavy – 110 grammes – and a whole day at *longuistes* requires considerable stamina. The *boule* needs to be tough and durable, since it takes a lot of punishment over the season and Monsieur Bedot added laughingly that for the players it was the same. He said: '*Boules* is a serious affair and it is also time-consuming. All the villages have tournaments throughout the summer months. I usually play three or four times a week. Our wives get pretty fed up with us, but every now and then we pacify them by giving them a good lunch!'

Begging my pardon, Monsieur Bedot reached for my bread-basket from which he selected a crusty roll. Placing the roll and a sugar-lump from my saucer side by side on the tablecloth he carefully explained the scoring method, shifting the roll and the sugar-lump and then my half-eaten *croissant* which he removed delicately from my plate, to show the results of a good and a bad throw. And then, grasping my untouched portion of *baguette*, he charged up and down the room between the tables in a vigorous demonstration of *longuistes* and its all-important throwing technique. He repeated this performance several times and might have continued longer, but for the arrival of a German couple who gaped in blank astonishment at Monsieur Bedot who had frozen momentarily in the classic pose of an Olympic discus-thrower to which his tweed cap added an air of jaunty *éclat*. In a moment he had regained his composure and, beaming at the speechless Germans, he deposited the *baguette* and the crusty roll in my bread-basket, wished me a hearty *bon appétit* and disappeared into the kitchen.

At Arles and Aigues-Mortes, when I watched *boules* being played by several groups of men at the same time, I had often wondered how each player managed to keep track of which *boule* belonged to himself or his opponents. From a distance the *boules* looked identical. But Monsieur Bedot later explained that some of them were of slightly different colours to the usual pewter or silver-grey, and in any case each player's *boules* were numbered or, as he said, 'just like the *taureaux*', they had a special marking which identified them and their owner.

In the Camargue it was often remarked that *boules*, bulls and the Course were the Trinity. Among the villagers at Les Saintes-Maries, as elsewhere, the fascination for *boules* and *taureaux* went hand in hand. On the delta's *manades*, I found that horses and bulls were the *gardians'* ruling passion.

At Le Simbèu, over the years I had learned a great deal about the *manade* life from Henri Aubanel, who wrote in his first book published more than thirty years ago: '*Je suis manadier! Cri de joie, d'amour, de contentement, d'accomplissement! Je suis manadier de taureaux sauvages.*' Monsieur Aubanel's exclamation of joy, love, contentment and accomplishment – his passion for the wild black bulls of the Camargue – expressed the *manadier's* sentiments completely and with a simplicity which is typical of them all. Almost the first thing Monsieur Aubanel said when we met was: '*L'élévage de taureaux, c'est ma passion!*' Bull-rearing, I soon discovered, was more than a mere fascination – it was Aubanel's whole *raison d'être*.

It was an uncertain way of life, fraught with continual risk and, on some occasions, danger. The bulls were hardy and yet susceptible to hazards and infections, such as the winter snow and ice and cattle-disease, which the *manadiers* like Henri Aubanel dreaded. The German occupation decimated the bulls: in February 1944, the year when Le Simbèu was destroyed, Monsieur Aubanel's herd numbered 178 beasts. By 1945, it had been reduced to thirty-seven, with a mere handful of calves.

In *La Camargue*, Aubanel's friend, Michel-Droit, recounted a terrible tragedy, still spoken of to this day, when in the winter of 1929 no fewer than seventy bulls and cows belonging to Fernand Granon died of hunger, thirst and cold, trapped on a frozen island near the Bois des Rièges in the Vaccarès lake, from which it had proved impossible to rescue them.

Over the 1951–2 winter, an epidemic of *fièvre aphteuse*, foot-and-mouth disease, killed forty-six of the Aubanel herd in the space of two months. This was the plague whose name the *manadiers* dared not mention among themselves: an unforgettable event which Henri Aubanel described in his second book, *Camarguaises: un gardian en hiver*. The high mortality rate caused by this epidemic, it appears, caught the *manade* unprepared, for, as Aubanel wrote, 'as a rule, the fever is less dangerous to animals, like those of the Camargue, accustomed to spend their lives in the open at liberty'.

Over the centuries, the number of the *manades* has fluctuated considerably. Writing almost 450 years ago, in 1551, a landowner from Arles, Pierre de Quiqueran de Beaujeu, noted in his important chronicle, *Provence Louée*, that there were 16,000 bulls roaming the Camargue – a large number, he observed wryly, which equated with their fierce temper – and some 4,000 horses, all of them in a wild or semi-wild state. Thousands of bulls were slaughtered by the German troops in the Second World War for food and 'sport', which over three years reduced the bulls' numbers to an all-time low; but by 1961 they had increased to a healthy 6,000 and a decade later this figure had nearly doubled, proof of the beasts' immense resilience and a tribute to the *manadiers*' and their herdsmen's care. I have no precise figure for the horses: the Camargue strain, however, continues to flourish and there are probably nowadays about 1,000 of them scattered throughout the delta, including the *manades* further west in the Petite Camargue.

The Camargue *manades* are something like an equivalent of the Spanish bull-farms, the *cortijos* and the word *manade* itself corresponds to the Spanish *manada* which in Spanish-speaking countries – for example, Argentina – is used to describe the herds of cattle or broken and unbroken horses on the *estancias*. Just as the roads dividing the pampas' vast acreages have been fenced by their proprietors, so, too, on a much smaller scale has the Camargue. The famous *manadier*, Alphonse Jalabert, now aged ninety-two, told me: 'Before 1900 when I was born, there were very few *manades* and lots of open ground. Since then, the situation has been reversed and the Camargue has been split up into much smaller units. In 1925, the manades began to be fenced off. Until then, you could ride all day and never see so much as a strand of wire. You might say that the wire-fences were a sign of the times and the beginning of the Camargue as we know it today.'

Stendhal, in 1838, compared the Camargue to Holland and described it as an equilateral triangle, each side 7 leagues (about 13 kilometres) long. In 1961, Michel-Droit estimated 'the real Camargue' covered an area of some 289 square miles in old measurement, with Arles at its apex and the triangle completed by the Mediterranean shore between the mouths of the Greater and Lesser Rhône. Michel-Droit gave the bull-pastures including the *sansouires* – the marshes which most people associate with the delta – as 139 square miles; and marshland and lagoons comprising 73 square miles – 15 square miles of smaller *étangs* and 34 square miles for the largest single lake the Etang de Vaccarès. This is what is known as the Ile de la Camargue. But the Petite Camargue to the west and the Grand Plan du Bourg to the east which lies between the Greater Rhône and the Crau must also be considered and these cover 193 and 77 square miles respectively.

A detailed map of the *manades*, drawn by Gérard Gadiot in

1962, listed over 100: an English journalist, Carol Dix, stated in 1975 that in the Petite Camargue, the Crau and the Greater Camargue at her time of writing, there were 'fifty-five *manades* and, it is estimated, twelve thousand bulls'. But the official list of the *Manades de Taureaux Camargues*, printed in the August 1991 issue of the *Camargue Magazine* at Nîmes, includes ninety-four – a figure which suggests that, instead of showing a marked decrease which might have been expected due to industrial and agricultural redevelopment which continues to threaten the Camargue's wetlands, the number of *manades* over the past thirty years has remained fairly stable.

Again and again, in *Je suis manadier*, Henri Aubanel has spoken of his love for the ranching life and, above all, the bulls – '*mes bêtes . . . mes grandes amies*' – among which he hopes to end his days. Monsieur Aubanel, during our many conversations, told me, often overcome by emotion, how much he owed his father-in-law, the Marquis. And indeed, as Michel-Droit has written: 'There is a little of Baroncelli in all true Camargue *manadiers*. and in every *genuine* gardian.' Here, I think, Michel-Droit meant something more than the inspiring example set by Baroncelli whose strenuous efforts to improve and purify his blood-stock won the Camarguais' respect. In fact I have heard it stated on good authority that, long before Folco de Baroncelli established himself at Les Saintes-Maries in the last decade of the nineteenth century, the pure-blood Camargue bull was already a thing of the past and had been so for about fifty years. In the very year Folco was born, 1869, a renowned *manadier* from the Mas de la Beluge, in the Eastern Camargue, Joseph Yonnet, had introduced seven Spanish cows which founded a Spanish-Camargue cross-strain of *toros de combat* bred for the *corrida*. Michel-Droit instead referred to Baroncelli's stalwart character: 'Faith, passion, an uncompromising fidelity to the country and its traditions and a freshness of spirit. . . .' Many now believe that Baroncelli's influence on the *gardian*'s world had been 'moral' and 'spiritual' and its chief benefits were a renewed sense of community pride and purpose, besides practical dedication to their craft. As Michel-Droit remarked so eloquently: 'To think of the *manadier* as a simple stock-breeder, and the *gardian* as a commonplace cowherd would . . . be a serious mistake. Their craft, in truth, contains a particle of priesthood, and the way in which they practise this, a breath of poetry, which the Marquis knew how to raise to the highest degree'.

The *manadier's* work, Roy Campbell wrote in *Taurine Provence*, is the absolute antithesis of the modern world (this was 1932) in which 'the human being has no self left apart from his or her mere utility as a working machine. . . . The only thing in modern life that can and will beat this tendency is the life of equestrians and cattlemen.' Campbell's words echoed Mistral's which half-a-century earlier had spurned the looming shadow of industrialization across the Rhôneland; and Richard Aldington's attacks on the evils of 'machine-worship' in Mistral's biography. In the Camargue of today, their relevance has never been greater and they underline the vital importance to the Camargue's ecosystem, as well as its traditions, of the *manades'* continued existence in viable terms. You can almost hear the shriek of the pen-nib on the page, as Campbell burst out – again in *Taurine Provence*: 'The reasons for this are obvious, because the cattleman is not like the turf-hoeing peasant or the city worker. His work comes in sharp, momentary feats of skill. The rest of the time he can be thinking, playing his guitar, creating fine poetry or making love. . . . The eyesight of the cattleman is the finest in the world. . . . It is vision that is the sense most closely associated with poetry, art and culture of any kind, the most far-ranging and perfect of all our senses.'

On the *manades* which comprise large areas of *sansouires* and salt-water lagoons, where the land is unsuitable for any other form of agriculture other than grazing, the bulls require several hectares per beast for adequate sustenance; whereas on the richer pastures of La Crau and around Le Cailar, the ratio of bulls to grazing is, by comparison, far more modest. I have been given sometimes widely differing estimates for the actual area of grazing needed by the bull living in the marshes: 'between 1 and 2 hectares', one *manadier* told me; while another, equally experienced man was convinced that the area might be as great as 4 hectares. This, in turn, would suggest that an average herd of, say 100 *taureaux* – bulls, cows and weaned calves of perhaps two or three years old, *doublens* and *ternens* – requires *sansouires* pasture covering anything from about 100–400 hectares, about the equivalent in Britain of a 250–1,000 acre farm.

As long as these *manades* survive, so does the marshland and all the rich diversity of wildlife it contains. Marcel Mailhan, the President of the Camargue Bull-Breeders' Association (Eléveurs de Taureaux de Camargue) observed: 'The *manadiers* don't carry on with this precarious life simply in order to make money. For many of us, the financial returns are poor – some of the *manades* are hard pressed to break even. For us *manadiers*, the real riches are liberty, the excitement of our vocation, the fascination for the bulls and horses and our intense love for the land.' By maintaing their breeding herds of bulls and the traditions such as the Course Camarguaise and *gardian* festivals which go with them, the *manadiers* play an essential, indeed, absolutely critical role in preserving the birds, animals, insects and flora of these magnificent wetlands – the greatest in Western Europe and part of a wetlands-chain which extends from Senegal to Scandinavia.

The *manades'* marshlands are the kingdom of the bull and they present the onlooker with an immense panorama which, seen from the depths of the Camargue may appear as vast as the plains of Patagonia. Often it is these huge spaces of marsh and sky, like the gaucho's *pája y cielo* – the wilderness of grass and sky – which linger in the mind. And yet the microcosm of Camargue life must never be forgotten: tiny creatures and things whose effect on the region is quite disproportionate to their size, but whose collective influence may be very significant. The mosquito, for example, which had infected the Camarguais with malaria in Daudet's time, and whose bites I have frequently cursed as I stood in the hot sun drawing a troop of horses at the reed-beds by a lagoon, is a staple food of several species of birds. If mosquitoes were eradicated completely, these birds would almost certainly leave the Camargue for good. This, in turn, would produce long-term results which might be ultimately

detrimental to other species. Even the white coats of the mature
Camargue horses, it is now belived, were evolved partly as a
protection against biting insects and parasites. The horses' long
constantly switching tails are useful as well as beautiful; and the
animals often stand head to tail in the summer, flicking away
mosquitoes and horseflies while they forage for grass, while the
dark brown or grey foals rely for protection on their thick,
woolly hair. Unlike the Argentine's *estancieros*, the Camargue
manadiers never dock their horses' tails: 'After all,' as one of the
gardians remarked, 'it would be like cutting off a man's arm.'

Another example of the miniature are the tiny red shrimps or
'sea-monkeys' which flamingoes feed upon and which give the
birds their reddish-pink colour. In zoos, flamingoes are fed with
carrots for the same purpose; and without the 'sea-monkeys' the
flamant-rose of the Camargue, presumably, would be *rose* no
longer!

More sinister, in the marshes where wildfowling formerly
helped to eke out the *gardians*' living, but in modern times has
become big business attracting sportsmen in their thousands to
shoot ducks and geese, the huge quantities of lead pellets falling
into the lagoons are ingested by ducks; and these wipe out large
numbers of birds as effectively as a blast of Number 4 or 5 shot,
straight from a gun-barrel. Of course, the numbers of ducks
killed in flight is much greater. The Camargue's six-month
shooting season is tolerated, not only because shooting is very
popular, but also because the income generated helps to preserve
the marshes (the *manades*, too) from rice-cultivation and other
encroachments which pose a permanent threat to the Camargue.
But the shooters' 'lead-rain' is a hazard to wildlife every bit as
real as the acid-rain which erodes our towns and cities.

Apart from the Course Camarguaise, for which the *manade*'s
most spirited fledging bulls are selected, the most important
ceremony involving the *manadier* and his *gardians* is the branding
of weaned calves, the *ferrade*. It makes an exciting spectacle and
takes place all over the Camargue between early spring and
autumn. The *ferrade* may be a workaday (though never

perfunctory) affair, carried out in private; or, more often, it becomes an occasion for festivity and a lavish luncheon held out of doors, with *pastis* and wine flowing freely. The local village *clubs taurins* often join in; and as well as their members, the *manadier* may invite tourists or paying guests anxious to witness the Camargue's version of this ancient rite whose origins are steeped in Mithraic sun-worship and early Cretan or Minoan culture.

About a dozen *gardians* on horseback gallop into the herd and, steering the beasts with their tridents, drive out a few calves – usually not more than three or four – which career towards the spectators, tensed and expectant, gathered round the fire. The atmosphere grows very lively with the shouts of the *gardians*, the bellowing cattle, the calves' frightened lowing, the drumming hooves and clouds of dust kicked up by bulls and horses rushing by. As they approach the fire, a *gardian* on foot grabs the yearling calf, or *anouble*, by its horns and, sometimes helped by another *gardian* who has dismounted at the run, hurls the calf on its side and together the men rope its thrashing legs tight, while the *manadier* stamps the calf's rump with a heavy-shafted branding-iron pulled red-hot and smoking from the flames. Michel-Droit wrote: 'This is known as the *grasiho*, a vivid word which describes the sizzling flesh and charred hair rising from the scar in an acrid smoke.' Before the calf is released, the *manadier* cuts its ear, or sometimes both ears, in a notched motif which, like the brand-mark, identifies the animal with its owner.

At the Baroncelli Museum im Les Saintes-Maries, I saw the charts of branding-marks drawn by the late Gérard Gadiot, who from 1939 had been the Secretary-Treasurer, Archivist and latterly Secretary of the five-centuries-old Confrérie de Saint-George, the *gardians*' brotherhood. Gadiot's framed charts, drawn in Indian ink, gave fifty-one bull-brands and fifty for Camargue horses. The bull diagrams included the *escoussuros*, the ear-notches, and the colours – like racing-colours – associated with the various *manades*. The shield-marking used by Le Simbèu, for example, took the form of the Baroncelli coat of arms: a classic shield outline divided from top-left to bottom-right by five diagonals. This mark was also used for the Aubanel *rosse*, its Camargue-horse herd. The brand, which a blacksmith worked by hand, was like the one I had seen at the Palais du Roure which had the Marquis' initials burned onto its wooden haft. And the famous blacksmith at Le Cailar, Monsieur Bonfort, was shown in a photograph putting the finishing touches to a Baroncelli shielded brand at his forge. Other brands simply took the form of the *manadier*'s surname – 'R' for Jacques Reynaud, 'F' for Fernand Feraud, for instance – while a few were more imaginative. Cacharel, the *manade* of Denys Colomb de Daunant, had a brand made of the Félibrige's seven-pointed star; the *manade* Fabre-Mailhan's symbol was the cross of Les Saintes-Maries – tridents, an anchor and a heart; while the *manadier* from La Sauvagine, Paul Autheman, was identified by a single resting flamingo.

The sixteenth-century *ferrades* were described by an Arles landowner, Pierre de Quiqueran de Beaujeu, whose family resided at the Grand Mas de Beaujeu and a house in the rue des Arènes, Arles, which later became a convent of nursing-sisters. The *ferrades* followed an already long-established pattern which was similar to that of the present day – except, of course, for the *gardians*' dress, the horses' harness and the tridents. The modern versions of harness and the crescent-shaped iron blade of the trident have altered only slightly, however. For all practical purposes, one might say, hardly at all. But the public *ferrades* of today probably will never again match in size and splendour the great branding ceremonies which Pierre Véran witnessed in 1760 and 1813. When at the latter, Véran 'counted more than five hundred and thirty-two wagons, six hundred horses, one hundred bulls and six thousand people'.

In 1851, in *Pictures of Travel in the South of France*, Alexandre Dumas deplored the brutal treatment of bull-calves by the *gardians* and the *ferrade*'s branding and bloody ear-notching displays which he denounced as obnoxious and degrading butchery performed by hooligans. (These were not Dumas's actual words, but it was, effectively, what he had implied.) The sight of so much blood-letting offended Dumas' refined *bourgeois* sensibilities. I cannot recall whether he was present at a *bistournage* when the three-year-old bulls, or *ternens* – those with enough aggression and fiery temperament to be chosen for the Course – are castrated. This practice, he would have almost certainly condemned. But it had been a *gardian* thrusting his trident-blade into a bull's sensitive nostrils which, in crude though appropriate slang, really got up Dumas' nose.

Many of these apparently coarse practices were modified after Baroncelli's coming. He endowed the *gardian*'s profession with a renewed self-esteem and helped to refine it. It is also fair to state, I think, that Baroncelli raised the *gardian*'s skills and respect for the animals in his charge to a higher plane – an achievement which in a sense paralleled Mistral's revival of the Provençal language.

Living on the Raoux and the Feraud *manades* after the First World War, Roy Campbell learned to use the trident to 'capsize a galloping bull with less danger of breaking its legs than a lazo'. And Campbell was taught to deflect a bull's headlong charge, leaving the beast bloody-nosed but otherwise undamaged, so that he made 'half a ton of animal-projectile ricochet off the trident, like a pebble from the water'.

Almost as spectacular as the *ferrade* and in some ways even more exciting, is the *abrivado* when a party of *gardians* on horseback drive the *cocarde*-bulls through the streets of a town or village to the arena before the Course. The *abrivado* usually takes place in mid-morning. The number of bulls and horsemen varies somewhat, depending on the occasion: Michel-Droit has observed that 'Ten *gardians* are needed to conduct half a dozen bulls in this manner.' Three riders lead the *abrivado* in this instance, with two on either side and three at the rear. In this way the *gardians* strive to keep the bulls together in a bunch and control their speed. The crowds lining the streets, in turn, try to distract the horsemen by shouting and waving and sometimes by letting off fireworks, the object being to make a bull escape from the circle of riders. This is known as the *escapado*, which can lead to accidents but is nevertheless a good-natured test of the *gardians*' prowess and is regarded as part of the entertainment. I have seen as many as sixteen *gardians* at a time, and as few as half a dozen. Occasionally, in the free-for-all which occurs, a bull will break away, or blunder into one of the horsemen in its path. This was how Marie-Caroline Aubanel had been injured; and I have seen some dramatic photographs taken by Michel Naval, which show a bull mounting a *gardian*'s horse, bringing the animal to its knees and throwing its rider, while some of the braver spectators hung onto the bull's tail in an effort to drag it away.

In days gone by, I was told, newly-married girls would rush out and try to touch a bull's testicles as a daring act which, if successfully accomplished, passed on some of the bull's courage and virility to any boy-child they might bear in the future. Of course, this was pure Mithraism, like the habit of men who worshipped Mithras to allow the fresh hot blood from a bull sacrificed at the god's altar to run down over their neck and shoulders and thus become imbued with its strength and other noble virtues.

The *bandido* is like the *abrivado* in reverse, so to speak, and follows the Course Camargue when the bulls are shepherded away from the arena by the *gardians*. Nowadays this is often dispensed with or, on occasions such as the *razeteurs*' ceremony

I described earlier at Tarascon when the *abrivado* had been staged merely to set the scene, the bulls are driven away in lorries.

22

Gods of the Marshes

Although it was but a shadow of its former self, at Le Simbèu the traditions and the essence of the *manade*'s lifestyle so dear to Folco de Baroncelli were still maintained by his son-in-law Henri Aubanel and his daughters. Here I learned something of the Camargue's great bull traditions: the bull's history and characteristics and the history of the Camargue's horses which are the indispensable ally of the *manadier* and his *gardians*.

Much of the information I gathered at various times over the years was imparted by Monsieur Aubanel during the quiet spells in spring and autumn when his work at Le Simbèu, or his duties as the Captain of the Nacioun Gardiano were less demanding. I used to visit the *mas* for lunch, or sometimes I spent an evening there and we had long talks after supper by the light of the oil-lamps when the table had been cleared away.

The midday meal at Le Simbèu, like supper, was a family affair. In days gone by, Henri and Riquette Aubanel would sit together with their backs to the fire, their three daughters and myself arranged two by two at either side of the polished dark walnut table and the *gardians* at the far end, nearest the door. The *gardians* of those days were an old grizzled fellow with watery blue eyes, whose name I forget, and a shy youth named Raymond Bechet. Except when spoken to, they seldom joined in the conversation: even so, the atmosphere was quite informal and the *gardians*, as soon as they finished eating, would push aside their plates and light a cigarette. Permission to smoke was neither sought nor required. Perhaps, save for this minor detail, the sense of *en famille* that existed was very like that of the farm lunches and harvest suppers at the Mas du Juge which Mistral described in *Mes Origines* nearly a century ago.

When I returned to Le Simbèu during my autumn stay at Les Saintes-Maries, I found the same warmth and the same eager hospitality. But alas there was something missing, too. Since Riquette Aubanel's death, the house seemed strangely empty. I missed her little, fluttering outbursts of laughter and her motherly presence, the often repeated anxious asides, as she made certain that I had second helpings of everything, that my chair was sufficiently comfortable, and so on. With quiet pride, Jacqueline told me that a street in Les Saintes-Maries was to be named after her mother the following year, as part of the Jour Baroncellien ceremonies after the pilgrimage in May. She murmured: 'Indeed, our mother was a saint. She was so kind, so full of goodness.' Among Madame Aubanel's many kind acts, I remembered one especially. My stepdaughter had been ill and one evening Madame Aubanel brought her sewing-basket and a lamp and, despite her failing eyesight, embroidered two tiny fragments of cloth, one blue and one red, each with a red cross and stitched them to an offertory-card of the Confrérie des Saintes. She handed me the card, embraced me and said: 'Take this *rélique* for the child. Tell your wife that I remember her in my prayers.'

Jacqueline and Marie-Caroline over lunch, urged their father to tell stories of the *gardian* life of Baroncelli's day; while their sister, Nerte, a genius of the stove, scuttled to and from the kitchen with ashets of succulent lamb, brussels sprouts and roast potatoes, and finally, the *pièce de résistance*, one of her mouth-watering chocolate puddings! Their brother, Pierre, a *manadier* and a professional cameraman, joined us having spent some months in Argentina, filming with the Aubanels' many-talented cousin Denys Colomb de Daunant. Le Simbèu's latest *gardian*

completed the lunch-party: Louis, a twenty-five-year-old *gitan* from Portugal – swarthy, saturnine, with a black moustache and wild, black eyes – who languished near the hearth and between the courses rolled thin, fast-burning cigarettes each of which he consumed, leaning back in his chair, in three or four long, deep inhalations.

Though he appeared to be in good spirits, Henri Aubanel looked pale and tired; but his memory was clear and vivid and his mischievous sense of humour was undiminished. He explained that, owing to ill-health, he had been forced to resign his position as the Nacioun Gardiano's Captain which he had held for many years. I had met Monsieur Aubanel's successor, André Dupuis, at the October pilgrimage several weeks before. Dupuis, cultivated and highly respected, had known Baroncelli-Javon in the late 1930s when 'the Marquis . . . was already very old, a small, wizened man [who] would leave a horse for me tied up at the station at Les Saintes so that I could come down for a weekend, or the holidays, and ride straight out and find him'.

It might have been as a gesture to these vanished times that Henri Aubanel now recited for me, faultlessly and with much emotion, the lines of Joseph D'Arbaud's stirring poem, 'La

Chanson des Tridents' ('The Song of the Tridents'). By the time he reached the sixth and final verse, Monsieur Aubanel's lip had begun to tremble and he appeared quite overcome. He had spoken D'Arbaud's poem in Provençal, as it was originally written. His sonorous words echoed about the airless, shadowed room filled with the more prosaic odours of cooked meat, tobacco and acrid smoke from the blaze of tamarisk-logs. The old gentleman rubbed his eyes and muttered an apology: 'Forgive me,' he said, 'but all this was my life, you know.'

The last words of D'Arbaud's poem rang in my ears as, for a few moments, we sat in silence. I thought of Baroncelli-Javon's taurine hymn, 'Lou Biòu', composed at the Mas de l'Amarée in March 1924, and its famous lines which translated run:

> I am the bull, roving from Asia
> As far as the forests of Liguria,
> Where I have reigned
> Over the Mediterranean peoples
> In joy, in art and in blood

The Marquis' poem not only celebrated the bull, but addressed it in an act of homage. Again and again, in the Camargue I had heard the bull referred to as kingly or god-like. There is no question that Baroncelli-Javon meant his lines, 'Where I have reigned/ Over the Mediterranean peoples' to be taken seriously; and the image of the bull as a god, which dates from the region's earliest civilization by Man, has been repeated endlessly by poets – for example, Geneviève Ribaud whose work, 'Le Taureau', won the Grand Prix de Poésie at the Bull-Festivals in Nîmes, in 1937. In her poem, the supernatural presence of the bull as a god predominated:

> *Animal fabuleux, tu restes notre idole,*
> *Car la race a garde croyance en toi, Taureau.*

(Literally, 'Fabulous creature, you remain our idol/ For the race has kept its belief in you, Bull.') And here, the bull-god is not distanced by the writer who used the informal, much more personal *tu* form rather than *vous* which emphasizes a sense of intimacy and affection, while throughout her poem the bull, 'Taureau', with a capital letter, implies a proper respect and even more than that, a feeling of awe.

Folco de Baroncelli-Javon, probably more than any *manadier* before or since, maintained an unyielding devotion to the bull's Mithraic origins and the cult-practices with which the sun-god Mithras was associated. He believed that the Camargue bulls were descended directly from Bos Primigenius which had migrated to the delta in the Quaternary Period, following the course of the Rhône. At the village of Solutre, near Mâcon on the River Saône west of the Jura Mountains, excavations revealed the skulls of Quaternary bulls with lyre-shaped horns like those of the Camargue species. Skeletons of horses were unearthed close to the bull remains and these suggest that the Camargue bulls and horses of today may have shared the same pastures in antiquity. The *manadiers*, including Henri Aubanel, believed in the common ancestry of their bulls and horses and, indeed, the animals' understanding of one another seemed extraordinary.

Such was Monsieur Aubanel's passion for bulls that, whenever he spoke of them – particularly when he remembered the feats of the *manade*'s great *cocarde*-bulls such as Vovo and Prouvenço – he came very close to tears.

That day, after lunch at Le Simbèu, we talked for several hours about bulls and horses and great *manadiers* and *gardians* of the past. And, from time to time, Monsieur Aubanel who, despite his years and an overflowing well of experiences too numerous to mention, quoted sayings and poems by members of the Nacioun Gardiano which he rendered without hesitation – not merely word-perfect, but also thoughtfully and with touching sensitivity – from memory.

He told me how, as a young *gardian* at L'Amarée, he had been deeply impressed by Baroncelli-Javon's dedication to bull-breeding which the Marquis defined, saying: 'You see, my boy, the races of horse and Camargue bull are exceptional; they bear no resemblance to any other. Strong, vigorous breeds, they were doomed to be forgotten. I rediscovered them at a moment in history when they were about to vanish forever; and I have devoted my life to restoring them to their original type.'

We spoke of our mutual friend, the *manadier* Alphonse Jalabert, to whom I had been introduced at Arles by Madame Dubosquet. When I recalled Jalabert's descriptions of the bull, Bramaïro, a great *dompteur*, or herd-leader, Monsieur Aubanel's eyes gleamed. He said: 'Such animals are rare, but wonderful to behold.' And it seemed he anticipated Alphonse Jalabert's very words which I did my best to reproduce now: 'This bull had immense intelligence. I tell you, he understood human speech. When another bull ran away and lost itself in the wilderness of tall rushes, far out in the depths of the *marais*, Bramaïro would go off by himself and find it. He would lead it all the way back to the enclosure. That was a great bull, I tell you.' More vivid even than that, were Jalabert's memories of his bull-horse, Guapa, a name derived from *guêpe* meaning a wasp – by inference, 'the stinger'. Guapa, like Bramaïro and another bull-horse, Veatto, had been the gods in Monsieur Jalabert's animal pantheon.

'On the command,' Jalabert exclaimed, 'Guapa would go like an arrow!' He made a rapid movement with his hands, striking the palms together as if to brush them clean, emphasizing the horse's speed and its instantaneous response. 'When Guapa got close to the bulls, he would start to tremble. His whole body vibrated with sheer excitement.' Here, Henri Aubanel interrupted me: 'Don't misunderstand this,' he said, 'It wasn't that the horse was afraid. It was simply his *joie de vivre* and the ancient scent of the bulls in his nostrils, the ancient instinct at work.' I told Monsieur Aubanel how Jalabert, for a few seconds, had lived the horse's part. He had extended his arms full-length in front of him; he had stiffened them, causing the muscles to twitch and tremble like the plucked strings of a guitar. His arms became like Guapa's forelegs. His loosely-held fingers were splayed like the horse's hooves. Jalabert lifted his head and turned it this way and that, his nostrils flared, making quick snuffling sounds which copied the horse's panting and rolling his eyes so that the whites showed like the eyes of a blind man. 'Like a centaur!' said Henri Aubanel. But I felt that it had been more than the fusion of man and horse. There in a café in the boulevard des Lices, Alphonse Jalabert had become not merely like Guapa, but Guapa himself.

The Camargue bull, in spite of its legendary power and resistance – the fact that it had been able to survive the Ice Age and re-establish itself, first in the primeval woodlands and afterwards in the marshes of the delta – was nevertheless threatened by the introduction of roads, railways and industry which compartmented and eroded the spaces over which it had been accustomed to roam for centuries. Monsieur Aubanel confirmed what I had previously read in Charles Naudot's classic treatise, *Camargue et gardians*, published in 1948. For countless decades *gardianage* consisted of little more than accompanying and guiding the migrating bulls over an unenclosed territory that stretched from Fos to the salt-marshes of the Aude and Montueux. But the railway and road-building changed all that: the forests of Les Pinèdes and Les Sylves were felled and many hectares of back-lying terrain along the branches of the Great and Lesser Rhône were drained for cereal crops and vineyards. The bulls which grazed over the remaining ground, which was still very extensive, had to be more rigorously guarded by the herdsmen and often they were driven into a corral, or *bouvau*, overnight.

With these changes, the *manadiers'* difficulties increased. In order that the bulls might adapt successfully to their regulated existence, the breeders were obliged to study the beasts' instincts and habits and master their secrets. It was this refined system of bull-rearing which Baroncelli-Javon brought to a high degree of perfection. In the words of Charles Naudot, the folklorist and *gardian*, Baroncelli had been among the first *manadiers* to realize that 'the wild creature accustomed to endure all weathers, tough and robust in its native surroundings, when removed from them became as fragile as glass'. In these changed conditions, as Henri Aubanel discovered time and again – notably in the winter of 1951–2 – the bulls were unable to throw off disease such as foot-and-mouth, which decimated them: whereas, in days gone by, in something closer to their original wild state, they managed to survive. The Camargue's bulls were not alone in this. There are many examples, world-wide; and not only animals but human beings also. We have to think only of the rain-forest Indians of Amazonia, or the forest tribes in Africa, for the comparisons between the wild, unfettered life and a life circumscribed by 'civilization' imposed from outside with its attendant dangers and unfamiliar restrictions, to appreciate the all too often deadly consequences of such interference with the natural cycle. Almost always it is the wild creatures, animal or human, that bear the brunt of suffering.

The lyre-shaped horns of the Camargue bull distinguish it immediately from the Spanish strain. I may be incorrect in saying so, but it appears to me that cows' horns are more graceful. As with all horned species, there are individual variations which help the *gardians* to recognize an animal from afar. Sometimes these are the result of an injury, or an inherent weakness. The bulls are seldom much affected, however, and one of the Camargue's greatest *cocarde*-bulls at the present day, Castor of the *manade* Laurent, has a deformed right horn as straight as a unicorn's, while the left horn is perfectly normal.

From an artist's point of view, sketching and painting the bulls as they graze among the *sansouire* is not really a practical proposition. The bulls react in different ways to the presence of someone approaching on foot. A small herd might watch with nervous curiosity before galloping away; but a *taureau* alone, perhaps, as Michel-Droit described, 'detaching itself from the slim shadow of a juniper bush . . . an obscure and powerful mass' is dangerous. The only sure way to approach the bulls at close range is on horseback. This was the method Pierre Aubanel used to photograph them with his precious Leica camera. I have never attempted to sketch the bulls when riding a horse and I know of no one who has made a habit of doing so. The wonderful studies of bulls made by artists such as Lelée and Pranishnikoff were worked up from thumbnail sketches made at various corrals: though it is just possible that Pranishnikoff, a very gifted horseman, may have drawn them from the saddle – a task for which he was well fitted, after his considerable experience as a military painter accustomed to portraying cavalry-charges in the heat of battle, in the 1860s.

Whenever he talked of bulls, almost in the same breath, Henri Aubanel would speak of the horses, for, here in the Camargue, the two are really indivisible. According to some authorities, the Camargue horse, the pure strain, originated in Asia like the bull; but others assert that it came from North Africa and was established there by Moorish and Saracen invaders. Whether the horses derived from Mediterranean Africa or Chinese Turkestan, like the bulls they have lived for centuries among the salt-marshes and lagoons and adapted to their semi-aquatic life better than any modern crosses, including the Camargue-Arab breed, which have never equalled their instinctive skills as bull-horses, their stamina or their fearlessness when confronted by large expanses of water. In all these respects, the white Camargue horses have proved unique; and, not surprisingly, they have been treasured by the *manadiers* and *gardians* for generations.

Like the bulls, the true Camargue horses are comparatively small; they never exceed about 14 hands and this height is attained when they reach an age of six or seven years. By the age of four or five the grey or dark-brown coat of the foals has turned pure creamy-white. Whereas the bulls – except the Camargue-Spanish crosses – have comparatively small feet, the horses' hooves are broad and so hard that they are hardly ever shod. The horses' hooves are, of course, adapted ideally to the marshes. Monsieur Aubanel and other *manadiers* and *gardians* I spoke to, said that the horses' sure-footedness was truly astonishing, like their homing instinct, and when they galloped across the parched *marais* in summer, or through the shallow lagoons where the water reached their stirrups, they never attempted to guide their mounts. The *gardians*, even so, had some terrible falls when their horses, by a million-to-one chance, struck a pot-hole or some hidden obstruction. But everyone agreed that such accidents were rare.

The Camargue horses with their deep-set eyes and long white lashes, their powerful necks and haunches and long, flowing manes and tails are perfect symbols of the white-capped waves which break along the Camargue's southern shore. Running wild and free, they appear as much creatures of the unbridled sea, the *mer déchaînée* of *gardian* poetry, as the vast, inundated plains of *sansouire*. It was as sea-gods that Mistral portrayed the horses in *Mireille*:

> A hundred steeds
> With manes like billows of the sea . . .
> Foam-coloured they are still!

In his poem, 'Horses on the Camargue', Roy Campbell echoed Mistral's assertion that, whether in fact or spirit, the Camargue horses had been spawned by the thunderous ocean waves. For, he wrote:

> Theirs is no earthly breed
> Who only haunt the verges of the earth
> And only on the sea's salt-herbage feed –
> Surely the great white breakers gave them birth.

This was how I had seen them first, as a boy of fifteen: white-coated, white-maned, spilling down the sand dunes in the opening sequences of *Crin-Blanc*, Albert Lamorisse's moving film of Denys Colomb de Daunant's story of a Camargue fisherboy and his wild stallion. It was the better part of thirty years afterwards when I saw the horses in reality; but I was not disappointed.

Once, returning to Le Simbèu, I had noticed a small herd of horses grazing close to Folco de Baroncelli-Javon's tomb. Less than 2 kilometres to the west, I had passed a herd of L'Amarée's bulls – a chain of black silhouettes far from the road. It seemed a perfect setting for the Marquis' grave: almost within sight of the bulls from which he had been for so many years inseparable; and with horses nearby whose coats by daylight shone brilliantly in the strong sun, and by night, caught the starlight's glimmer or the moonbeams which made them ethereal, like the ghosts of Baroncelli-Javon's celebrated stallions, Sultan, Le Prince and Lou Vibre.

23

Shepherds on Horseback

The visits I made to Le Simbèu were among the highlights of my autumn travels in the Rhôneland. In a sense they had brought these excursions full circle. Here, at the former Baroncelli *manade*, in the company of the Marquis' son-in-law and his granddaughters, I saw the links in the long chain of events completed at last – events which, like a series of filmed flashbacks, connected Mistral and the Félibrige poets of the upper Rhôneland and Baroncelli-Javon, and the Nacioun Gardiano's horsemen-poets of the Camargue.

At Le Simbèu, more than anywhere else, these images of 150 years had been gathered and revived by Henri Aubanel whose honest fervour imbued them with vivid realism.

Here in the Camargue – though not for the first time – I found the beautiful wild landscapes of the *gardians* and their poetry. I first met the *gardians*, as it were, *en masse*, at a Nacioun Gardiano luncheon which followed their Acampado Generalo, an Annual General Meeting held at the village of Gallargues, near Lunel, in April 1984. On this occasion, Monsieur Aubanel had invited me to join the *gardians* on horseback. But, since I cannot claim to be a competent rider and felt uncertain of my ability to control the spirited Camargue stallion which he offered me, with regret I decided it was wiser to decline. Instead I accepted Jacqueline's offer to drive me to Gallargues with her sisters, while Henri Aubanel went ahead alone.

I arrived at Le Simbèu shortly after 10 am, having walked from Les Saintes-Maries along the coast road in a tremendous storm of wind and rain. The rain battered me every step of the way, blowing horizontally off the foaming, green water which the gale had lashed to a frenzy. The sky was the colour of pewter: grey and unbroken, lowering above the dark *sansouire* marshes where I saw a few egrets with staring white plumage sheltering in the reeds near a *roubine*. Apart from the egrets and a gull or two which struggled to keep airborne, low above the waves, buffeted by the gale, the marshes revealed no other sign of life.

The drive to Gallargues was, to say the least, somewhat unnerving with Marie-Caroline at the wheel, driving like the devil, the sheet-rain crashing at the windscreen of the little car, its heater turned full on and the windows completely misted over and streaming with condensation. The girls in their best Arlésien dresses talked incessantly and every so often Marie-Caroline, to my horror, would turn her head, so that she almost faced backwards, to tell me the history of a *mas*, or a Cistercian tower, or to point out some bulls and horses which came and went at lightning speed as we hurtled along. Marie-Caroline drove with the instinct of a galloping horse: but it was more by luck than judgement, I felt, that we reached Gallargues in one piece and swept up the steep narrow streets of the village which ran like rivers in the deluge.

Even so, we arrived late and found the Nacioun Gardiano's meeting nearly over. A huge luncheon followed immediately at the Hôtel de Ville across the square and was attended by perhaps 150 *gardians*, their wives and children. The room had half a dozen long tressle-tables carefully laid, with white tablecloths and linen napkins and stainless steel cutlery. One each of the tables there were five or six 2-litre bottles of wine and many more of *pastis* and brandy on a serving-table at the side. At right-angles to the rest, at the far end of the room, was the head table where Henri Aubanel and the Gardiano's committee sat, with the *capoulié* of the Félibrige, René Jouveau and several guests of honour, including the writer, Michel-Droit who represented the Académie-Française.

All the women and girls were, as usual, in Arlésien costume and they appeared to take the proceedings seriously; most of them, though by no means all, observing the finer points of tradition – one of which, for example, forbade women in Arlésien costume to smoke. The *gardians* to a man were turned out in black velvet and moleskins and filed into the room wearing their rain-spattered grey or black sombreros – the soft felt *chapeau camarguais*, which Henri Aubanel reminded me must never be confused with the hard-crowned *chapeau andalous* of the Spanish *ganaderos*. In their lapels, many of the *guardians* sported a sprig of *saladelle* or a silver cicada, the badge of the Félibrige to which they belonged. I discovered then that, while in some respects the Nacioun Gardiano was the Camargue's equivalent of the Félibrige – for many *gardians* wrote poetry and songs, as well as prose-works – it was by no means uncommon for *gardians* to be members of both.

The luncheon itself began at half-past-one and it lasted for the better part of five hours! The menu consisted of eight courses and was, of course, printed entirely in Provençal. The translation I give here was provided for me at the time by Marie-Caroline Aubanel. We began with an *hors d'oeuvre* of delicious cold ham: *Cambajoun dou Pais Raiou*, or *Jambon cru du Pays*; then came *Teniho Santenco* and *Muscle de Bouzigue* – an enormous seafood salad consisting mainly of mussels. At this point, the notes written on my copy of the menu became a little confused: but, combining them with memory, the remainder of lunch comprised of roast kid, roast duck, *gardian* cheese from the Mas de Bruns, several helpings of a rich, sweet sponge-pudding soaked with alcohol of some nameless, but lethally potent variety and finally quantities of dark, bitter and absolutely necessary coffee! Between the roast kid and duck, to refresh our palate, there was another course, *Sepi à la Setori*; but what this *Sepi* consisted of apart from mushrooms, I cannot remember. In case the scale of the lunch is still too vague, I should add that all eight courses arrived in not merely generous, but quite gargantuan helpings many of which, besides the mind-altering dessert, were doubled and even trebled by my hungry neighbours.

As for the wine: 10 or 12 litres shared among a table of twenty thirsty *gardians* soon vanished and replacements were called for. And this heavy consumption did not include the glasses of stronger liquor which most of the guests drank in between. In those days I drank a little wine, but I quickly reached my limit and watched in amazement as gallons of wine were drained away on either side of me – not only by the 'young and ruthless' but by the 'old and toothless' in almost equal measure.

Throughout lunch, long impassioned speeches from the Gardiano committee, including an oration by Henri Aubanel, were relayed by microphones which the speakers held close to their mouths with deafening results. Many of the speeches were made in Provençal, which I could not understand, but even those in French echoed like thunder about the room, in a torrent of thickly-accented, jumbled sounds like the clashing waggons of a goods-train. All the speeches received enthusiastic ovations, which like the speeches themselves grew louder and more prolonged as the afternoon wore on. My neighbour on the left, a banker and an amateur *gardian* from Grasse, went off during the recital of a long poem and returned with a book which, there and then, he insisted that I accepted as a gift: 'This will help you to follow the verse,' he said, leafing through the pages. A page of French translation mirrored another in Provençal. The book was a perfect, partly uncut edition of *gardian* poetry – the *Flourilege de la Nacioun Gardiano*, dated 1932! Not only that: before returning to the table, the banker had had the book inscribed for me by Henri Aubanel who caught my eye and saluted me from across the room. Fifty-two years old, the little book might have come brand new from the shelves of the Librairie Roumanille.

However much the *gardians* loved and appreciated the region's literature, it must not be assumed that all of them were poets. But even those who wrote nothing shared the poets' spirit which stemmed partly, I believe, from their strong sense of vocation.

While many poems in the *Flourilege* collection evoked the *gardian* life and its scenery with great beauty, in simple phrases which touched the heart, the poetry itself was also an expression of something deeper. Perhaps it was something like religious faith: an underpinning of their lives made of an intense community spirit, a sense of brotherhood, the common experience of the work, its hazards and rewards and their jealously guarded freedom. As the *gardian* life mixed extremes of stillness and activity, so their poetry and writing combined nostalgia and melancholy yearnings with hot-blooded outbursts of passion.

The *gardian* societies, the Confrérie de Saint-George founded on 2 January 1512 and the more recent Nacioun Gardiano which Folco de Baroncelli-Javon established on 24 June 1904, each inclined to a different aspect of *gardianage*. The almost five centuries-old Confrérie was both a practical and a ceremonial affair, something like a guild which from its original core of only twenty-three members united the *gardian* brotherhood. The Nacioun Gardiano, designed to complement but in no way rival the Confrérie, also took part in parades and festivals but contributed mainly to the preservation and revival of *gardian* folklore and traditions, encouraged literature and art and improved (one might say, standardized) the *manadiers'* and herdsmen's dress, especially that adopted for public ceremonies. Early critics of Baroncelli-Javon dismissed these innovations as largely superficial. Nevertheless, like Mistral's Félibrige, the Nacioun Gardiano not only survived the catastrophic effects of two World Wars, and the immense social upheavals that followed in their wake, it actually gained support and increasing recognition. It has been rightly observed that, for such a small area, the Camargue's production of literature was exceptionally great – in quantity certainly, though, it must be admitted not always in quality. Its contribution to the literature of the Rhôneland as a whole has been significant; and, since the days of Mistral, Roumanille and Théodore Aubanel, the Camargue has offered the region's poets and writers a seemingly fathomless rich source of inspiration.

★

The Camargue's *gardians* have their equivalents in many other countries, not only among peoples of Latin origins. The *gardians'* work finds echoes among the *csikós*, horsemen-herders of the Hungarian plains, and the North American cowboys. In Spain, the *ganaderos* herd bulls using a lance not unlike the *gardian's* trident. A similar lance is used by the *buffalari*, the Italian drovers of water-buffaloes who participate in bull-games known as *giostras* which, like the Camargue's bull-games, are held in the local arenas. There are obvious similarities between the *gardians* and the *llaneros*, Venezuelan herdsmen living on the waterlogged plains along the Orinoco. In contrast, the *vaqueiros* of Brazil's parched Nordeste herd their half-starved, scraggy cattle in the blazing heat. Germaine Greer, who has travelled in Brazil and ridden with Camargue *gardians*, told me in a letter written several years ago that 'the *vaqueiros* have to serve their scrawny animals, feeding them in the dry with specially grown prickly pear by hand. . . . They have great pride and glamour, but they are really poor devils after all . . . . I loved the *gardians*, who were like the *vaqueiros*, shy show-offs and very fond of their Ricard.'

About the Mexican *vaqueiros* I know comparatively little: but of all these herdsmen from lands beyond the Camargue, perhaps the Argentine *gaucho* comes closest to the *gardian*. In terms of their freedom, equestrian and taurine skills, sense of identity and long-established tradition of literature and song, certainly there are many obvious comparisons between them. Like the *gardians*, the *gauchos* are both the masters and servants of their animals. While many *gauchos* have attached themselves more or less permanently to their *estancias*, at heart they are really nomads. In the Camargue, the closest the cattle-herders and shepherds come to the nomad life has been the *transhumance*, when great herds of cattle and flocks of sheep were driven to and from the grazing lands every year; but this has now largely died out, due to changes in land-use in the Camargue and the introduction of cars, lorries and the motor-roads which serve them. As a further comparison between the *gauchos* and the Camargue *gardians*: the *gardian*'s poetry I have read contains no real equivalent for Hernández' great *gaucho* epic, *Martín Fierro*, which portrays the glories and tragedy of a *gaucho*'s life in the nineteenth-century pampas. The herdsmen-poets of the Camargue instead have written eulogies dedicated to bulls, horses and the land which in many cases celebrate *gardian* life but never devote themselves exclusively to portraying a *gardian* hero. For this, we must turn to their prose works or else to the little-known realm of the Camargue cinema and the *gardian* films which form part of the genre begun in 1906 with the first production of *Mireille*.

In *La Camargue*, Michel-Droit introduced his chapter on *gardians* and *manadiers* very effectively by describing an evening he had spent at the Mas de L'Amarée with Baroncelli-Javon's former bailiff or *baïle-gardian*, the late René Barbut. He brought the old *gardian* to life, seated by the high stone-built Provençal fireplace in the fading light, his battered grey sombrero pushed back, 'his face dry and sunburnt, his eyes blue and shining' and the room filled with echoes of Barbut's 'high-pitched, rolling, thundering and chanting voice'. I might have written the same about Henri Aubanel at Le Simbèu: except that now, aged eighty, after a long spell of illness, Monsieur Aubanel's tanned features had paled to the waxen shade of old vellum, his hair was now pure white and his powerful voice had mellowed. Like Barbut, Henri Aubanel yielded to no one in his devotion to Baroncelli-Javon's memory; and, of course, compared to Barbut, his relationship with the

Marquis had been much closer and since his marriage to Riquette in 1933 was on far more intimate terms. Whereas René Barbut's recollections of Baroncelli-Javon had been enhanced by some of the Marquis' letters penned in his 'fine, sloping hand' which he handed Michel-Droit to read by the lamplight, those of Henri Aubanel came to me direct, in Aubanel's own words. Some of his descriptions were like those he had written in *Je suis manadier*: for example, his perceptive portrayal of the Marquis' face and his enigmatic smile.

Monsieur Aubanel said: 'His gaze burned with the fire of his very soul. His habit of fixing you with his glance was just as striking, gentle yet as piercing as a dart. His eyes smiled upon everything and everyone. And Baroncelli's smile! How difficult it was to comprehend, for the whole man was in this smile. It was a tolerant, all-seeing smile that might have been capable of causing hurt, save for its mitigating spell. It was the smile of a sage, a princely smile which confronted life and death alike and which nobody understood.' Michel-Droit wrote of René Barbut that he had 'truly lived the life of his dream, in this land of salt, sand and water, of mirages and mystery'. It was a dream which Henri Aubanel shared. As a poet with a poet's soul, he told me that in his youth he searched not only for liberty but for the greatness of which Man is capable and a higher awareness of spirit, here in the marshes whose way of life was far removed from the commonplace, materialistic world beyond. Aubanel said: 'I found this in the Camargue, where the peace brought by a life among wild creatures is unsurpassed by any other, save by the peace conferred by God!' A true disciple of Baroncelli-Javon and Mistral, a direct descendant of Théodore Aubanel, one of the seven founders of the Félibrige, it was only natural that all his life, Henri Aubanel's love for the Camargue had been matched by his love for the Provençal language, 'elegant . . . pure' which breathed 'the melodious rhythms of antiquity'.

Though twelve years older than Henri Aubanel, at ninety-two Alphonse Jalabert epitomized to me the traditional *gardian*'s image. Amazingly youthful still, Jalabert walked with a loose, swinging gait in unhurried, even strides. His long thin legs in faded jeans were slightly bowed, as if he had just left the saddle after a long day's ride. He wore his old scuffed brown-leather jerkin draped over his shoulders with its sleeves hanging loose and, as he walked, his arms swung loosely by his sides. His posture was marvellously erect and his constitution was strong. Only Jalabert's hearing now failed him and occasionally he put in the hearing-aid which he carried in a small grey plastic box secured by an elastic band. His false teeth also fitted rather too loosely so that his speech and mouth movements did not always synchronize. Years of exposure to the sun and wind had burned his skin the colour of old leather, with the same leathery sheen; his blue eyes glittered and were as clear and as luminous as water; and his breath smelled as fresh as the Camargue wind laced with sea-salt, grass and *sansouires*. Monsieur Jalabert spoke in simple, well-chosen phrases, the words coming in surges of concentrated energy like a pony as it breaks into a gallop spurred on by its rider. (Again and again I found these easy comparisons between the *gardians*, the bulls and horses – so close were the ties which bound them together, and so natural.) I felt attracted by Jalabert's youthful eagerness, his wild shy mannerisms and moments of hesitancy which worked on his features and in his bright penetrating gaze like cloud-changes – at times clear, hazed at others, always transient, yet somehow firm and resolute. This appears like a contradiction, but it is, nevertheless, how it was. He said: 'Life has treated me well, on the whole. Life is still good, save for three things: my hearing is imperfect and I don't find walking as easy as I used to.' The third difficulty had been Madame Jalabert's health which had forced them to move from the Camargue to the Arles' suburb of Trinquetaille. Although I have written as though Monsieur Jalabert and I had met in the Camargue, in fact our meetings took place in Arles, at the Café Malarte on the boulevard des Lices, before and after my stay at Les Saintes-Maries.

'I began my work as a trainee *gardian* – what we call a *gardianou* – on 1 February 1915 when I was a boy of fourteen,' he told me. 'My wages were 10 francs a month in those days. A single, small gold 10 franc piece! And I had my food besides that. This was at

L'Amarée, under Folco de Baroncelli. What was our food like, you ask? Well, there was usually soup, plenty of bread and fresh fruit such as melons. We ate whatever the kitchen provided. I drank only water. Wine, never! At that time, as far as I recall, nobody drank much wine – oh, except for one man who eventually became a Minister of the Interior, who used to drink a litre of wine every day. That was regarded as an appalling indulgence!'

Even now, as he remembered the litre-a-day Minister of the Interior, Monsieur Jalabert blinked and shrugged expressing a mixture of incredulity and disdain.

He went on: 'I slept out of doors with no sort of covering, just like the horses and the *taureaux*. On cold nights, perhaps, I was given a blanket. I never owned a watch and the time of day, in hours and minutes, didn't concern me in the least. The sun served as a clock. I rose with the dawn and I went to bed when night fell. My life in the Camargue in those days came as near as you'll ever get, I suppose, to a completely natural existence. My whole life centred on the animals and the land. At first, I had no horse of my own. I worked with the bulls and horses on foot, to begin with, until I got a horse. In a money sense, I was always poor. Later on, my wages rose to 60 francs a month and I managed to save a little. I stayed with the Marquis for five years and I went everywhere with him – to fêtes, on expeditions to town, even to the cinema. When I left the Marquis for another *manadier* who offered me more wages than he could afford to pay, I was sorry. It wasn't the money that lured me away, you understand. I needed a little extra by then in order to save and get myself established.'

It was then that Alphonse Jalabert told me about his beloved horses, Guapa and Veatto. He said: 'A *gardian* always wants a good mount. Any horseman who knows his business will feel the same. *C'est normal.* A good marriage between the horse's parents is vital. Good breeding is everything. What you're looking for is intelligence, courage and temperament. These are the main points. Our Camargue stallions cover about twenty-five or thirty mares. Compare that to the bull, mind you, which covers anything up to forty cows. By God, these bulls take some beating.'

Monsieur Jalabert spoke with affection of Henri Aubanel. He knew already that Monsieur Aubanel and I were friends of some years' standing and I think this encouraged him to open up and talk freely. Jalabert was a perfect gentleman and behaved with a charming, old-fashioned courtesy down to the smallest detail. He was also generous-hearted and very kind; but, like so many *gardians* and *manadiers* I have known, he was fundamentally quiet and retiring and not inclined 'to display his wares'. He had known the Marquis' daughters and many of Baroncelli-Javon's friends. He told me that the Marquis' daughter Nerte who had a profile like a Red Indian and wore her hair in two long plaits like a squaw (the *manadière*, Fanfonne Guillierme, did the same) had been a magnificent rider. She used to gallop at full-tilt across the *marais* on her bull-horse which was named Buffalo. Monsieur Jalabert remembered Jeanne de Flandreysy's visits to the Mas de L'Amarée and how she arrived there in great style, by car. But he could not recollect ever having seen Madame de Flandreysy *montée à cheval*. Yes, he agreed, there were many photographs of her seated side-saddle on a horse, including a romantic photograph I had seen at the Palais du Roure, with the Marquis standing by her side near a tiny marsh *étang* fringed with bull-rushes. In this photograph, the exchange of fond glances between Jeanne and the Marquis spoke volumes, although by that time their first flower of passion had died back and had been replaced by the first years of a long, unfailing friendship that only ended when Baroncelli-Javon died.

Now Alphonse Jalabert, like Henri Aubanel, had virtually retired. A *manadier* for decades in his own right, his two sons were also successful *manadiers*: one of them specializing in horse-rearing, Camargue strains and others of Portuguese and Spanish blood; and his other son a breeder of *toros de combat*, in the tradition of Joseph Yonnet – here again, bulls of crossed Camargue and Spanish blood, for the arena. Jalabert had been even younger than Folco de Baroncelli-Javon when he was carried out to see the bulls for the first time, a little boy of two or three years old at the most, on a visit to his uncle's *manade*. Much water had flowed under the bridge since 1903 and now, almost ninety years later, Monsieur Jalabert confronted a radically different world in which the Camargue's jealously-guarded lifestyle and its traditions were threatened increasingly by outside influences, above all technology and tourism which offered the certainty of long-term destruction of the old ways in exchange for the short-term benefits they conferred. As Carol Dix wrote in 1975: 'How could a romantic revival exist in post-war days? How could an association of men devoted to *not* progressing, calling each other nicknames and forever looking backwards, co-exist with the new baby, technology?' The spirit of the place and its people, it is true, remained, if not wholly intact or untarnished. This, more than anything, guaranteed the region's survival in one form or another.

Making a limp gesture that indicated something like proud resignation if not quite defiance, Jalabert said: 'Most of my old friends are dead and gone, *monsieur*. Now, I come here every Thursday afternoon to the Malarte and I sit here by the window and drink a cup of coffee, all by myself. I'm mostly quite alone, these days. There are none of the old faces here to greet me. *Mon Dieu*! Of course, I miss them. . . . But life must go on and, as far as I'm able, I try to live life to the full. Now I remember the old days in order to tell stories to my grandchildren. This gives me some reason to go on. I'm not quite defunct yet, as you can see. I can still teach the children a few things about good horseman-ship, show them a few points. My little grandson, who is eleven, is awfully keen. He thinks that I'm as old as a dinosaur and when he introduces me, he always says: "This is my grandfather, who is ninety-two!" He has no idea what being ninety-two is like, of course, and I just seem unbelievably ancient, like an old leafless tamarisk clinging for dear life to its scrap of earth.'

Monsieur Jalabert's words brought to mind a remark made years ago by an elderly lady, a famous author and traveller, who confessed to us that she was quite ready – more than that, actually impatient – to die. But, alas, she said, the moment of death cannot be hurried, no matter how hard one wished for it to happen. She put it like this: 'It's like being on board an old-fashioned steam-train at Victoria Station at the beginning of another long journey. You're standing at the window, which you have let down by its leather strap, and all your friends are there to wish you goodbye from the platform. You wave back at them and call out, "Bye-bye, bye-bye," but the blasted train never moves! That is what waiting for death feels like.'

For Monsieur Jalabert, it wasn't being old that mattered as much as the lack of companionship that age brought in its wake: not the absence of money, but the void left by absent friends.

One of the most interesting stories which Alphonse Jalabert told me concerned the making of *Crin-Blanc* (a.k.a. *Wild Stallion*), the film directed by Albert Lamorisse in 1953 which won the Grand Prix du Festival International de Cannes and effectively put the Camargue on the map after the war. Lamorisse's beautiful film was based on the tale of a wild, white Camargue stallion, Crin-Blanc, and Folco, the ten-year-old orphan, a little fisher-boy from the marshes, who befriended the horse which a party of *gardians* had failed to capture. The plot had been derived from a story-line conceived by Denys Colomb de Daunant and much of the film was shot on de Daunant's *manade*, Cacharel, on the borders of the Parc Naturel Régional de Camargue to the north of Les Saintes-Maries. Monsieur Jalabert's story focussed on the film's main highlights, a fierce battle between Crin-Blanc and another young stallion for the leadership of the herd.

Monsieur Jalabert said: 'Twenty times, Lamorisse and Denys de Daunant tried and failed to stage the fight. Again and again, something went wrong. The main problem was, they could not make Crin-Blanc and any of the other stallions they put into the corral with him fight to order. It seemed the fight scene which Lamorisse wanted so badly was doomed. At that time, Crin-Blanc belonged to Denys Colomb de Daunant, by the way. Finally, one of Lamorisse's colleagues, Fernand Ferraud, explained the situation to me. I brought one of my stallions, a mean brute named Coquet, to Cacharel and we tried again. The stallions were pretty evenly matched. Crin-Blanc was seven years of age and Coquet was six or seven. Coquet was the meaner horse of the two. He was really *méchant* and very wild. Coquet's mean streak was due to the fact that he'd dropped only one testicle. The other testicle stayed inside him. This always makes a horse vicious-tempered. Same thing with a dog. We put one of Denys de Daunant's mares into the corral and then we put first one stallion, then the other in beside her. As soon as one of the stallions showed signs of getting excited, we brought him out. We carried on like that for about three hours. By that time, Crin-Blanc and Coquet were both very worked up and ready to do battle. We led out the mare and put the two stallions together in the corral. Then the fun started in real earnest, I can tell you! The stallions went for each other, screaming with fury! They bit and kicked and reared like mad things. The noise of their squeals and angry screams, the fierce neighing and the hoof-beats was absolutely terrific. Lamorisse had three cameras running all the time, getting pictures from different angles. Nothing you see was faked, except the sound-track which had to be added later in the studios. The racket made by the fighting stallions was too loud for Lamorisse's recording equipment, and the noise came out in a blur. That didn't matter. It was easy enough to fix. We stood there, praying that the pictures would come out all right. It was the only chance Lamorisse would get and he had to make the most of it.'

In return for his services, Denys Colomb de Daunant had offered Alphonse Jalabert a substantial fee, but he said that he would rather take Crin-Blanc instead, and that was agreed. No money passed between the *manadiers*. Nor, for some reason, was Jalabert credited in the film, which he did not mind although several of his friends thought it rather unfair. Crin-Blanc was never ridden afterwards and some years later Alphonse Jalabert sold the stallion to another *manadier*, Marcel Mailhan. Crin-Blanc died at Mailhan's *manade*, aged seventeen, ten years after the film appeared, in 1963.

I have seen people flinch in horror at the battle-scene between Coquet and Crin-Blanc and many times I have heard the outraged question asked: was it really necessary, for the sake of realism, for the sake of effect in what is, after all, only a film, that the horses should have been tormented and then allowed to inflict such bloody injuries on one another? It may appear all the more strange and inexplicable since both Alphonse Jalabert and Denys Colomb de Daunant are not only strong and hardy, but also essentially gentle men, nature-lovers as well as artists. But it must also be borne in mind that both are Camarguais, *manadiers*, and their whole ethos is rooted in the Camargue where beauty and harshness are indivisible and where one without the other destroys the essence of the region's identity. The stallions' battle, had it taken place in the wild, would have almost certainly ended in death. It is true that the battle-scenes for the film had been staged. To that extent, it might be argued, they were artificially contrived. But there was nothing artificial, however, about the battle itself. In *Crin-Blanc*, the film, the wounds you see were quite real – like the blood from the savage bites gouged out of the stallions' necks and sides – and were even more bloody in the still-photographs enlarged from the film negative. It is possible that anyone who disapproves of these scenes might also disapprove of the Course Camarguaise, for there, too, the bulls are taunted (it has been said, tormented) by the *razeteurs* and indeed, very occasionally, a bull is hurt by the teeth of the *razeteur's* comb or when it hurls itself at the barricades in hot pursuit. I can appreciate better the criticisms made of the *mise-à-mort* bull-fights of the *corrida*, despite its *aficionados'* informed claim that the *corrida* is an art, whereas the Course is by contrast a 'sporting contest'. The danger in these ostensibly humane arguments lies in their tendency to interfere with nature. What is seen by the arena's spectators is really an extension of what occurs naturally in the wild, except that there the struggle is between the animals themselves and Man is only very rarely involved.

This was a facet of the Camargue I had seen and accepted, as it was, for years since I first went there. The advice I was once given by the *manadier*, Hubert Yonnet, had guided me through-out, especially the unforgettable remarks which Yonnet made in

1988 at Arles: 'If you ever wish to write about our life in the Camargue, *monsieur*, try to record everything you have seen and heard, as truthfully as possible. Do not play the role of the censor. Also you mustn't allow yourself to be carried away by too much sentiment. The life can be desperately hard and unforgiving: I won't deny that. But this is the life that shapes us and makes us what we are. You'll find enough hardship and poetry without the need to manufacture them. Above all, *mon ami*, never, I beg you, give the impression that you know more than you do, for then you will simply make a fool of yourself. Even the oldest of the *gardians* and *manadiers* goes to his grave having learned only a fraction of the Camargue's mysteries.

'And, as for the ways of the bulls and the horses, a man would need several lifetimes to understand all there is to know. That is why we Camarguais are so reserved. From the cradle, we have been taught to keep our mouths shut and our eyes open. For only thus may real knowledge and understanding be acquired.'

24

Moving Pictures of the Camargue

Whenever I hear the opening bars of *Crin-Blanc*'s film-score, – the fanfare and the strumming guitar rhythms – and see the first sequences of horses plunging down the sand-dunes, kicking up the sand, with their manes and tails streaming in the sea-breeze, I experience the same thrill, the same shock of pleasure that made my blood tingle as a boy.

I had longed for years to meet the film's creator, Denys Colomb de Daunant. One evening, he came to the Hôtel L'Abrivado with his charming wife, Monique, and together we drove to a *mas* owned by a friend of the de Daunants', Madame Anik Nou, where we were joined for dinner by Madame Bellon, the Director of the Parc Naturel Régional. Madame Nou provided an excellent meal and her house, which lay well to the north of Les Saintes-Maries, was elegant, comfortable and filled with wonderful furnishings including her late husband's big-game trophies from the Belgian Congo. We dined in a room hazed with the smoke from a wood-fire, in front of which stretched her dreaming gun-dogs, while the strong night wind in the chimney made a sound like the rumble of distant thunder. This was a memorable occasion, but most of all I remember the drive to Madame Nou's house: the starlit night, the road in the car headlights, the dark dashboard-lit interior of the car and

Denys Colomb de Daunant's bearded profile in dim silhouette, as he told me the story of how *Crin-Blanc* came to be written.

Using a favourite expression, he began: '*Effectivement*, I scribbled the first outline very rapidly, very late one night. An earlier idea, the story of a youngster and a bull, hadn't worked out satisfactorily. This was a disaster. Then I got the notion of a boy and his passion for a horse and the thing quickly came together. The first strike of the idea is what really matters. I don't bother about the style or the development until much later on. I allow my hand to be only a servant of my brain and my emotions, and I get the first impressions down on paper as fast as possible while they remain fresh. I already knew Albert Lamorisse's work. Such a tragedy when he was killed in a helicopter crash in Iran fifteen years ago! He was an excellent organizer, a brilliant director. He worked with a small crew. Basically it was himself and two assistants and, for most of the time, just one camera. The stallion fight was more complex and then he used two or three cameras, I think. You say the strong light added to the film's dramatic effect, am I right? Indeed that is so. Black-and-white achieved a better result than Technicolor. *Crin-Blanc* was a very true film, but it was also to an extent, a fantasy. We left the ending wide-open, for instance, with the boy, Folco, and *Crin-Blanc* swimming out to sea in search of the island – *où les enfants et les chevaux sont toujours des amis*. That's how Lamorisse phrased it, I think. Nobody knows for certain whether they ever reached the island, or whether they drowned. After all, it was *une île merveilleuse*, an imaginary paradise. Whether they got there, or whether the island actually existed, doesn't matter. The black-and-white treatment removed our film from what is strictly natural, natural colours and all that. We were after realism certainly: but in making a work of art, you want to go a stage further. We tried not merely to copy nature, but, if you like, to transcend it. Lamorisse got the intense effect of light and shadow by using a weak filter which was less absorbent than the ultra-violet filters people sometimes use to film the Camargue. This gave a big blast of light and very powerful contrasts. I'm delighted that you feel it has worked so well.'

I noticed that de Daunant's voice, even at moments when he spoke passionately, was as gentle as his eyes which the American journalist William Davenport once described as 'the eyes of a mystic . . . as warm as the fire in the grate'. Seated in the back of their car, Monique de Daunant seldom interrupted her - husband's flow of words and ideas. The bond between them was very tangible, and I realized how perfectly the couple were matched. Madame de Daunant, like Mistral's Marie-Louise, understood the artist's needs and how best to serve – better than that, to complement them.

De Daunant continued: 'You will have gathered no doubt that we did not employ professional actors. Alain Emery who played Folco, was ten years old in 1952. He soon got the hang of what Lamorisse wanted. He behaved very naturally in front of the camera. A child-actor might have been self-conscious, though in a different way. Alain wasn't frightened by the lens and he soon forgot about its leering gaze like a Cyclops that followed him everywhere. We had to prepare him differently for his scenes to an actor, to whom you explain in advance what is required and who puts on his role very much as one puts on one's clothes. Instead, Lamorisse guided Alain Emery and the others – the old poacher, Clan-Clan, for example, who played the boy's grandfather – as he went along. It was a two-way track. Sometimes the lad's expression, or his sudden reaction to something totally unexpected, would give Albert Lamorisse another idea, a new slant on the scene. That was the charm, the satisfaction of filming with untaught, unpractised ama-teurs. . . . *Crin-Blanc* did surprisingly well at the time, but nowadays it appears dated. Filming techniques have changed since then, and the equipment has been improved. Some people say that *Crin-Blanc* is naïve, or else it's too long [the film runs for 47 minutes]. . . . Well, let them have their say! I disagree about the length which, to me, seems about right; and, if the film appears naïve, so much the better, for it was just that sort of innocence we tried to achieve – the innocence of the youngster and the untouched life he led in the Camargue.'

In *La Camargue*, Michel-Droit has recorded that, in making

Crin-Blanc, Denys Colomb de Daunant, it was felt by some Camarguais, had 'played the sorcerer's apprentice'. His critics believed that the film had attracted unwelcome attention to the delta and was in some measure responsible for opening-up and exposing the Camargue to the outside world of tourism and wholesale commercial exploitation. When I posed this question, de Daunant answered, after a moment's thought, in very much the same words he had used when replying to Michel-Droit in 1960. Unrepentant, harbouring no feelings of guilt or remorse, he said: 'How could we expect to hide the Camargue away from the twentieth century's gaze? To imagine this is possible would be absurd, just as it would be unforgivably selfish and egoistical of us to attempt such a thing! Far preferable, don't you agree, that the Camargue should be revealed to the world with our approval than without it. And, as I told Michel-Droit, even if the tourists descend on Les Saintes-Maries in tens of thousands, we have only to go a kilometre or two into the *marais* to regain our peace and privacy, and, besides, how many would follow us?'

Neither Denys Colomb de Daunant nor Michel-Droit, perhaps, had foreseen the immense numbers of visitors or the changes they have wrought. Even so, in principle at least, I share Michel-Droit's opinion that de Daunant's view, then and now, is 'both wise and convincing'. Monsieur de Daunant's hair and beard have turned snow-white since those far-off days, but his versatility and his creative energy remain undiminished. If anything, they are greater and even more diverse than they were. *Crin-Blanc* was followed by a sequel, entitled *Braco* – the story of a boy's adventures in the Camargue by night, and the Camargue wildlife after dark. It was an intriguing idea, but the film did not achieve the success, or maintain a cult-following like its predecessor. When I met Denys de Daunant, he was working on a film-project set in Argentina, where he had spent three months with Pierre Aubanel, for whose camera-work he has a high regard. At Madame Nou's, he showed me his latest book of colour still-photographs, an extraordinary experimental work for which he used the camera like a paintbrush, washing the colour images like watercolours, by moving the camera at the instant of exposure so that the images were left partly blurred, partly sharp-edged, like a 'stopped' colour-wash. The photographs gave an effect of tremendous power and vitality, but at the same time they were mysterious, fugitive and undefined; some of the images were almost surreal, while others might be best described as 'impressionistic'. How de Daunant had achieved these strange effects, I cannot say. His camera, I gathered, was fitted with a motor-drive, and he had played very freely with various lenses of differing focal-length and had bent the rules of exposure more than a little, besides. But there was more to this than simply technical experiment. He sought to push the frontiers of still-photography further than merely using his camera as an extension of the human eye which, put simplistically, regarded its subject, blinked and captured the image – as still and uninvolved with the creative process as the eye in the photographer's head. Agitating the hand–held camera was a kind of photographic jazz, which relied on hit-and-miss improvisations. This was instinctive rather than calculated work. Again the camera was relegated to a servant's role, like the hand, the pen, which transferred de Daunant's creative impulses to paper. I think the only real difference between his *approach* to writing and photography lay in the actual working-up – in the case of still-photography, literally the development of the material. Denys Colomb de Daunant's 'jazz' photographs were selected from hundreds of negatives. I may be wildly wrong: but I should have imagined the ratio of success to failures using this intuitive, one might say 'pot-luck' method must have been very high. It was this restless urge to experiment and again and again create anew by untried means, that made artists like de Daunant so difficult to classify – and, of course, in turn, this was what made them so interesting.

I heard de Daunant described as a showman and an opportunist by those who, I suspect very strongly, neither knew nor took the trouble to understand his work. I doubt that such criticisms bothered him: besides, de Daunant had been in good company. In *Provence and the Riviera*, Alan Houghton Brodrick while praising Mistral also wrote of him as 'an adroit showman knowing all the uses of publicity' and scorned 'the ballyhoo with which [Mistral] advertised his works'.

While nobody who knows anything about Frédéric Mistral would deny for a moment that he shunned the limelight, it must be just as obvious that Mistral never sought publicity for himself as such. If he took the centre of the stage on occasions, it was because he saw in this the possibility of promoting the Provençal revival to which so much of his life and work was dedicated. He preferred the seclusion of Maillane to the literary life of Paris. As someone said, he chose to labour in the engine-room. But even in this capacity, he made his presence felt and he was quite prepared to take the helm when necessary. All this is very different from the behaviour of a man who allows his personality and his reliance on self-promotion and its attendant 'bally-hoo' to interfere with his real vocation.

To a large extent, I believe, Denys Colomb de Daunant's attitude has been similar to Mistral's and, for that matter, Baroncelli's. De Daunant was, and is, a traditionalist, a poet, a cavalier and a *manadier*. His passion for these rivals that of Henri Aubanel, Alphonse Jalabert, Marcel Mailhan, Jacques Bon, Hubert Yonnet and other great Camargue figures; and de Daunant's first duty, as he told William Davenport in 1973, has been 'to raise and preserve the bulls that are the oldest symbol of our way of life'.

Until then, I had not fully realized the importance of the Camargue cinema and knew little about its long and fascinating history. I discovered much more when I returned to Arles. Before leaving the Camargue and Les Saintes-Maries, I spent the days drawing and painting on the shore, or sketching the *sansouire* plains of L'Amarée and the marshes near Le Simbèu and Cacharel. In the village itself, I visited the Baroncelli Museum many times to look at the displays of pictures by René-Georges, Hermann-Paul, Ivan Pranishnikoff and Brayer; and sometimes when the weather was fine, I climbed the steep winding staircase to the Museum's roof-terrace and stayed there, gazing at the sunlit marsh landscapes and the sea. I visited Pranishnikoff's grave in the village cemetery, his little house which, in Michel Gay's words, has been 'transformed by commerce' and adjoins a chemist's shop in a cobbled street near the church, the rue Victor Hugo; and nearby the rue *Pranisnikoff* as it is now known, renamed and respelled in the artist's memory.

On the morning of my departure, I rose at six and went out and stood on the terrace to watch the sun rise. There was a great red flush across the sea where the line of bright water met the massed grey and dark-blue banks of cloud. I saw the flash of a lighthouse in the distance and the hard, pale white glow from the street-lamps lining the harbour walk. The sea was calm: the waves rolling and unrolling like a vast greenish-grey carpet fringed with curling white tassels of foam as they advanced and retreated and advanced again. A tiny fishing vessel bobbed at the horizon and I saw the wavering light of a motor bicycle on the shore road coming from the direction of Le Simbèu.

Monsieur Bedot had very kindly offered to drive me to Arles. 'This will be no trouble, *monsieur*,' he assured me, 'for today I have to go in any case to Tarascon, where the association of *boules*-players is holding a lunch-time meeting. Arles is on my way and there's no inconvenience involved.'

After breakfast, my packing done, I walked down to the shore and sat there for an hour, letting my thoughts wander. And then, the good, kind Monsieur Bedot came and found me and said it was time to be going. Madame Bedot embraced me and presented me with a bottle of red wine and a tiny gold pin for my wife, which her daughter had made in the shape of the village symbol, 'Faith, Hope and Love'. The little ceremony was deeply touching and sincere. In the excitement, I forgot to return my bedroom key and only discovered this when we stopped at a petrol-station half-way to Arles. But Monsieur Bedot merely shrugged and beamed like Bernard Miles, dismissing my momentary anxiety with a cheerful, *'C'est pas grave!'* which was his usual response to any minor problem.

As we raced along past the village of Albaron, with its church-spire and cottage roofs just visible through a cluster of

trees, Bedot waved at the open fields and announced: 'I was born
just over there.' For a moment, I thought he meant that he had
been born in Albaron and I asked him where the house was.
Bedot roared with laughter and lifted both his hands from the
steering wheel so that the car made a juddering swerve towards
the ditch: 'No! No! my dear sir,' he said, struggling to recover
his composure, 'I did not say that I was born in a house. My
mother reached her time while she was working back there in
the meadow. She gave a shriek of pain and clasped her stomach,
like this' – again the car veered ditchwards as he demonstrated –
'and she dropped me among the grass, just like a mare giving
birth to its foal! *Bon!* I arrived like a *poulain*, like a baby-horse.
No fuss whatever! Ah, yes, my dear mother was a truly wonderful
woman. . . . A true daughter of the Camargue!'

At Arles, several days later, I took up the subject of the
Camargue cinema once again, this time with Chantal Franco
and Jean-Pierre Morize, an enthusiastic, talented young couple
who run the Cinéma le Méjan from their offices on the east bank
of the Rhône.

The couple specialized in promoting classic films, including
many of the old pre-war favourites. They had shown few, if any
films shot in the Camargue and grew excited and deeply
interested when I mentioned the earliest of the silent films, Alice
Guy-Blachet and Louis Feuillade's production of *Mireille*, which
was screened for the first time in 1906. I had by then obtained a
copy of an illustrated booklet titled, *Camargue, terre de cinéma*,
published to commemorate the pioneer film-maker, Joë
Hamman, by the Musée Camarguais and the Parc Naturel
Régional de Camargue. It had been the park's Director,
Madame Bellon, and Denys Colomb de Daunant who turned
my thoughts in this direction. The Camargue cinema made a
fascinating study and I regretted my lack of background
knowledge which prevented me from pursuing it much further.

I suggested to Chantal Franco and Jean-Pierre Morize that
they might consider the possibility of arranging a season of
Camargue films at the Cinéma le Méjan in 1993, to mark the

fiftieth anniversary of Folco de Baroncelli-Javon's death. This seemed very appropriate in many ways: not only because the Marquis and Jeanne de Flandreysy had been involved with the production of *Mireille*, but also because Folco's younger brother, Jacques de Baroncelli, had directed several important films of the Camargue *genre*, including *La Femme et le pantin* (1929), *L'Arlésienne* (1930) based on Daudet's three-act play which had been abandoned when Daudet turned to fiction, *Gitanes* (1932) and *Le Roi de Camargue* (1934).

According to Evelyne Duret, the main feature films shot in the Camargue can be divided into several groups. Those inspired by the Rhôneland's literature included *Mireille*, of which at least three versions exist: apart from the Guy-Blachet-Feuillade production in 1906, the story was filmed again in 1920 by Ernest Servaes and in 1933 by René Gaveau. Daudet's *L'Arlésienne* had been the subject of three re-makes after Albert Capellani's pioneer silent in 1909: filmed in 1922 by André Antoine, in 1930 by Jacques de Baroncelli and again in 1941 by Marc Allegret. *Mireille*, Mistral's classic, and two works by Jean Aicard, *Notre-Dame d'amour* and *Le Roi de Camargue*, were stories of star-crossed lovers. *L'Arlésienne* was, compared to the innocence of *Mireille*'s juvenile love, more sophisticated and mature; a melodramatic tale of a *gardian*, Frédéri, who found himself torn between his affection for the sweet, gentle, socially-acceptable Vivette whom his family adored, and his passion for the Arlésienne, 'a stranger of doubtful virtue', a classic scenario of the conflict between good and evil. These undemanding story-lines and the basic moral dilemma they depended upon for dramatic effect achieved popularity. In a sense, they were little more than cryptic, allegorical narratives, like the New Testament parables.

A further group of films featured *gardians* and gipsies: for example, Jacques de Baroncelli's *Gitanes* (1932) and *Cartacalha, reine des gitans* filmed by Léon Mathot in 1941, and Jacqueline Audry's *La Caraque blonde*, in 1952. The *gardians* and gipsy heroes, though immensely popular with contemporary audiences, tended to appear, like Daudet's Vivette and her rival, the Arlésienne, as all too readily identifiable representatives of good and evil and lacked the nuances of character necessary for real credibility – in other words, the possibility for goodness, heroism, temptation and even wickedness to manifest themselves in one individual's behaviour. Like the gipsy characters, the *gardians* in these films were distinguished like the 'goodies' and 'baddies' of B-Westerns who wore either a white or a black sombrero depending on whether they were heroes or villains. There had been the *gardian* hero who appealed to maidens in distress and who redressed wrongs, emerging as the inevitable victor in the finale. The *gardian* anti-hero, corrupted by jealousy and malice, was epitomized by Mistral's character, Ourrias, in *Mireille*. As Andre Bouix, one of the older generation of *gardians*, observed, in the silent-film dramas it wasn't enough that a man should find himself cuckolded by his wife and a friend, he would give his wife's lover a thrashing and then gallop off and drown himself in the Rhône.

Again, the Camargue wilderness had been used by film directors and scriptwriters as a background for dramas set in the American prairies, the Argentine pampas, the Russian steppes and Africa. Among examples of the Wild West film sagas of the silent era, the most notable were those by Jean Durand – *Le Railway de la mort, Cent dollars mort ou vif* and *La Prairie en feu*, shot between 1910–11 in which Joë Hamman starred – and Hamman's own film series of 1912–14, *Arizona Bill*. The idea of the Camargue as a wonderland, an alternative to the sordid temptations and jaded blandishments of city life, came much later and made a direct appeal to the disillusioned post-Second War audiences who craved for nostalgic reminders of their innocent, vanished youth in times of change. This period produced such films as *Crin-Blanc* and almost thirty years later Marcel Jullian's *L'Eté de nos quinze jours* (1980) where, in contrast to Lamorisse's work, the Camargue was seen as a temporary refuge, a world away from Paris – a mythical desert of dreams and simple delights peopled by *gardians*, wild bulls and horses. Evelyne Duret has noted exceptions to the escapist formula, *La Caraque blonde* and *Chien de Pique* (1960) which focussed on the

conflict between the Camargue's *manadiers* and the new genera-
·tion of agricultural businessmen who sought to develop the
delta's potential as a rice-growing area; and Georges Rouquier's
Le Sel de la terre (1950), which portrayed the Camargue after the
Second War in a decade of flux – social and economic revolution
highlighted by industrial development and the mechanization of
agriculture which threatened the traditional lives of fishermen,
shepherds and *manadiers* and indeed the Camargue's very
existence as a separate region in Provence.

These serious films by Jacqueline Audry, Yves Allegret and
Georges Rouquier stood apart from the *genre* of Camargue
cinema as a whole. The delta's image portrayed briefly by
Claude Lelouch in *Un Homme et une femme* (1966) and other
post-war productions, was still the romantic, atmospheric,
predominantly visual one of bronzed herdsmen galloping their
white stallions through showers of sun-drenched spray; or else,
like José Giovanni's *Le Gitan* (1975), they returned to popular
themes grounded in the Camargue's history and folklore.
Including modern television documentaries and wildlife films,
literally hundreds of films have been made in the Camargue, or
made about it.

Of the many writers, directors, producers and actors concerned with the Camargue cinema, perhaps the most outstanding, certainly one of the most influential figures has been the
prolific Joë Hamman. Born in Paris in 1883, Jean Hamman as he
was then known, travelled with his father, an art-dealer, to the
United States in 1903. There he visited Dakota and other parts of
the West and immersed himself in the cowboys' world of
cattle-ranching, Indians and the prairies. During this period, Joë
Hamman was befriended by Buffalo Bill Cody and many of the
Red Indian chiefs. After returning to Paris, Hamman met Folco
de Baroncelli-Javon and when the Marquis attended Buffalo
Bill's Wild West Show in Paris in 1905, Hamman introduced
him to the Sioux and acted as his interpreter.

In turn, Folco de Baroncelli-Javon introduced Hamman to the
Camargue whose wild scenery and virgin landscapes thrilled
him, reminding him of the Western plains, so that in July 1906,

he wrote to Baroncelli-Javon that '*c'est absolument le Far-West cette Camargue!*' This was the beginning of Joë Hamman's long association with the delta which lasted uninterrupted for almost seventy years until his death in 1974. As a writer, actor, director, production-assistant, producer and co-ordinator, Joë Hamman was involved with more than 100 films, including Jean Durand's silent Wild West adventure-stories made before the First World War and the film he made in 1950 with the writer and *gardian*, René Baranger, *Aux Pays des étangs clairs*. In Dakota and the Camargue, Joë Hamman became a skilled horseman and was many times photographed astride his lively American mustang as well as stallions of the Camargue breed. Under the direction of Jean Durand, Ernest Servaes, Henri Fescourt and René Gaveau, he developed as a competent actor of film-roles which allowed him to show off his equestrian skills. A gifted artist, he painted many Camargue scenes with *gardians* and *cabanes*, a number of which have been preserved in the Musée Baroncelli at Les Saintes-Maries and the Palais du Roure in Avignon, where I first saw them. Hamman's drawings and paintings which were naïve and colourful, were used to illustrate several books about the Camargue. He painted murals, as Lelée had done, for hotels and restaurants; and he edited a humorous periodical, *La Boîte à sel* ('The Salt-Cellar') and wrote a variety of autobiographical sketches, the best of which is, without doubt, *Du Far-West à Montmartre*, a work quoted and much praised by Gérard

Gadiot in his excellent, discursive study of *gardian* life, *En
Camargue*.

It was while staying at the luxurious Hôtel Jules-César as a guest
of its owner Michel Albanac that I rubbed shoulders with
another breed of film-maker, an Italian-American producer and
his American girlfriend who had broken their journey to dine
here on their way to Avignon. To say that I 'rubbed shoulders'
with the pair is somewhat exaggerated: in reality, we occupied
neighbouring tables in the Jules-César's exclusive, far-famed
restaurant, Lou Marquès. After my meeting with Chantal
Franco and Jean-Pierre Morize, I returned to the Jules-César
where I bathed in surroundings almost worthy of the emperor
after whom the hotel is named and afterwards ate a meal of
near-imperial dimensions and quality.

Dinner began with a *tranche* of pressed, perfectly-cooled
vegetables. After that came a delicately prepared *jambonette*,
with slivers of chicken and spinach-mousse shaped like a
miniature green volcano. Then followed a dessert made of
whipped chocolate which contained several other toothsome
flavourings which the chef, I was told, kept a strictly guarded
secret only to be revealed on pain of death! After the whipped
chocolate *surprise*, at a discreet interval, a plate of tiny variegated
strawberries appeared, vermilion, ruby-red and crimson, which
tasted piquant and delicious. The wine-list, which I was shown
earlier, was both superior and comprehensive. This, and other
dinners I ate at the Jules-César, might have given me the taste for
luxury living which honesty compels me to admit I don't
possess, although I cannot go so far as to claim, as the Victorian
hunter-naturalist Selous once did after a sumptuous meal at the
London Savoy that, given a choice, he actually preferred to most
things a few hunks of cold roast moose and a pot of strong tea!
That would have seemed excessive; but I dare say I could have
stayed for a week at a modest hotel in Arles for the price of one of
the Jules-César's memorable dinners.

A bottle of rich, dark-red Burgundy nestled in a wicker-
basket lined with a snow-white napkin by the American film-

producer's table. The producer, whose mop of back-combed iron-grey hair exactly matched the colour of his expensive tweed jacket, sipped his glass of wine, fastidiously savouring each mouthful. He and his lady companion wore matching polo-neck sweaters with high, tight-fitting collars, his in navy and hers in bright scarlet.

The producer slumped in his thickly-padded chair, sipping his Burgundy, listening to his attractive young companion's flow of loud conversation, chuckling politely at her jokes and keeping her glass filled as she drank steadily and deeply. The lady's crisp, nasal West Coast accent penetrated the carpeted silence of the dining-room and grew louder the more she imbibed. She talked at some length about the neglected virtues of the sea-bass. 'Did you know,' she intoned, dropping her voice half an octave, 'that the sea-bass is also called the sea-wolf, the sea-dace, the blackfish, the bluefish and the rock-bass?' The producer replied wearily that he did not, in a way that also said he did not really care. Undaunted, the woman continued: 'The sea-bass is common in European waters and on the East Coast waters of the US. The sea-bass is a serranoid food-fish according to Webster's Dictionary, but what the hell serranoid is I can't tell you. *Don't ask me that!*' She gulped down the remains of her wine, which a waiter instantly replenished. 'All I know is that sea-bass tastes damned good, but it has to be cooked just right. Have they got sea-bass here, do you suppose? Could you please ask someone? You're the walking Linguaphone round here, dammit! My French is just so fundamentally awful.'

The producer shook his head indulgently and chuckled. The woman burst into a fit of giggling. 'I guess we're the last of the Old Hollywood Romantics,' she said. 'We're here in France having a fine, wild time and what are we talking about, my God! We're talking about serranoid food-fish! Now don't you think that's a little ridiculous?' The producer nodded and chuckled. 'How is your tenderloin?' he enquired, touching the wine-glass to his lips. He reached for the bottle but was beaten to the basket by a pouncing waiter who topped up his friend's glass. I noticed that the colour of her sweater now merged with her glowing cheeks as the Burgundy began to take effect. 'This tenderloin reminds me of your new sofa,' she said. 'I feel exactly as if I am eating your sofa . . . your lovely, soft leather-covered sofa. . . . You know, I've never seen a sofa that size anywhere else. But then, the sitting-room at your new house must be eighty feet long . . . or maybe it's a hundred. Yeah, I guess such a vast room needs a vast sofa . . . A small sofa would look out of place.' She collapsed into another fit of giggling. '*Place*! My God, did you hear what I said just now? I said, *place*! Dammit, here I am, talking about fish again!'

The producer nibbled his steak and sipped his wine with a delicacy that seemed at odds with his heavy build and his heavily-jowled Roman features. He listened to his girlfriend's serranoidal chatter and her adenoidal drawl, fielding her many intimate questions about his various film-projects 'in development', his plans for building a new beach-house in California and his partners' marriages, with gentle, practised dexterity, hypnotizing her with his predatory-eyed Italianate charm. His powerful boardroom presence blended perfectly with his sleepy-voiced bedroom manner.

The couple seemed totally disinterested by their surroundings. When the producer sighed and remarked that the following morning they would have to drive to Avignon, he said this without enthusiasm as if it were a necessary, but tiresome chore. 'All I need to know about Avignon,' said the woman, holding out her empty glass for another refill, 'is whether we can park the car somewhere near our hotel. Is it as difficult to find a parking-lot in Avignon as it is here in Arles? Whenever I visit a Roman city, I get so nervous about finding a car-space. Do you know if the Romans had similar problems? I mean, can you imagine Caesar's wife trying to park her damned chariot outside the Colosseum?' She covered her face with her hands in mock-horror. She said: 'No, I guess not! But you've got to ask the manager before we leave here. If the parking-situation at Avignon is as crazy as Arles, I don't wanna go there. . . . I can find all the parking-problems I need in Santa Monica.'

As I rose from my table, my heel snagged a cord which connected the electric lamps on the producer's table and mine with the main socket a few feet away and plunged our corner of the room momentarily into semi-darkness.

While one of the waiters dived for the socket-outlet and felt for the wrenched-out plug under one of the dessert-trolleys by the wall, I hovered embarrassed until the lights came on again. There was no need for alarm, however, and the producer's girlfriend merely remarked: 'But how romantic! Maybe we can finish our dinner by candlelight? Did you arrange this little surprise specially for me? You're such a delightful, old-fashioned thing sometimes.'

When the lamp flickered into life by her elbow, she didn't seem to notice and, though it might have been my imagination playing tricks, I could have sworn that the producer winked at me.

The American movie-mogul and his lady and the world they represented could have been hardly further removed from the world of Joë Hamman and *Crin-Blanc*. A lover of sea-bass and leather sofas, the woman in scarlet neither knew nor cared about Mistral or Baroncelli, though she might have learned much to her advantage from Jeanne de Flandreysy – as indeed the producer might have, had their paths through time and life coincided. There was something of the sea-bass in Jeanne's nature, I reflected: both were serranoidal creatures – saw-toothed and, unless handled with caution, capable of inflicting a vicious bite when least expected.

25

Flowers in the Sky

I awoke in my small hotel-bedroom in Avignon, dragged from a deep sleep and a confused dream about the Jules-César – of being arrested by the Arles' *gendarmerie* for terrorist activities in a blacked-out dining-room. In my dream, the producer and his girlfriend were also being detained by the police on charges relating to parking offences and I had heard the woman's nasal screams: 'Take your hands off me, you damned sea-bass!' But it was the noise of the waking city that aroused me: a rumbling dust-cart and the clashing of empty bins, the roar of a passing car and a workman's shovel scraping the cobblestones where the street below my window was under repair.

I switched on the television set to catch the breakfast news.

Terry Waite and an American hostage had been released. 'A great day for the hostages families,' said the bland, unsmiling newscaster. 'And now to Yugoslavia where more villages have been devasted.' On another channel, the gap-toothed presenter of a food programme was interviewing the resident chef, a fat, pasty-faced youth with a crumpled white chef's hat and a long pony-tail who explained a few of the hundreds of things one can do with clementines. The chef said that this year's clementine harvest in Spain, Algeria and Morocco had been excellent. I noted once again, the Frenchman's fascination for North Africa;

and it was as if, gazing at a clementine which lay cupped in his hand like a gipsy's crystal ball, the chef saw visions of Bedouin and camels, desert strongholds and mysterious palm-fringed oases. '*Elles sont tout magnifiques, ces clémentines!*' the chef exclaimed and rubbed the fruit on his lapel before bowling it under-arm at the startled presenter who, to my mild satisfaction, fluffed the catch.

Here in Avignon, like Arles and other towns and cities throughout France, the North African immigrant workers were viewed with grave suspicion. In this sense, they were part of the gipsies' *demi-monde*. They integrated more successfully when of mixed parentage – when they had a French father and an Algerian mother, let us say – but they tended to be ostracized, like the *gitans* or the Palestinians living in Jerusalem, and were seldom seen except by themselves, or together in groups, performing the menial tasks reserved for them, or shopping in the street markets with their wives and children.

Leila, the chambermaid at the Hôtel de la Muette in Arles, had been the child of a mixed marriage. But the hotel's owners, the DePlancks, were broad-minded people and Leila was totally accepted and respected by them. This she deserved, for she was a hard worker, punctual and very tidy both in her work and in her appearance. During the school holidays, her little daughter Zorah usually accompanied her and helped Leila to carry the day's supply of fresh bedding and bathroom-towels to and from the bedroom. Little Zorah always reminded me of Matisse's famous model, also named Zorah, whom he painted on the terrace of her Tangiers' bordello in 1912–13. There, the comparison ended, however, for Matisse's Zorah had been a prostitute, while Leila's sweet-smiling daughter was a picture of innocence with her large, liquid, dark eyes and her angelic face which told the child's thoughts as clearly as a watch-face marks the hours and minutes. Sometimes, on a wet morning, when I worked late in my room, there would be a timid knock at the door which I often left slightly ajar to make a through-draught between it and the open window, and Zorah would appear half-hidden by her huge, unwieldly soft bundle of towels. She would lay the towels carefully on my unmade bed and smilingly whisper: '*Pardon. Vos serviettes, monsieur.*' At such critical moments, I noticed that Leila was never very far away and I often glimpsed her in the corridor shadows, leaning on her broom while Zorah did the honours.

Now at Avignon, on the last day of my autumn travels, I already felt these impressions begin to slip away. It seemed like an age had passed since I sat in the Aubanels' kitchen in the Camargue, since I stood on the roof of the Musée Baroncelli at Les Saintes-Maries and gazed across the marshlands beyond the Etang des Launes to L'Amarée and the glittering arc of the sea. I remembered my friends' voices, the sharp tang of the ozone, the blinding glare of the Camargue sunlight on the village roofs and the sharper glare from the waves. I remembered the other days before that, when I scrambled the hills of Fontvieille near Daudet's Mill and with Michel Gay searched for Roumanille's birthplace and the poet's grave at Saint-Rémy. Images came flooding back of Tarascon and the *razeteurs* in the rain and the long bus-ride through the Nîmes' suburbs to Aigues-Mortes. And I pictured Aix-en-Provence and its bubbling fountains like cake-stands with their tiers of dripping water like lace doilies. Just as unforgettable had been Les Baux in the evening twilight: the damp night air scented with wood-smoke and full of the soft cooing of Monsieur Macchia's doves. And yet, it felt as though all these impressions had been received, strange as it may appear, at secondhand: as if they had been told to me by someone else, or perhaps I had read about them in a book. All these and a host of other experiences had been consigned safely to the thick green notebook which lay on top of my suitcase. To relive them, I had only to pick up the book and turn its pages: and yet, even so, the impressions seemed no more tangible than reflections in a mirror. I feared that to attempt to write about them, in the end, might be like attempting to describe one's dreams.

Even the streets of Arles, where I had spent a month and where it was impossible to walk without recognizing, or being recognized by familiar, friendly faces, receded into the dimming haze of memory and floated there as provokingly real, and yet as tantalizingly insubstantial as a Camargue mirage in summer.

That morning, I said my farewells to Madame Bosqui and Madame Barnicaud at the Palais du Roure and passed the remainder of the day sheltering in odd corners and in Avignon's twisting back-streets from a fresh onslaught of *mistral* wind which scoured the city. Much of the time I spent merely looking, otherwise I sketched and painted one or two rough wash-drawings – one of a tumbledown house, another of Saint-Agricol's church which was still *en travaux* and, judging by the hive of inactivity surrounding the building, would be for some considerable time to come. I made a pencil sketch of Mistral's bust near the Roure and one of the head of a little nun, a *nonette*, at a corner of the Palais du Roure itself, five metres above the street, which at first I had mistaken for the Devil until Madame Bosqui, who happened to pass by at that moment shepherding along a crocodile of chattering school-children, pointed out my error.

All day long the cold *mistral* blew with a terrific force and by late evening it was still blowing as hard as ever when a taxi arrived at my hotel to carry me and my baggage to the station.

The great sloping cobbled space in front of the Palais des Papes was crowded with Avignonais and a sprinkling of late-autumn visitors who had braved the cold wind to attend a festival in celebration of a new Beaujolais. The chief attractions, I was told, were an almost limitless supply of free wine and the rock-band which played Beatles and Rolling Stones hits at a deafening pitch through loudspeakers relayed from the group's massive amplifiers.

I remembered Daudet's brief description of a fête at Maillane on Sunday, when he had tramped from Fontvieille in the wind and rain to spend the day with Frédéric Mistral. Mistral had been reading from his manuscript of *Calendal*, 'the sad tale told of a maiden made mad with love', but for Mistral the cheerful cries of the village procession, the blue and grey penitents in their hooded cloaks, the farm-labourers holding aloft 'pink banners with golden flowers; big wooden saints . . . porcelain saints coloured like idols with huge bouquets in their hands' in the end proved an irresistible temptation. Mistral put his manuscript aside, jumped to his feet and told Daudet: 'That's enough of poetry! . . . We must go and see the festival.' And out they went into the windy village street, where they joined the procession: 'the wind blowing it, the candles and sunshine lighting it, and the psalms, the litanies and the wild pealing of the bells accompanying it'.

As the taxi drew away from the fringes of the crowd, the music faded and a salvo of red, blue and green rockets flashed skywards and rained down explosions of gold and silver stars in huge clouds above the Palais des Papes. Mistral's impulsive invitation, 'We must go and see the festival,' for a moment seemed to echo down through the darkness. But, after all, I reflected that was a spectral voice from the irretrievable past – more than a hundred and twenty years ago – and instead I left the crowded square, the fireworks, the wine festival and Avignon behind, and caught the night-train home.

Bibliography

Aicard, J.: *Poèmes de Provence*, 1873.

——: *Roi de Camargue*, 1891.

Ajalbert, J.: *L'En-avant de Mistral*, Paris 1931.

Albalat, A.: *Frédéric Mistral, sa vie, son œuvre*, Paris 1907.

Albaric, A.: *Les Saintes-Maries-de-la-Mer*, Aigues-Mortes 1978.

Aldington, R.: *Introduction to Mistral*, London 1956.

André, M.: *La Vie harmonieuse de Mistral*, Paris 1926.

Apollinaire, G.: *Le Bestiaire ou cortège d'Orphée*, Paris 1911.

Arène, P.: *Croquis parisiens et provençaux*, Avignon 1983.

Aubanel, H.: *Je suis manadier*, Paris 1957.

——: *Camarguaises: un gardian en hiver*, Avignon 1982.

Aubanel, T.: *La Miougrano entre-duberto*, Avignon 1944.

Audouard, Y.: *Camargue*, Lausanne 1965.

——: *Les Lions d'Arles*, Paris 1990.

Auvergne, J.: *Fontvieille*, 1908.

Avienus, R. F.: *Orae Maritimae: les régions maritimes*, Paris 1843.

Backhouse, H.: *Among the gauchos*, London N. D. (c. 1950).

Baranger, R.: *Un An de gardianage en Camargue*, Avignon 1936.

——: *Cavaliers de Camargue*, Paris 1958.

——: *Camargue d'aujourd'hui*, Paris 1962.

Barrès, M.: *Le Jardin de Bérénice*, Paris 1921.

Benoit, F.: *La Camargue*, Paris 1933.

——: *L'Immersion des reliques*, Paris 1935.

——: *La Provence et le comtat venaissin*, Paris 1949

Baroncelli-Javon, F. de: *Babali*, Avignon 1890.

——:*Blad de luno*, Avignon 1910.

——: *Les Bohémiens*, Paris 1910.

——: *L'Elévage en Camargue: le taureau*, Drome 1931.

——: *Sous la tiaré d'Avignon*, Lyon 1935

——: *La Cavalo de Gregori XI*, Lyon 1937.

Bicheron, L.: *Camargue taurine*, Paris 1974.

Bonaparte-Wyse, W.: *Li Parpaioun blu*, Avignon 1868.

Bone, G.: *Days in Old Spain*, London 1942.

Bonnet, B.: *Un Paysan du Midi, vie d'enfant*, Paris 1895.

Bonnet, M.: *L'Empire du soleil: la Provence de Frédéric Mistral*,
  Monaco 1986.

Bonnet, N.: *Moun cacho-maio*, Avignon 1902.

Bosco, H.: *Malicroix*, Paris 1948.

Bosqui, M.: *Mistral par l'image*, Nîmes 1986.

Brion, M.: *Provence*, London 1956.

Brodrick, A. H. (ed.): *Provence and the Riviera*, London 1952.

Burnand, T. & Oberthür, J.: *Toute la Camargue*, Paris 1938.

Cabanne, P.: *Le Midi des peintres*, Paris 1964.

Cali, F.: *Provence, Land of Enchantment*, London 1965.

Campbell, R.: *Taurine Provence*, London 1932.

——: *Collected Poems*, London 1949.

——: *Light on a Dark Horse*, London 1951.

Cendrars, B.: *Sutter's Gold*, London 1925.

——: *L'homme foudroyé*, Paris 1945.

——: *Confessions of Dan Yack*, London 1990.

Cervantes-Saavedra, M.de: *Nouvelles exemplaires*, Lausanne 1744.

Chabanis, C.: (Guy Chambelland): *Jeanne de Flandreysy: ou la passion
  de la gloire*, Paris 1964

Chabaud, F. L.: *Auguste Chabaud, mon père*, Marseille 1956.

Chamson, A.: *Roux le bandit*, Paris 1925 (trans. London 1958).

Chapman, F. M.: *Camps and Cruises of an Ornithologist*, London
  1908.

Charles-Roux, C., Flandreysy, J. & Mellier, E.: *Livre d'or de la
  Camargue*, Paris 1916.

Châtel, G.: *La Selle gardiane et le harnachement camarguais*, Nîmes
  1988.

Clébert, J.-P.: *Rêver de la Camargue*, Paris 1956.

——: *Gypsies*, London 1963.

——: *Provence Antique*, Paris 1966, 1970 (2 volumes).

Clérambault, G. G. de: *La Passion érotique des étoffes chez la femme*,
  Paris 1908.

Collier, B.: *To Meet the Spring*, London 1937.

——: *I Wore my Linen Trousers*, London 1941.

Cunningham, C.: *What I Saw in Hungary*, London 1932.

D'Arbaud, J.: *La Caraque*, Paris 1914.

——: *Nouvè gardien*, 1923.

——: *La Bête du Vaccarès*, Paris 1926.

——: *La Sauvagine*, Paris 1929.

Daudet, A.: *Le Petit Chose*, Paris 1868.

——: *Lettres de mon moulin*, Paris 1869 (trans. London 1984).

——: *Les Aventures prodigieuses de Tartarin de Tarascon*, Paris 1872, 1937 (trans. London 1969).

——: *Le Nabab*, Paris 1877.

——: *Nouma Roumestan*, Paris 1881.

——: *Le Trésor d'Arlatan*, Paris 1897.

Davenport, W.: 'France's Wild Watery South', *National Geographic*, Washington, May 1973.

Day, S. R.: *Where the Mistral Blows*, London 1923.

D'Elly, E. R.: *La Camargue gardiane*, Paris 1938.

Denizet, F.: *La Camargue: son passé, son avenir*, Marseille 1931.

De Daunant, D. C.: *Braco*, Paris 1954.

De Daunant, D. C.: & Proal, J.: *Camargue*, 1955.

Des Vallières, J.: *Le Chevalier de la Camargue*, Paris 1956.

——: *Folco de Baroncelli*, Paris 1990.

Dibon, H.: *Folco de Baroncelli*, Nîmes 1982.

Dix, C.: *The Camargue*, London 1975.

Dorval, Y.: *La Nature et ses merveilles: les parcs naturels français*, Paris 1974.

Drouet, G.: *Le Cheval Camargue*, Marseille 1910.

Dumas, A.: *Pictures of Travel in the South of France*, London 1851.

Durand, L.: *Pirates et barbaresques en Mediterranée*, Avignon 1975.

Downer, C. A.: *Mistral, Poet and Leader in Provence*, New York 1901.

Droit, M.: *La Camargue*, Paris 1961.

Durand, J.: *André Bouix, gardian de Camargue*, Paris 1986.

Duret, E.: *Cabanes de Camargue*, Cavaillon 1983.

——: *Camargue, terre de cinéma*, 1984.

Edwards, T.: *The Lion of Arles: a Portrait of Mistral and his Circle*, New York 1964.

Enlart, C.: *Manuel d'archéologie française*, Paris 1927.

Flandreysy, J. de & Bouzanquet, G.: *Le Taureau Camargue*, Paris 1925.

Forrest, A. S.: *A Tour through Old Provence*, London 1911.

Florescu, A. I.: *Réflexions et témoinages sur l'histoire et la civilisation roumaine*, Arles 1990.

Flower, J. & Waites, C.: *Provence*, London 1987.

Gadiot, G.: *En Camargue: taureaux, chevaux et gardians*, Paris 1968.

Gaillard, L.: *La Vie quotidienne des ouvriers provençaux en XIXme siècle*, Paris 1981.

Gallett, E.: *Les Flamants roses de Camargue*, Lausanne 1949.

Gerard, J.: *The Life and Adventures of Jules Gerard – the Lion Killer*, London 1855.

——: *Lion Hunting and Sporting Life in Algeria*, London 1856.

Gangneux, G.: *Les Saintes-Maries-de-la-Mer de 1675 à 1792*, Nîmes 1988.

Galtier, C.: *Entre Provence et Languedoc: les vanniers de Vallabrègues*, Grenoble 1980.

Gaut, J.-B.: *Souneto et sounaio*, Aix 1874.

Gélu, V.: *Lou Garagai*, Marseille 1872.

Gasquet, J.: *Cézanne: a Memoir with Conversations*, London 1991.

Gasquet, M.: *Une Enfance provençale*, 1926.

Gay, M.: *Léo Lelée: un angevin chez les félibres*, Nîmes 1989.

——: *Fontvieille*, Nîmes 1990.

——: *Ivan Pranishnikoff*, Nîmes 1991.

Genevoix, M.: *Introduction to Wildenstein & Co. Ltd Exhibition Catalogue, Yves Brayer*, London 1971.

Giono, J.: 'The Man who Planted Hope and Grew Happiness', in *Vogue*, London, March 1955.

Girard, J.-C.: *Le Cheval Camargue*, Nîmes N.D.

Girard, M.: *La Crau*, Avignon 1894.

Giraud, J.: *Les Baroncellis d'Avignon*, Avignon 1957.

Girdlestone, C. M.: *Dreamer and Striver: the Poetry of Frédéric Mistral*, London 1937.

Giusti, A.: *Arles*, Florence 1981.

Godefroy, E. N.: *Provence Historique*, vol. III, 1953.

Gostling, F. M.: *The Auvergne and its People*, London 1911.

Graham, R. B. C.: 'La Camargue', in *His People*, London 1906.

Guignard, J.: *Yves Brayer, catalogue raisonné*, 1970.

Gwynne, P.: *The Guadalquivir*, London 1912.

Hamman, J.: *Du Far-West à Montmartre*, Paris 1962.

Hanbury-Tenison, R.: *White Horses over France*, London 1985.

Headlam, C.: *Provence and Languedoc*, London 1912.

Hériat, P. *et al*: *Paul Surtel*, Carpentras 1987.

Hernández, J.: *The Gaucho, Martín Fierro* (trans. Walter Owen), New York 1936.

Hoffmann, L.: 'An Ecological Sketch of the Camargue', in *British Birds*, September 1958.

Hugo, J.: *Avant d'oublier*, Paris 1976.

James, H.: *A Little Tour in France*, London 1987.

Jaloux, E.: *Fumées dans la campagne*, Paris 1918.

Jasmin, J. B.: *Las Papillotos de Jasmin, coiffeur*, Agen 1835–42.
Jean, V.: *Au pays d'Arles*, 1908.
John, A.: *Chiaroscuro*, London 1952.
Johnson, A.: *Camargue flamingoes*, Slimbridge 1973.
Jouveau, M.: *Le Fils de Tartarin*, Villedieu-Vaison 1906.
——: *Eléments de grammaire provençale*, Marseille 1907.
Jouveau, R.: *La Cansoun de l'agneau-blanc*, 1970.
——: *Histoire du Félibrige*, 1970, 1977.
Jouveau, M.-T.: *Joseph D'Arbaud*, Nîmes 1984.
Kammerman, E. L.: 'The Camargue, Land of Cowboys and Gypsies', *National Geographic*, May 1956.
Krippner, M.: *Discovering the Camargue*, London 1960.
Laclotte, M.: *L'École d'Avignon*, Paris 1960.
Lamorisse, A.: *Crin-Blanc*, Paris 1953.
Languedoc: *Histoire du Languedoc de 1900 à nos jours*, 1980.
Lanoux, A.: *Yves Brayer*, Paris 1975.
Lartilleux, H.: *Géographie des chemins de fer français* (Tome I), Paris 1959.
Lasteyrie, R. de: *L'Architecture religieuse en France à l'époque romane*, Paris 1912.
Lenthéric, C.: *La Grèce et l'Orient en Provence*, Paris 1878.
——: *La Provence maritime, ancienne et moderne*, Paris 1880.
——: *La région du Bas-Rhône*, Paris 1881.
——: *Les Villes mortes du Golfe de Lyon*, Paris 1898.
Lyall, A.: *Companion Guide to the South of France*, London 1986.
Maclean, A.: *Caravan to Vaccarès*, London 1970
Mariéton, P.: *La Terre provençale*, 1888.
Matisse, H.: *Jazz*, Paris 1947.
——: *Matisse in Morocco*, Washington 1990: studies by Jack Cowart, John Elderfield *et al.*
Mauron, M.: *La Transhumance*, Paris 1952.
——: *La Camargue des Camarguais*, Paris 1972.
——: *Le Taureau, ce dieu qui combat*, Nîmes 1991.
Maurras, C.: Introduction to D'Arbaud, *La Bête du Vaccarès*, 1926.
Mayle, P.: *A Year in Provence*, London 1989.
Mazars, P.: *Yves Brayer, Aquarelles*, Neuchâtel 1978.
McQuillan, M.: *Van Gogh*, London 1989.
Mistral, F.: *Mireille*, Avignon 1859 (trans. 1867).
——: *Calendal*, Avignon 1867.
——: *Les Iles d'or*, Avignon 1876.
——: *Le Trésor du Félibrige*, Aix-en-Provence 1878–1886.

——: *Nerte*, Paris 1884.

——: *La Reine Jeanne*, Paris 1890.

——: *Le Poème du Rhône*, Paris 1897.

——: *Mes Origines: mémoires et récits*, Paris 1906 (published as *Memoirs of Mistral*, London 1907).

——: *La Genèsi*, Paris 1910.

——: *Les Olivades*, Paris 1912.

Montherlant, H. de: *The Matadors*, London 1957.

More, C. & More, J.: *A Taste of Provence*, London 1988.

Moyal, M.: *On the Road to Pastures new*, London 1956

Nacioun Gardiano: *Flourilege de la Nacioun Gardiano* (collected poems by twenty-four contributors including d'Arbaud and Baroncelli-Javon), Montpellier 1932.

Naudot, C.: *Camargue et gardians*, (1948); Anduze 1977.

Niel, N.: *L'Art du costume d'Arles*, privately printed, Arles 1989.

Nostradamus, M. de: *Prophecies of Present Time* by D. Pitt Francis, London 1984.

Oakley, A.: *The Heart of Provence*, New York 1936.

Oldham, R. D.: 'Earth Movements in the Rhône Delta', in *Nature*, April 1930.

Pagnol, M.: *Jean de Florette*, Monte Carlo 1962.

——: *Manon des sources*, Monte Carlo 1962.

Papetti, Y. *et al*: *La Passion des étoffes*, Paris 1990.

Parsons, C.: *A Bull called Marius*, London 1970.

Passa, M.: *Camargue, mon pays*, Salin-de-Giraud 1976.

Peyre, S.-A.: *Frédéric Mistral*, Paris 1959.

Price, W. L.: *Tauromachia, or the Bullfights of Spain*, London 1852.

Quigley, H.: *The Land of the Rhône*, London 1927.

Quiqueran de Beaujeu, P. de: *Provence louée*, Arles 1551.

Reval, G.: *La Côte d'Azur*, Grenoble 1934.

Renoir, J.: *Renoir my Father*, London 1962.

Rieu, C.: *Le Parrié: cant dóu terraire*, Marseille 1904.

Ripert, E.: *Le Chemin blanc*, Paris 1904.

——: *La Renaissance provençale*, Paris 1917.

——: *La Versification de Mistral*, Paris 1917.

——: *La Félibrige*, Paris 1924.

——: *Mireille mes amours . . .* , Paris 1930.

Robson, E. I.: *A Wayfarer in Provence*, London 1926.

Roumieux, L.: *La Rampelado*, Avignon 1876.

Ruvigny, Marquis de (ed.): *Titled Nobility of Europe*, London 1914.

Salem, M.: *A la gloire de la 'Bouvino'*, Uzès 1965.

Schulenburg, W. von der: *Eine Winterfahrt durch die Provence*, Berlin 1910.

Solignac, H.: *Auguste Chabaud*, Nîmes 1989.

Stendhal (Henri Beyle): *Mémoires d'un touriste*, Paris 1838.

Stone, I.: *Lust for Life*, London 1989.

Turnbull, P.: *Provence*, London 1972.

Théron, R.: 'Bouto-sello!' (poem), 1960: in *Li Nouvello de Prouvenco*, No. 11, Avignon April 1991.

Unger, H.-J.: *Die Literatur der Camargue*, Munich 1969.

Van Gogh, V.: *Correspondance complète de Vincent Van Gogh*, Paris 1960.

Varille, M.: *Trois de Camargue: D'Arbaud, Baroncelli-Javon et Hermann-Paul*, Lyon 1954.

Vaux de Foletier, F. de: *Les Tziganes dans l'ancienne France*, Paris 1960.

——: *Les Fêtes des Saintes-Maries-de-la-Mer*, Paris 1973.

——: *Les Mondes des Tsiganes*, Paris 1983.

Venture, R.: *Arles*, Avignon 1989.

Véran, J.: *La Jeunesse de Mistral*, Paris 1930.

Viallés, A.: 'Camargue, the Cowboy Country of Southern France', in *National Geographic*, Washington, July 1922.

Vigny, A. de: *Poèmes, antiques et modernes*, 1914.

——: *Œuvres complètes*, 1965.

Villeneuve, Comte de: *Statistique du département des Bouches-des-Rhône*, Marseille 1824–9.

Vincent, J.: *Frédéric Mistral*, Paris 1917.

Virgil: *The Aeneid*, London 1757.

Voretzsch, K.: *Frédéric Mistral*, Halle 1928.

Weber, K.: *Camargue, un pays sauvage en péril*, 1972.

Weber, K. & Hoffmann, L.: *Camargue, the Soul of a Wilderness*, London 1968.

Whelpton, B.: *Painters' Provence*, London 1970.

White, F.: *West of the Rhône*, London 1964.

Yeates, G. K.: *Bird Life in Two Deltas*, London 1946.

——: 'Flamingo City', in *Country Life*, London 1950.

Note: Apart from general works in English, which may be found in any good public library, most of the books I have listed are available for study at the library of the Institut Français, South Kensington, London, the Palais du Roure in Avignon and the Médiathèque in Arles.

Glossary of
Provençal and French Terms

abrivado: the ceremony when bulls are led by *gardians* from the
  corral, or *bouvau*, to the arena for the Course Camarguaise.
aïoli: mayonnaise flavoured with garlic, used for *bouillabaisse*, fish
  and snails.
l'amarée: a plum-tree, the *prunier* Sainte-Lucie, after which the first
  Baroncelli *mas* was named.
anouble: a yearling bull calf.
arrastre: the carrying-out of a bull's carcass from the arena after a
  mise-à-mort contest.
baccalauréat: school leaving certificate.
baïle: foreman, or head-*gardian*, as in *baïle-gardian*.
banderillero: matador who implants the *banderillas*, the darts trimmed
  with ribbons, in the bull's neck.
bandido: the ceremony when *cocarde*-bulls are led away from the
  arena by *gardians* after the Course. As in the *abrivado*, in the
  bandido the bulls are driven by *gardians* through the streets of a
  town or a village.
biòu, lou: the bull.
bistournage: the castration-ceremony performed on three-year-old
  cocarde-bulls.
bouillabaisse: fish-stew of many varieties, flavoured with garlic.
boules: the popular game where metal balls are thrown by the
  players at a mark.
bouvau, bouvaou: a bull-corral.
cabane: the *gardian's* traditional thatched hut, consisting of one or
  two rooms, oriented so that its rounded north-gable faces the
  prevailing wind, the *mistral*.
cacharel: a species of wild duck.
capoulié: the head of the Félibrige.
chivau: a horse.
Club Taurin: the club consisting of *aficionados* or amateurs of the

Midi's bull-games. The local clubs throughout the region have been gathered to form a *fédération*.

cocarde: the device strung between a bull's horns which *razeteurs* attempt to slash free with their metal comb during the Course.

corrida: a bull-fight to the death, the *mise-à-mort* Spanish-style contest.

Coupo Santo: the Provençal hymn, Mistral's poem delivered in 1867 to acknowledge the silver loving-cup first used at Saint-Rémy and paid for by a public subscription raised in Catalonia by Victor Balaguer and other Catalonian poets.

Course Libre: the contest also known as the Course Camarguaise or the Course à la Cocarde; the Provençal bloodless equivalent of the *corrida*.

crochet: the *razeteur*'s metal comb.

diestro: a matador.

doublen: a two-year-old bull calf.

dountaire: the *dompteur*, a herd-leader of bulls, sometimes called the *simbèu*.

draille: a pathway, or land-route followed by herdsmen.

élévage: the raising, literally, or breeding of bulls and horses.

engano: *salicornia*, or marsh-samphire, glasswort.

escalassoun: the *échelier*, a wooden post about 7 metres high, with steppings of wood or iron, used by *gardians* to survey the marshes. It is usually found near a *mas* or a *cabane*.

escapado: the bull's escape from the encircling *gardians* during an *abrivado*, encouraged by the spectators.

escoussuro: the notch cut in a bull's ear to identify the *manade* to which it belongs.

estocade: the death-blow, or thrust, which ends a *mise-à-mort* bull-fight.

étang: the shallow lake or salt-water lagoon found in the Camargue marshes.

étrier: stirrup(s).

félibre: a member of the society of Provençal poets founded by Mistral in 1854.

Félibrige: the society of Provençal poets which Mistral and Roumanille founded at Font-Ségugne on 21 May 1854 from an original membership of seven poets. This word, like the term, *félibre*, has no precise or definitive translation.

ferrade: a bull-branding ceremony held at a *manade*.

fièvre (aphteuse): foot-and-mouth disease.

gardian: a herdsman with the responsibility for protecting a number of bulls or horses in his care. The *gardeur*, usually an impecunious horseman, lacks the *gardian*'s knowledge and experience of the craft. The *gardianou* is an apprentice *gardian*.

gaso, gaze: a stretch of shallow water.

Gitan: the name commonly, though in this sense incorrectly, applied to gipsies as a whole in the Camargue.

grasiho: an onomatopoeic term meaning the burning, sizzling noise of the hot-iron on a bull's hide during the *ferrade*.

langue d'oc: the language of the Midi, also called Provençal, which Mistral sought to revive and restore in an as nearly as possible pure form.

Malagroy: a large lagoon to the west of Les Saintes-Maries.

manade: a herd of bulls and cows; the ranch on which they are reared. Cf. the *cortijó* or *ganaderia* of Andalusia.

manadier: the owner of a bull-herd; a rancher and stock-breeder.

marais: the marsh-lands of the Camargue.

marquès, lou: a name by which the Marquis Folco de Baroncelli-Javon was commonly known.

mas: a Provençal country-house; a farmhouse, e.g. the Mas du Juge.

mistral, mistrau: the cold, strong northwest wind which blows for much of the year across the Mediterranean provinces of France.

Mithras: the Persian god identified with the sun; the god associated with bull-games and taurine ceremonies.

mourven: Phoenician juniper found on the Bois-des-Rièges, islands in the Etang de Vaccarès north of Les Saintes-Maries.

muselado: the ceremony of weaning, by muzzling, a yearling bull calf. A wooden guard, the *mourrau*, is attached to the calf's nose to prevent it suckling and thus encourage it to graze.

Nacioun Gardiano: the society of Camargue *gardians* established by Folco de Baroncelli-Javon in 1904.

novillade: a *course de toros* arranged for young bulls; hence *novillos*, young bulls which sometimes appear in the *corrida mixte*.

paseo: matadors' entry at the start of a *corrida*.

pastis: alcoholic drink flavoured with aniseed.

pélote: master or proprietor of, for example, a Camargue *manade*.

peones: the matador's assistants.

plan: a makeshift arena for the Course consisting of waggons drawn up in a circle; a village arena.

quatren: a four-year-old bull.

querençia: a place in the arena, often close to the barricades, where

an exhausted bull seeks refuge. Here the bull may receive its final
  death-blow.

quite: the action of distracting a bull during its attack in the *mise-à-
  mort* bull-fight.

radeau: a sand-bank, or islet.

razet: the effective distance, which may be long or short, judged
  by the moving *razeteur* during the Course, by which the *cocarde*
  may be successfully removed at a stroke.

razeteur: the contestant dressed in white who attempts to slash the
  cocarde from a bull's horns during the Course Camarguaise.

Rièges: lovely forested islands in the Vaccarès lake where
  Phoenician junipers grow to a height of 5 or 6 metres. .

roubine: a narrow irrigation canal in the Camargue.

rouille: hot garnish used for *bouillabaisse* made of several quarters of
  garlic pounded in a mortar with a whole chilli-pod; generally
  known as 'the rust'.

rosse, rosses: *li rosso* in Provençal; a herd of Camargue horses.

Saintin: a resident of Les Saintes-Maries-de-la-Mer.

saladelle: the statice, or sea-lavender; a frail-looking bluish flower of
  the *marais*, the emblem of the Nacioun Gardiano.

sansouire(s): an expanse of alluvial soil covered with salt-vegetation
  such as *engano*.

sauvagine: a collective term for wild animals or flocks of wild birds,
  e.g. wildfowl, in the Camargue.

seden: the *gardian*'s lazo made from plaited strands of horsehair.

selle, selo: a saddle, usually one of the traditional Camargue type
  with a high cantle.

simbèu, le: literally, the symbol. A name given to the leading bull,
  or bulls, the herd-*dompteurs*. The Baroncelli-Aubanel *manade* near
  Les Saintes-Maries.

tau: a complete, that is to say, uncastrated bull.

taureau, toro: bull. The collective term for a mixed herd is *taureaux*.
  Toro is used for the Camargue-Spanish cross, the *toro de combat*
  bred for the *corrida*.

ternen: a three-year-old bull calf.

traje de luces: the matador's 'suit of light'.

tramontane: a cold, blighting north wind.

transhumance: the traditional migration of sheep to and from the
  lower Alpine pastures.

trident: the three-toothed, or three-pronged iron fork mounted on a
  shaft of chestnut wood about 2 metres long, used by the *gardians*

to guide or control bulls and horses. The iron blade is shaped like a crescent-moon and is of a design which has varied very little over the centuries.

vannier: the traditional, nomadic basket-weaver associated with Vallabrègues; this was the trade followed by Mistral's youthful hero, Vincent, in *Mireille*.

vedel: calf.

véronique: a two-handed pass made with the matador's cape.

vibre, lou: the beaver.

Vovo: the celebrated *cocarde*-bull bred by the Baroncelli-Aubanel *manade*.

Index